Right (clockwise from top left) Tina Turner; Elvis Presley; John Lennon; Boy George; Mick Jagger and Keith Richard; Eric Clapton.

Title page 'Freewheeling' Bob Dylan.

Contents page Stevie Nicks, whose remarkable voice has contributed greatly to the success of Fleetwood Mac.

Pages 6-7 Clash crashing out the latest sounds.

THIS BOOK WAS DEVISED AND PRODUCED BY
MULTIMEDIA PUBLICATIONS (UK) LTD

EDITOR: RICHARD ROSENFELD
ASSISTANT EDITOR: SYDNEY FRANCIS
PRODUCTION: ARNON ORBACH
DESIGN: IVOR CLAYDON/BOB HOOK SUNSET DESIGN CO.,
PICTURE RESEARCH: DEBBIE GELLER, VIRGINIA LANDRY, MICK ALEXANDER

COPYRIGHT © MULTIMEDIA PUBLICATIONS (UK) LTD 1985

FIRST PUBLISHED IN THE UNITED STATES OF AMERICA 1985 BY
GALLERY BOOKS, AN IMPRINT OF W. H. SMITH PUBLISHERS INC.,
112 MADISON AVENUE, NEW YORK, NY 10016

ISBN 0 8317 2784 5

TYPSET BY ROWLAND PHOTOTYPESETTING, (LONDON) LTD
ORIGINATION BY IMAGO
PRINTED IN ITALY BY SAGDOS

Encyclopedia of
ROCK⚡POP
Stars

GALLERY BOOKS
An Imprint of W. H. Smith Publishers Inc.
112 Madison Avenue
New York City 10016

Encyclopedia of ROCK/POP Stars

Ritchie Marsh and Sam Johnson

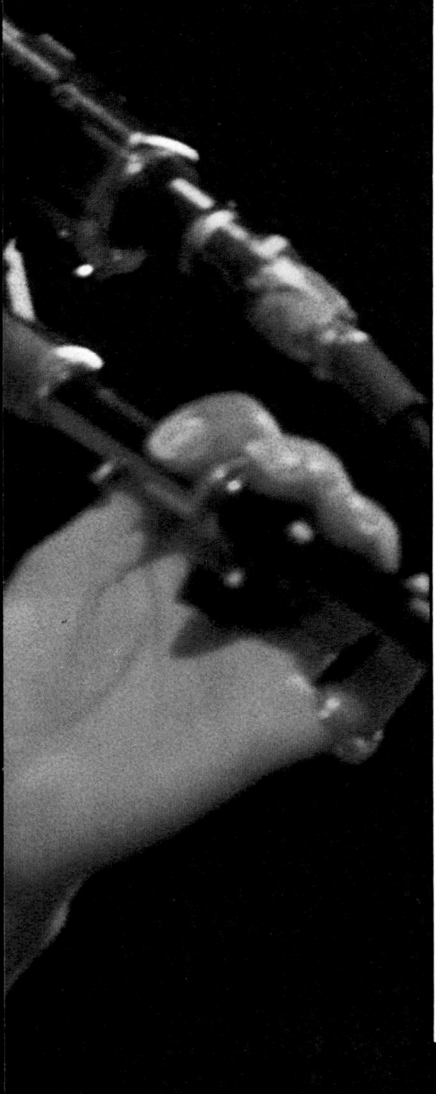

CONTENTS

1956 Rock'n'Roll and Kiss Curls   Page 8

1957 Long Live the King   Page 12

1958 Rebel Rousers   Page 18

1959 Teen Dream   Page 22

1960 Year of the Twist   Page 28

1961 Spector of Things to Come   Page 32

1962 'Times they are a-changin'   Page 38

1963 Mersey Mania   Page 48

1964 Invasion of the US   Page 54

1965 Stones Satisfaction   Page 60

1966 Gasoline Alley   Page 66

1967 Acid Rockers   Page 72

1968 Bubblegum and Blues   Page 80

1969 Woodstock Goes Pop   Page 84

1970 Beatles Break Up   Page 92

1971 Osmonditis   Page 98

1972 Soul and Glitter   Page 104

1973 Soft Rock   Page 110

1974 Rock'n'Roll Revival   Page 116

1975 Emergence of Reggae   Page 120

1976 Breaking New Ground   Page 126

1977 Punk Classics   Page 136

1978 Like a Bat Out of Hell   Page 142

1979 Headline Stoppers   Page 148

1980 Women At The Top   Page 154

1981 Heavy Metal Melodies   Page 160

1982 Video Madness   Page 166

1983 Moneyspinners   Page 172

1984 Second US Invasion   Page 182

Index

Rock 'n' Roll and Kiss Curls

1956

Although rock'n'roll made a certain impact in 1955, it was not until the following year that the music freed itself from the novelty tag and announced that it was here to stay. The first hero of rock'n'roll was a somewhat unlikely figure: Bill Haley. He had served a thorough musical apprenticeship in both country music and blues, eventually coming up with a hybrid sound set to an amplified shuffle in which the backbeat was given special prominence. By 1955, Haley was already 30 years old, and his chubby face, cheerful grin and 'kiss curl' seem hardly the stuff of teen rebellion in hindsight – but that was exactly what he sparked off.

Jungle fever

His big break came when one of his tunes was played over the opening credits of *Blackboard Jungle*, a mild teenage-rebellion film. The most controversial moment in the film comes when the caring teacher has his old jazz records smashed up by his unruly class. The success of the film carried the song along with it and, by the end of 1955, "Rock Around the Clock" had topped the charts in the United States and Britain, despite being little more than a novelty record. A new generation had sprung up that was hungry for a new sound and the lyrics of Haley's corny song touched a chord, while the beat moved feet.

Another film, *Rock Around the Clock*, cemented Haley's success. It was the first rock film, had virtually no story and worked purely as a vehicle for the groups appearing in it. These included Haley and his Comets, the Platters, and Freddie Bell and the Bell Boys. The film caused riots when it was shown in the UK.

Right Bo Diddley with his flashy rectangular guitar. Diddley's popularity was based on unabashed vulgarity and the characteristic "Diddley Beat".
Far right Bassist Bill Black provides back-up to the King of Rock'n'Roll, Elvis Presley.

Enter 'the Pelvis'

Haley may have been rock's first star, but he was nothing more than a minor prophet compared to the messiah emerging in Memphis. Legend has it that the young Elvis Presley entered Sam Phillips' studio in order to record a song for his mother's birthday. Whatever the truth, it is certainly true that he was soon making records that drove mothers to try to lock up their sons and, especially, their daughters. Presley had been exposed to much the same influences as Haley – R&B, blues, raw country – but whereas Haley paraded a style, Presley presented a complete synthesis. He lived and breathed rock'n'roll and, perhaps more importantly, he 'sneered' it out and moved with his music in such a flagrantly sexual manner as to call down all the impotent rage of the establishment on his own head.

By the beginning of 1956 Presley was with RCA, having been lured away from Phillips' Sun label with a payment of $35 000, a transfer fee unheard of in those days. It was justified almost instantly as his first single for RCA, "Heartbreak Hotel", raced to the top of the charts, displacing Les Baxter's "Poor People of Paris" and announcing that rock'n'roll had voted itself a king.

Sweet Gene Vincent

Naturally, there were pretenders to the throne. The most convincing at the start was Gene Vincent, a brooding and menacing presence in black leather with a badly smashed leg, courtesy of an old motorcycle crash. Vincent and his group the Blue Caps scored an instant hit with their first single – "Be-Bop-A-Lula". Another newcomer with impressive vitality and flamboyance was the pianist Little Richard, who helped himself to a string of seminal rock'n'roll hits ("Tutti-Frutti", "Rip It Up", "Good Golly Miss Molly").

Below Gene Vincent whose vibrant "Be-Bop-A-Lula" (1956) made him a star in Britain. On stage, Vincent exaggerated his limp — the result of a bike smash.

ROCK'N'ROLL COUNTDOWN

In its earliest days, rock'n'roll was too diverse a music to sustain trends in the modern sense. Performers were springing up all over the United States (there was very little of worth happening in the UK) playing variations on a theme. As well as Presley, Vincent, Haley and Richard, there was the crazed R&B/soul stomp of James Brown, the sweet harmonies of the 'doo-wop' groups, the witty teen anthems of Chuck Berry, the patented guitar shuffle of Bo Diddley and even the limp covers of Pat Boone. Each of these artists tended to work in isolation on what had been very much a regional music scene with little crossover. As we have seen, Bill Haley led the music into the international market, but it was Elvis Presley who defined and even personified rock'n'roll.

Play it again, Sam

Although Presley conjured up much of his own magic, he was assisted greatly in his endeavors by Sam Phillips, who in many ways set the trend for classic rock in his own Sun studio. It was Phillips who made the classic statement: 'If I could find a white man who had the Negro sound and the Negro feel, I could make a billion dollars.' Phillips did just that (although he lost out on the billion dollars) and if Elvis walked into Sun of his own accord, it was Phillips who heard the magic in his voice and eventually suggested he tried singing 'some blues' – and the rest is history.

Yet Phillips repeated the formula many times after Elvis had gone to RCA, proving that he possessed a very fine ear and a studio technique unparalleled in achieving a fresh, live feel. After Presley, Phillips quickly discovered Carl Perkins and the partnership produced an instant rock classic in "Blue Suede Shoes" in 1956. Perkins suffered a crippling accident that kept him out of the public eye for a year and damaged his career irreparably, but Phillips picked up the pieces once more and produced further classic recordings with such new talents as Jerry Lee Lewis ("Whole Lotta Shakin' Goin' On") and Johnny Cash ("I Walk the Line").

Sam Phillips, therefore, was a major influence on the growth of rock'n'roll. He pioneered a studio sound that has stood the test of time and has been re-created many times when rock has been in one of its cyclical pursuits of effective simplicity. He virtually invented the concept of studio mystique, whereby bands fly to all parts of the globe in pursuit of 'that sound'. His name endures.

1956 Diary

January

Elvis Presley makes his national TV debut on *The Dorsey Brothers Show*.

Reaching Number 12, Bill Haley and the Comets' *Rock Around The Clock* LP becomes the first rock'n'roll entry listed in the Top Fifteen Pop Album charts.

February

In the UK best-sellers chart all Top Ten records are American.

In Cleveland, Ohio, police invoke an ordinance from 1931 banning people under 18 years of age from dancing in public, unless accompanied by an adult.

Carl Perkins' "Blue Suede Shoes" and Bill Haley's "See You Later Alligator" enter the US pop charts.

March

Colonel Tom Parker (of 'Colonel Tom Parker and his Dancing Turkeys circus troupe' fame) becomes Elvis Presley's manager.

Eleven teenagers are arrested and the venue's license is revoked during Alan Freed's three-day rock'n'roll show at the Stage Theater in Hartford, Connecticut. At license hearings, psychiatrist Dr Francis J Braceland testifies that rock'n'roll is 'a communicable disease . . . tribalistic and cannibalistic'.

Asa Carter, executive secretary of the North Alabama White Citizens Council, blames the NAACP for introducing rock'n'roll to white teenagers and launches a campaign to pressure radio stations into banning the 'immoral' music.

April

Elvis Presley earns $5000 for one appearance on *The Milton Berle Show*. However, he is less popular at his Las Vegas debut – his scheduled two-week run is cancelled after just one week owing to poor attendances.

CBS Radio premieres the first national rock'n'roll show, *Rock'n'Roll Dance Party*, hosted by Alan Freed. One week later, ABC airs its *Rhythm On Parade*.

Paramount signs up Elvis Presley for a three-film contract.

May

Both Carl Perkins' "Blue Suede Shoes" and Elvis Presley's "Heartbreak Hotel" appear in the US Top Tens for pop, R&B, and country and western simultaneously.

In an article entitled 'Teenagers' Hero', *Time* magazine explains the secret of Elvis Presley's appeal: 'His movements suggest, in a word, sex.'

An unidentified disc jockey coins the nickname 'Elvis the Pelvis'.

June

Gene Vincent's "Be-Bop-A-Lula" is released by Capitol Records, who originally noticed the singer when he won first prize in a Los Angeles talent contest.

The Biggest Rock'n'Roll Show of 1956, which includes performances by Bill Haley, the Platters and Clyde McPhatter, is the target of bomb scares, threats and insults when it tours in the American South.

Sales of Elvis Presley records average 50 000 a day, accounting for more than half of RCA Victor's turnover.

July

A press report announces that rock'n'roll music is banned in Asbury Park, New Jersey, where it is assumed to be responsible for June's riots.

Elvis fans are disappointed when he appears on *The Steve Allen Show* and Allen forbids Presley to dance, arranging for him to croon "Hound Dog" to a real basset hound instead. The following day NBC is picketed by crowds of teenagers, whose signs proclaim: 'We want the real Elvis.'

Ed Sullivan, who previously had vowed never to have Elvis Presley on his show, signs up the singer for three guest appearances.

August

The Five Satins release "In the Still of the Night"; it will go on to sell over 15 million copies.

Frankie Lymon & the Teenagers and Fats Domino are among the featured acts at Alan Freed's *Second Annual Rock'n'Roll Show* at Brooklyn's Paramount Theater.

Washington, DC, disc jockey Bob Rickman forms the Society for the Prevention of Cruelty to Elvis.

September

As predicted by the national press, violence breaks out at British cinemas where Bill Haley's film *Rock Around the Clock* is showing; local committees ban the film in some areas. Meanwhile, Haley has five hits in the UK Top Thirty.

Elvis Presley buys his mother a pink Cadillac.

Fats Domino's "Blueberry Hill" enters the pop charts. The singer/pianist will eventually sell over 65 million records and earn 15 gold discs.

October

With 856 327 advance orders, Elvis Presley's "Love Me Tender" becomes the first record ever to enter the US charts at Number 2.

20th Century-Fox announces plans for a new rock'n'roll movie – *Do Re Mi*, starring Fats Domino and Little Richard.

The first British rock'n'roll star, ex-bellboy Tommy Steele, enters the British charts with his first hit "Rock with the Caveman".

November

Elvis Presley's debut film, *Love Me Tender*, opens in New York.

Band leader Tommy Dorsey is found dead, the result of an accident, in his Connecticut home.

Johnny Cash enters the US charts with "I Walk the Line", released on Sun Records.

December

Shake, Rattle and Roll, a film featuring Fats Domino, goes on release.

Mickey and Sylvia make their chart debut with "Love Is Strange". It will be their biggest hit as a duo (reaching Number 13), but Sylvia Robinson will return to the charts in 1973 with the Top Ten hit "Pillow Talk".

Four Sun Records stars, Elvis Presley, Carl Perkins, Jerry Lee Lewis and Johnny Cash, record an impromptu session together; it will not be released until 1981.

Far left Bill Haley (second left) and the Comets. With his jaunty rocking anthems, like "Rock Around the Clock" (1955) and "See You Later Alligator" (1955), and his impish kiss-curl, Haley introduced many white audiences to the sound of rock'n'roll for the first time. **Center** Gene Vincent and the Blue Caps performing in the 1956 rock movie *The Girl Can't Help It* which starred Jayne Mansfield and Tom Ewell. The film also featured a typically energetic performance from Little Richard *(left)* whose whooping vocal style was to be a primary influence on the young Paul McCartney.

Long Live the King

1957

By 1957, the fiery flame of the new rock was already being tempered by sophistication. Elvis Presley dominated the singles charts in the United States with a series of tracks that were appreciably smoother than the material he had cut at Sun. Big business had already claimed 'the King', and his career was a carefully ordered series of average to appalling films, by which he got massive exposure and sold truckloads of records without having to go on tour. The Colonel Tom Parker recipe for success was undeniably effective and destructive to his protégé's talent: by denying him a live audience to whip up into a frenzy, Parker killed off much of the creative nervous tension that fueled Elvis' greatness. Nevertheless, in 1957 Elvis still had plenty in reserve: "All Shook Up", "Teddy Bear" and "Jailhouse Rock" were powerful performances. But they weren't dangerous. That was left to a newcomer: Jerry Lee Lewis.

The Killer

Presley's success had spawned a thousand imitators, a few of whom pressed a genuine claim to fame, while the rest made up the numbers for a short time. Jerry Lee Lewis fitted into neither of these categories, nor indeed into any other. He was rock's first genuine wild man (with the possible exception of Screamin' Jay Hawkins and his coffin routine) and he is certainly the one who has lasted longest.

Lewis played professionally from the age of 15, soaking up elements of country swing, R&B and piano boogie. He headed for Sam Phillips and demanded to be heard. He was heard, and his second visit to the studio produced "Whole Lotta Shakin'", a classic piano-led stomper with lyrics that were, at the very least, suggestive. Lewis' career was seriously damaged in 1958, however, when it was discovered that he had married his 14-year-old (third) cousin. It was perhaps fortunate for 'the King' that 'the Killer' suffered this untimely demise, otherwise it could have meant the end of Elvis' reign.

Below **Frankie Lymon and the Teenagers. Lymon's sweat'n'squeaky flutings brought the sound of doo-wop music to a wider audience on both sides of the Atlantic through hits such as "Why Do Fools Fall In Love?" (1956). The Teenagers broke up in 1957 and Lymon died of a drug overdose a decade later.**

Buddy boy

The two other most promising newcomers of 1957 both displayed a more sophisticated approach to songwriting that signaled the transformation of the wild energy of rock'n'roll into the sweeter melodies of pop music. Buddy Holly, from Lubbock in Texas, had a clear vision of the sound he wanted, and traveled to Norman Petty's small studio in New Mexico to get it with his group, the Crickets. The first release from the ensuing session was "That'll Be the Day", which went into the top five on both sides of the Atlantic.

From the start, Holly presented a more vulnerable persona than his contemporaries, epitomized by his unflattering horn-rimmed spectacles, and his songs were mainly quests for the true and everlasting love, rather than celebrations of youthful sexuality. "Peggy Sue", "Rave On" and "It Doesn't Matter Anymore" followed that first hit in rapid succession, and when one considers both the size and the quality of his songbook (not to mention his influence on the Beatles alone) it is all the more astonishing, as well as saddening, that he died at the age of 22.

Brotherly love

The second newcomers of 1957 were also concerned with true love and all its trials and tribulations. Don and Phil Everly were born into a family of respected country singers and looked set to continue the tradition when they signed for the Cadence label (also the home of rising pop star Andy Williams) in 1957. However, the aspiring duo met Boudleaux Bryant, a veteran country and western songwriter who was peddling a tune called "Bye Bye Love", which had already been turned down by a number of other acts. The Everly Brothers snapped it up and it gave them a Number 2 hit record.

Bryant went on to write many of the Everlys' early hits, all of which laid the accent on melody so that the brothers' exquisite and instinctive two-part harmonies could come into their own. The Everlys went on to a five-year run of hits before dissolving in acrimony (later to reform), but most of the great sixties bands did not forget them.

The Everly Brothers. Genuine blood brothers from Kentucky, Don (right) and Phil (left) had been brought up in show business, singing on their parents' country and western radio show in the forties. The perfection of their voices fused on record was not always managed in real life: they parted acrimoniously and had a less than satisfactory reunion in the eighties.

DOO-WOP DELIGHT

A style of music flourished in the years between the middle and late fifties that at the time had no name and, with the exception of a handful of acts, threw up no household names. The music has come to be called doo-wop because that was one of the phrases the backing singers would fall back on. It could have been called almost anything. Doo-wop was basically the preserve of black vocal harmony groups and its roots went back to much earlier in the century.

Disc jockey Alan Freed was the man responsible for the wider success of the genre, which by the mid fifties had responded to the changing times by incorporating hefty R&B backing sounds and more vigorous soul/gospel inflected vocals. The scene abounded with one-hit wonders with records by such groups as the Orioles, the Crows and the Penguins Frankie Lymon & the Teenagers came close to longevity with a string of hits including "Why Do Fools Fall in Love?" and "I'm Not a Juvenile Delinquent", but they are chiefly remembered because Frankie's sweet soprano peaked at the age of 13 and because he died tragically young in 1968, aged 25.

. . . don't talk back

The two big names on the scene were the Platters and the Coasters. The Platters were the brainchild of Buck Ram, a veteran of doo-wop who had previously worked with the legendary Ink Spots. Under Ram's guidance and usually working with material he had composed, the Platters enjoyed consistent hits throughout the late fifties with songs such as "Only You", "My Prayer" and "The Great Pretender", the last of which was the first doo-wop record to make the top of the pop charts.

The Coasters were a much tougher outfit from the West Coast, who had the great good fortune to have Jerry Leiber and Mike Stoller as their writers/producers. The combination turned out a series of singles in the late fifties – "Searchin'", "Yakety Yak" and "Charlie Brown" – which combined great vocals, neat tunes and beautifully observed lyrics.

The doo-wop strain eventually died out around 1963-4, but not before it had mutated into something very like soul music, which is another story.

Buddy Holly and the Crickets (Joe Mauldin, bass, and Jerry Allison, drums). With his horn-rimmed spectacles and boy-next-door looks, Holly provided the perfect antidote to the pure, snarling sex symbol that was embodied by Elvis Presley, Gene Vincent and other contemporaries. His chirpily palatable version of rock'n'roll, typified by numbers like "Peggy Sue" (1957) and "It Doesn't Matter Anymore" (1959), lit up the airwaves. It was not until his death in a plane crash at the age of 22 that his name became known to all.

Diary

January

Warner Brothers release their *Rock, Rock, Rock* movie starring La Vern Baker and Chuck Berry.

On *The Steve Allen Show* ex-fight champ Joe Louis introduces singer Solomon Burke, who performs Louis' composition "You Can Run But You Can't Hide".

Elvis Presley takes the US Army pre-induction exam – and passes.

The Cavern Club, later to become the home-base for the Beatles, opens in a cellar in Liverpool, England.

February

Bill Haley and the Comets arrive at Southampton, England, by boat and board a chartered train to London's Waterloo Station, where they are greeted by 4000 cheering fans.

The Coasters record "Young Blood", written and produced by Jerry Leiber and Mike Stoller.

Columbia's *Don't Knock the Rock* movie premieres in New York. The film, which debates the 'ethics' of rock'n'roll, features Little Richard, Bill Haley, the Platters, Fats Domino, Gene Vincent and Alan Freed.

March

Chess Records of Chicago release Muddy Waters' "I Got My Mojo Workin" and Chuck Berry's "School Days".

Samuel Cardinal Stitch, head of the Catholic Archdiocese of Chicago, bans rock'n'roll from all Catholic schools and 'recreations' in his district, on the grounds that it provides 'encouragement to behave in a hedonistic manner'.

Mass hysteria occurs at *The Alan Freed Show* at the Paramount Theater, New York, featuring the Platters and Frankie Lymon & the Teenagers. Eleven teenagers are rushed to hospital.

Right Vocal harmony group the Platters, featuring the lustrous tones of Zola Taylor. The Platters produced a succession of elegant hits, including "The Great Pretender" (1956), but they are best remembered for their appearances in films like *Rock Around the Clock*.

Opposite, top Jerry Lee Lewis thumps his piano in a scene from the 1958 rock movie *High School Confidential*. Jerry Lee's extravagant lifestyle and behavior, along with his extraordinary keyboard technique (he would play with elbows, feet and any other part of the anatomy), earned him a reputation as the wild man of rock.

Opposite, bottom The Coasters, who introduced humor into pop music.

April

Singer Andy Williams enters the US charts with "Butterfly".

Sixteen-year-old Ricky Nelson's first record, "Teenager's Romance", is released. Already well known in America from his appearances on his parents' TV show, *The Adventures of Ozzy and Harriet,* Nelson will sell 60 000 copies of the song within three days.

May

Alan Freed premieres his half-hour television program, *The Alan Freed Show*, on ABC-TV.

Buddy Holly and the Crickets' first record, "That'll Be The Day", is released.

Four British skiffle groups have songs in the UK Top Twenty, led by Lonnie Donegan's "Cumberland Gap". In Liverpool, 16-year-old John Lennon leads skiffle band the Quarrymen.

"Love Letters in the Sand" by Pat Boone enters the US charts.

John Beverly, alias Sid Vicious, born 10 May.

June

Teen-age Records release "Angels Cried"/"The Cow Jumped Over the Moon", first single by the Isley Brothers. The record proves to be a total failure.

Jerry Lee Lewis has his first chart success with "Whole Lotta Shakin' Goin' On", which was recorded in one impromptu take at Sun Studios.

Paul Anka enters the US charts with his own composition "Diana".

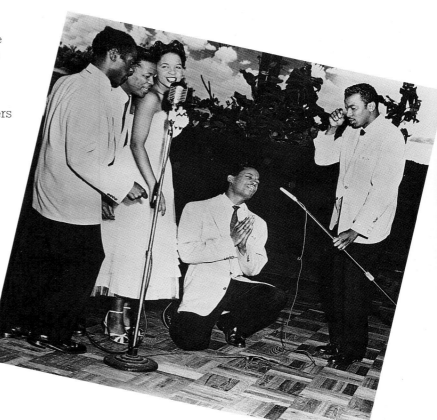

July

John Lennon, 16, meets 14-year-old Paul McCartney at a Liverpool church picnic, where John's band the Quarrymen are playing.

The Bobbettes' first release, "Mr Lee", enters the US pop charts. The song, about their high school principal, will be the trio's only Top Forty hit. Three years and several flops later, they will record a follow-up with the title, "I Shot Mr Lee".

Fourteen-year-old Jim Morrison, future lead singer with the Doors, quits Albuquerque public school.

August

Frankie Lymon quits the Teenagers.

The Everly Brothers play their forthcoming release, "Wake Up Little Susie", on *The Ed Sullivan Show*.

American Bandstand makes its national debut on ABC-TV. It started as a local hit-parade show in Philadelphia, hosted by Dick Clark, in 1956.

September

CBS-TV premieres *The Big Record*, a record-hop style show, hosted by Patti Page.

Colonel Tom Parker demands $60 000 for one appearance by Elvis Presley on *The Dean Martin Show*. The offer is declined.

October

After a concert in Sydney, Australia, Little Richard announces that he is giving up rock'n'roll. His reason: 'If you want to live for the Lord, you can't rock'n'roll, too. God doesn't like it.'

Sam Cooke has his first US hit when "You Send Me" enters the pop charts.

Buddy Holly, aged 21, celebrates one million sales of "That'll Be the Day".

November

Jerry Lee Lewis' "Great Balls of Fire" is released.

Jamboree premieres in Hollywood. The film features Jerry Lee Lewis, Fats Domino, Connie Francis and Frankie Avalon.

Elvis Presley announces that he won't work outside the United States.

December

Elvis' Christmas Album is released and immediately sparks controversy over the propriety of a rock'n'roll star singing religious songs. The record is banned by many radio stations.

"The Stroll" by the Diamonds is released and starts a fad for the dance of that name.

Donny Osmond born 9 December, in Ogden, Utah.

Rebel Rousers

1958

When all is said and done, 1958 was not a great year for rock'n'roll. It was, of course, the year that Elvis Presley started his army service. It was also the year that Jerry Lee Lewis, the most potent and original of the young pretenders, made a bride of his young cousin and laid himself open to attacks from the righteous-minded, effectively demolishing his mainstream career. Later the next year, Chuck Berry suffered a similar fate and actually spent two years in jail. Little Richard's rich vein of hits was about to dry up as he turned to religion. It seemed that the moral majority had finally instituted a backlash against this new kind of music.

Just like Eddie
So what new talent came rushing forward to fill the void? At the tougher end of the rock'n'roll spectrum, two new figures emerged. The first was Eddie Cochran, who achieved international fame in 1958 with his single "Summertime Blues". Cochran's was to be a tragically brief career, but of the handful of records he put out, several have become rock standards, covered by a multitude of artists. The second newcomer was Duane Eddy, one of the earliest guitar heroes. Eddy's trademark was the 'twanging' guitar, seemingly based on a couple of slack bass strings, which thrilled a wide audience for some years – the 1958 favorite was "Rebel Rouser" – before the inflexibility of the formula led to an inevitable decline in popularity.

Teen dream idols
The signs that appearance was considered increasingly more important than content were confirmed in 1958 by the arrival of several good-looking young men with little discernible talent. Foremost among these were ex-child TV star Ricky Nelson, Fabian and Frankie Avalon. Bobby Darin made a promising start, including the perky "Queen Of The Hop", but he swiftly mellowed his approach and diluted his talents in search of a wider audience. Finally, the year was notable for the appearance of a record by Link Wray – "Rumble" – in which one can hear the first stirrings of heavy rock.

ROCKABILLY REBELS

From the time that Elvis Presley burst on to a disbelieving audience, until the end of the decade, the most important and fiendishly alive white rock'n'roll was called rockabilly. As the name implies, it was a fusion of rock'n'roll, as practised by Bill Haley, and the hillbilly sounds of the Southern states, as popularized at Nashville's Grand Ole Opry. As Presley proved in his original Sun recordings, it was a music of awesome energy, despite the fact that it was initially drumless. Presley's matchless voice was accompanied only by his own rhythm guitar, Scotty Moore's lively lead runs and Bill Black's upright bass figures. The only added ingredient was the echo that was deliberately encouraged by the use of studios with bathroom acoustics.

The first wild men
Rockabilly was a spontaneous explosion of youthful energy, a celebration of a new status that was deliberately couched in terms no adult could hope to understand. Mick Jagger at his most vocally opaque never sounded as crazed or indecipherable as Gene Vincent on "Be-Bop-a-Lula". Even Roy Orbison, best remembered for his yearning pop gems of the sixties, started life as an angry young man in Sam Phillips' studio, cutting the likes of "Ooby Dooby". When the punk revolution started turning over rocks in the mid seventies, what should crawl out but a rockabilly revival, inspired on the one hand by new groups such as the Cramps and on the other by original artists who had never gone away, like Ray Campi and Sleepy La Beef.

Right **For many devotees, Eddie Cochran was the personification of pure rock'n'roll. His spirited singing and frenetic guitar created classics like "Summertime Blues" (1958) and "C'mon Everybody". He died in a car crash aged just 21.**

1958 *Diary*

January

New US chart entries include Frankie Avalon's "De De Dinah", and Paul Anka's "You Are My Destiny".

Gibson patents its 'Flying V' electric guitar, which will become a favorite among posturing rock guitarists.

St Louis radio station KWKS stages its *Record Breaking Week*, in which every rock'n'roll record in their library is played for a 'farewell spin' before being smashed to pieces on-mike.

Danny and the Juniors' "At the Hop" reaches Number 1 in the American pop charts.

February

The American Research Bureau reports that *American Bandstand* is currently the top-ranked daytime TV show, drawing an average of 8 400 000 viewers a day.

"Book of Love" by the Monotones is released. The song, based on a Pepsodent toothpaste TV commercial, will reach the top five in the US charts.

The government of Iran bans rock'n'roll music on the grounds of its being against the concepts of Islam, and because rock'n'roll dancing is injurious to the hips.

The Dick Clark Show, a Saturday night rock'n'roll program, premieres on ABC-TV. Guests include Jerry Lee Lewis, Pat Boone and Connie Francis.

March

Big Records release "Our Song", the first record by teenage duo Tom and Jerry – alias Paul Simon and Art Garfunkel.

Gary Numan born 8 March, in London.

Elvis Presley reports for duty in the US Army.

April

Lawrie Records release "I Wonder Why"/"Teen Angel", the first record by New York band Dion and the Belmonts, named after Belmont Avenue in the Bronx.

Carole King's first record, "The Right Girl", is released.

A wax model of British rock'n'roller Tommy Steele is unveiled at Madame Tussauds in London.

May

Teenagers allegedly attack police with stones and bottles outside the Boston Arena following an Alan Freed rock'n'roll show. Although no arrests are made, the police add charges of rape, narcotics possession and stabbings to their allegations, and blame Freed's on-stage remark, 'the police don't want you to have any fun here', for the incident. Freed is later indicted for inciting unlawful destruction.

Jerry Lee Lewis arrives in Britain for a 37-date tour, accompanied by his 14-year-old bride Myra. Against his manager's advice, he reveals all the facts about his marriage when questioned by the press. The British public is outraged, and four days later London's *Evening Star* newspaper calls for his immediate deportation. That night, at his third concert, he is booed from the stage. He returns to America the following day.

Because They're Young.
Duane Eddy provided the film's title music that became a world-wide instrumental hit.

June

Jerry Lee Lewis takes out a full-page ad in *Billboard* and, in an open letter, explains the circumstances of his second divorce and third marriage. He finishes by expressing his hope that his public will not turn against him because of a hostile press.

British pop music show *Oh Boy!* airs on television for the first time.

While on tour in Italy, the Platters are granted an audience with Pope Pius XII, who gives each member of the band a gold medal.

July

Alan Freed's *The Big Beat* premieres on ABC-TV. Chuck Berry is among the first guests.

Billboard reports on new findings by the Esso Gas Research Center, which claim that listening to rock'n'roll on a car radio can cost motorists money; the rhythm causes the driver to jiggle the gas pedal, thus wasting fuel.

At Number 1 in the US charts is the Coasters' hit record "Yakety Yak".

August

Buddy Holly meets Maria Elena Santiago and the couple are married in Lubbock, Texas, two weeks after they meet.

Billboard inaugurates its Hot 100 record chart.

George Harrison joins the Quarrymen, fronted by John Lennon, at a gig at Liverpool's Casbah Club.

September

Elvis Presley leaves for Germany where he is to join his army unit.

New US pop chart entries include: Fabian's "Got the Feeling", Bo Diddley's "Say Man", and the Isley Brothers' "Shout".

The Teddy Bears' "To Know Him is to Love Him" is released. The song was composed by 18-year-old Phil Spector, who took the title from the inscription on his father's tombstone.

October

Billboard reports that 'payola' – bribes to disc jockeys by record companies – is already a wide-spread practice and growing rapidly.

James Brown's "Try Me" is released.

November

Hank Ballard and the Midnighters record the original "The Twist" in King Studios, Cincinnati.

Cliff Richard and the Drifters make their variety stage debut.

The cha-cha is hailed as the latest dance craze.

December

Billboard's year-end survey of 1958 lists the top-selling single as Domenico Modugno's "Volare", and the original cast album of *My Fair Lady* as best-selling LP.

Last year's Christmas hit, Bobby Helms' "Jingle Bell Rock", reappears in the charts. It will do so again at Christmas in 1960, 1961 and 1962.

Alan Freed's *Christmas Rock'n'Roll Spectacular* opens in New York. Seventeen acts will perform during the show's ten-day run, including Chuck Berry, Frankie Avalon and Bo Diddley; headlining on the last five nights are the Everly Brothers.

BBC-TV's new pop program, *Dig This*, premieres. It will be taken off the air within three months.

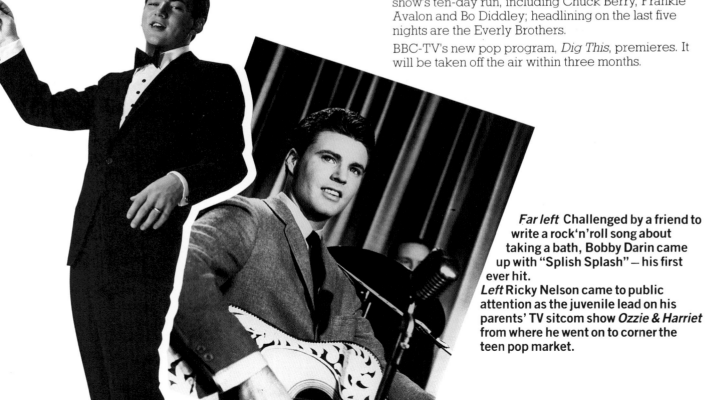

Far left Challenged by a friend to write a rock'n'roll song about taking a bath, Bobby Darin came up with "Splish Splash" — his first ever hit.
Left Ricky Nelson came to public attention as the juvenile lead on his parents' TV sitcom show *Ozzie & Harriet* from where he went on to corner the teen pop market.

Teen Dream

If 1958 had been a less than satisfactory year for rock'n'roll, the following year threatened to be worse. At the beginning of February, Buddy Holly, Ritchie Valens and the Big Bopper were killed in a plane crash, and at the end of the year a huge payola (the offering of bribes and inducements to disc jockeys) scandal rocked the music scene and in particular Alan Freed, one of rock's most vociferous and important champions, who was hounded off the airwaves. It was also the year when the various major record companies re-asserted themselves, having temporarily lost control of a wildly evolving new music scene to thrusting independents. The raw energy that had characterized rock'n'roll was tamed and packaged by an industry decreeing that if the new sounds were a fad, then they should be a lucrative one.

High school graduates

Yet it was impossible that a phenomenon that had fired the imagination of the young to such an extent could fail to throw up interesting newcomers. Two such were Jan Berry and Dean Torrance, better known as Jan and Dean. The two had played in groups together throughout their schooldays and decided to carry on when they left. After an erratic early career, which included Dean doing national service (it was not confined to Presley, despite indications to the contrary) and a strange Top Ten hit called "Jennie Lee", which was credited to Jan and Arnie, Jan and Dean finally hit their stride with "Baby Talk" and went on to chronicle the speed and sun of Californian life in a way that pre-dated and influenced the Beach Boys. "Dead Man's Curve" was their best song.

Right The Crossfires were just one of a mass of surfing instrumental combos playing around the LA club area in the early sixties. Later on, they changed their name to the Turtles with enormously successful results.
Center With songs like "Who's Sorry Now?" (1958), Connie Francis captured the heart of a generation and sold more records than any other female artist in pop history.
Far right Surfing flatheads, Jan and Dean, set the aspirations of young California to music.

Johnny be good?

Another vastly entertaining outfit to come to prominence in 1959 was Johnny and the Hurricanes from Toledo, Ohio. Johnny Paris specialized in a dirty tenor sax sound, which was well complemented by guitar and organ on a number of chart smashes of uncommon virility – "Crossfire", "Red River Rock", "Beatnik Fly". It could never be claimed that Johnny and his merry men were an innovative force in rock'n'roll since most of their tunes were based on old standards, but the energy they brought to the job in hand was commendable. Furthermore, when last heard of, Johnny Paris was still belting it out to live audiences, waiting for his time to come again.

Bachelor boys

In the UK, there was at last a stirring of activity. Cliff Richard had produced a rock'n'roll record of some merit in "Move It" and he ended the year in some style with a pair of chart toppers – "Living Doll" and "Travellin' Light". Other contenders included Marty Wilde, Adam Faith and Billy Fury, the last of whom showed real promise until ill-health began to retard his career.

DREAM DATES

As a result of the record companies' decision to clean up the sound and the image of rock'n'roll, the years around the turn of the decade became synonymous with the heyday of the teen idol. Joining the already well-established figures of Ricky Nelson, Fabian and Frankie Avalon, were Bobby Rydell, Paul Anka (who at least wrote his own songs) and a host of pretty/handsome faces from the film colony and California. Foremost among this latter group was Annette Funicello, star of a slew of inane 'beach party' movies and wobbly singer of their accompanying songs. She recorded for Walt Disney's record label and it certainly sounded like it.

Flying Vee

The most successful of this new breed of movie pop star, apart from Ricky Nelson who was at least shored up by James Burton's guitar playing, was Bobby Vee, a Buddy Holly sound-alike with none of that singer's innate qualities. The female examples of this genre are not so well remembered, but honorable mentions go to Connie Francis, who remained the top girl vocalist in the United States for some years, and Brenda Lee, an ex-country singer who had a run of hits.

1959 Diary

January

Coral Records releases what will be Buddy Holly's last record before his death, "It Doesn't Matter Anymore"/"Rainin' In My Heart".

The Kingston Trio receive their first gold disc for "Tom Dooley".

The Chipmunks' novelty record, "Chipmunk Song", tops the US pop charts.

February

Buddy Holly, Ritchie Valens and the Big Bopper are killed when their tour plane crashes in Clear Lake, Iowa. That night the show goes on with the Crickets and Dion and the Belmonts performing. Fabian and Paul Anka will finish off the tour as headliners.

Private Elvis Presley makes an unscheduled singing appearance at Paris night club, the Lido.

Coral Records brings out a Buddy Holly memorial album, *The Buddy Holly Story*.

March

Ian McCulloch (Echo and the Bunnymen) born 5 March, in Liverpool.

Elvis Presley's "I Need Your Love Tonight"/"A Fool Such as I" is released by RCA Records. Advance orders are in excess of one million, and a gold record is shipped to Elvis in Germany, where he is stationed.

The re-formed Drifters' "There Goes My Baby" is released. It is the group's first record with new lead singer Ben E. King, replacement for Clyde McPhatter.

April

"Puppy Love", the first record by 13-year-old Dolly Parton, is released. *Billboard's* review comments: 'She sounds about 12 years old.'

Your Hit Parade, a pop music show that has been running since April 1935 (on radio, then later on TV), is broadcast for the last time.

May

Chubby Checker has his first US chart entry with his record "The Class".

Ray Charles, B B King, and the Drifters headline at one of rock's first outdoor festivals, in Atlanta, Georgia.

Far left With songs like "Diana" (1957), Paul Anka appealed to all teenagers going through the agonies of adolescence. Unlike many of his teen dream contemporaries, Anka possessed enduring talent.

Left Annette Funicello was the very epitome of American girlhood and her performances in paper-thin films such as *Muscle Beach Party* captured the 'sun'n'fun mood of the times.

June

New Hot 100 entries include: the Flamingoes' "I Only Have Eyes For You", Sam Cooke's "Only Sixteen" and the Drifters' "There Goes My Baby".

Bob Zimmerman graduates from Hibbing High School, Hibbing, Minnesota. In September he will enter the University of Minnesota and begin performing in campus coffee houses under the name Bob Dylan.

July

Billie Holiday, 44, dies from a liver ailment in a New York City hospital shortly after being arrested for a small quantity of heroin.

New chart entries in the United States are the Eternals' "Rockin' in the Jungle" and the Shirelles' "Dedicated to the One I Love".

August

All four male members of singing quintet the Platters are arrested in a Cincinatti hotel and charged with aiding and abetting prostitution; the four young women found with them are charged with prostitution. In December all eight will be acquitted.

Bobby Darin signs a six-year film contract with Paramount.

Chuck Berry is arrested and charged with violation of the Mann Act – the transportation of a minor across a state line for immoral purposes.

Left His army service behind him, Elvis Presley was steered by manager "Colonel" Tom Parker away from live performances into cheap budget movies.
Above Britain's first rock'n'roller Tommy Steele later switched to a middle-of-the-road career in musicals.

Above Cliff Richard in the film *Expresso Bongo* (1959). Though he played a surly, lip-curling rebel in this movie, Cliff's later image became progressively more wholesome.

September

Bobby Darin hit "Mack the Knife" is banned by CBS Radio in New York, after two teenagers are stabbed to death by a 17-year-old.

Frankie Avalon, Annette Funicello, Freddie Cannon, the Coasters, Duane Eddy, Jan and Dean and Bobby Rydell are the featured acts at Dick Clark's Michigan State Fair stage show.

October

Neil Sedaka's "Oh, Carol" enters the US pop charts. The song was written by him for colleague Carole King.

Tommy Fecenda's novelty record, "High School USA" enters the charts. Dozens of different versions are released, mentioning different high schools for different cities and states.

Well-bred English singing star Petula Clark flies to Paris to star in a French TV show scheduled to be broadcast in the New Year.

November

During a government investigation into the record company practice 'payola', Alan Freed refuses to sign an affidavit stating that he never accepted payola, or bribes. Within a week he will be fired by WABC Radio, ABC-TV and WNEW-TV.

Liverpool group the Quarrymen disband and then re-form as the Silver Beatles.

December

Gene Vincent, neatly dressed in suit and tie, arrives at London's Heathrow Airport to appear on Jack Good's *Boy Meets Girl* TV show. Good, at the airport to meet him, quickly hustles the singer into a black leather jacket and silver medallion before any of his fans can see him. He also insists that Vincent exaggerate his limp while walking past his fans.

Elvis Presley's former bass guitarist, Bill Black, has his first chart success with "Smokie-Part 2".

Year of the Twist

1960

It can fairly be said that 1960 was the year of the Twist. The original twist merchant was Chubby Checker, who seized his chance for fame when asked to perform the song at short notice on Dick Clark's all-powerful *American Bandstand*. The twist craze swept the United States, and any songs that promised to cater for its not-too-difficult steps were virtually guaranteed success in the charts. Sam Cooke made a very good twist record in "Twisting the Night Away", as did the Isley Brothers with "Twist and Shout". The rest were mainly of variable quality, ranging from the bad to the truly awful, with the honorable exception of Gary US Bonds' ("Twist-Twist Senora" and "Dear Lady Twist").

Raunch'n'roll

Somewhat more exciting and certainly longer-lasting was the impact of Ike and Tina Turner, who scored their first chart success in 1960 with "A Fool in Love". Ike Turner had a blues pedigree stretching back to the fifties, and the combination of his instrumental and arranging prowess with his wife's raunchy vocals and even raunchier stage antics was powerful enough to keep them afloat through several changes of fashion. On a somewhat different emotional plane, Roy Orbison shot to fame on the back of a series of singles whose romantic pessimism has seldom, if ever, been surpassed. "It's Over" probably marks the height of his inner torture.

Apart from the newcomers, the year was a good one for Elvis Presley, who racked up three Number 1 hits throughout the year, the Everly Brothers and the evergreen Drifters. Bryan Hyland had a smash hit with "Itsy Bitsy Teenie Weenie Yellow Polka Dot Bikini" and actually survived the experience, going on to other hits in later years.

Apache rising

It was a much better year for rock'n'roll in the UK. As a result of being picked up as Cliff Richard's backing band for a UK tour, the Shadows gained themselves a shot at the big time, which they seized with alacrity. The focal point of the group was uncompromisingly bespectacled Hank B Marvin, a most unlikely guitar hero who was probably responsible for the sales of more cheap and garish guitars (with tremolo arm, of course) than anybody in rock, before or since. The rapid rise of the Shadows with their toe-tapping instrumentals was confirmed when "Apache" pitched its tent at the top of the UK charts in the summer of 1960.

The other major UK success of the year was Fred Heath, who wisely changed his name to Johnny Kidd and, with his excellent group the Pirates, produced a most satisfying slice of teen angst in "Shaking All Over". It proved to be his finest hour, but it was one to relish.

Far left Neil Sedaka. A classically-trained pianist, Sedaka soon made a name for himself as a composer of pop melodies such as "Stupid Cupid", a hit for Connie Francis in 1958.
Left Ike and Tina Turner began their recording career in the late fifties but it was not until "Proud Mary" (1971), that they enjoyed their first US Top Ten hit.
Below Chubby Checker — real name Ernest Evans — pioneered the free-style, partnerless dance craze, the Twist, with a series of identical-sounding hits.

BRILL CREAM

When the record companies started packaging teen idols for mass public consumption, they were able to provide their svelte young men and women with everything – except songs to sing. With the exception of those such as Paul Anka who were capable of writing their own material, the vast majority of this new breed of star could no sooner write a song than a symphony. Therefore a demand was created for an almost limitless supply of pop songs to keep the production lines rolling. Fortunately for both artists and listeners, a large part of this demand was met by an extraordinary assembly of talent contained within the famous Brill Building on New York's Broadway.

Pop factory

The Brill Building was, in effect, a superior battery farm where songs were hatched at an alarming rate by teams of writers shut away in small dark rooms. The astonishing fact about all this was that the teams comprised some of the best pop composers of all time, many of whom later made it to household-name status. The prime movers behind the Brill Building phenomenon were Don Kirshner and Al Nevins, whose company, Aldon Music, was set up specifically to plug the song gap. Among the early crop of songwriters unearthed by Aldon were such names as Carole King, Gerry Goffin, Neil Diamond, Neil Sedaka, Cynthia Weil and Barry Mann. In as much as songwriting can ever be a nine-to-five job, it was in the Brill Building, with the participants working usually in pairs, hunched over pianos tossing around melodic and lyric ideas until a complete song came together.

The resulting songs fueled the careers of groups from the Drifters to the Shirelles, of artists from Bobby Vee to Little Eva. Apart from the Aldon teams, there were other denizens of the building of equal talent, including Burt Bacharach and Hal David (early hitmakers for Dionne Warwick and Gene Pitney) and the group of writers gathered round the legendary Leiber and Stoller. It was only after the shattering impact of the Beatles that it became fashionable, if not *de rigueur*, for pop stars to write their own material. It was to the lasting credit of Kirshner and his ilk that what filled the early sixties gap was of such consistent, sometimes transcendent, quality.

1960 Diary

January

Elvis Presley is promoted to the rank of sergeant.

Despite injuries from a recent car crash, bass guitarist Jet Harris flies with his fellow Shadows to America to support Cliff Richard on his US tour. Cliff will be congratulated by Elvis' manager, Colonel Tom Parker, after one of the shows.

February

Fabian takes acting lessons in preparation for his new career as a movie star.

Jesse Belvin, R&B singer/songwriter, dies in a car crash in Los Angeles, aged 20. A successful solo artist, as well as a member of various doo-wop groups, he also co-wrote the Penguins' hit "Earth Angel".

Pat Boone receives a gold LP for *Pat Boone's Great Hits*, which includes the singles "Love Letters in the Sand" and "April Love".

March

Elvis Presley is released from the army. He makes his first and only visit to Britain when he signs autographs at Prestwick Airport while waiting to change planes for his return home to the United States.

The Everly Brothers' "Cathy's Clown" enters the Hot 100; it will eventually reach Number 1.

Adam Faith tops the UK charts with "Poor Me".

April

Elvis Presley's first post-army release, "Stuck on You", enters the US charts.

Eddie Cochran is killed in a car crash in Wiltshire, England. Fellow passenger Gene Vincent also suffers serious injuries.

The National Association of Record Merchandisers presents its first annual awards night in Las Vegas. Elvis is named as best-selling male artist and Connie Francis is top-selling female.

Elvis Presley's film *GI Blues* is released.

Left Elvis Presley strums a South Seas love song in a scene from *Blue Hawaii.* Released in 1961, this was the eighth of Elvis' 30 plus movies, and its tepid songs, including such forgettable oddities as "Ku-U-I-Po", "Ito Eats" and "Slicin' Island", showed how far from his rocking roots the 'King' had come in five short years.

Below Johnny Kidd and the Pirates — from left: Mick Green, Kidd, Frank Farley and Johnny Spence.

May

In Hollywood, Fabian begins his acting career, working on *High Times* with Bing Crosby and *North to Alaska* with John Wayne.

Frank Sinatra and Elvis Presley swap hits on ABC-TV's *Timex Spectacular*: Elvis sings "Witchcraft" and Sinatra croons "Love Me Tender".

June

"Alley-Oop" by the Hollywood Argyles enters the US charts. The song's producer is the notorious pop opportunist Kim Fowley.

The Kingston Trio Show, to be aired six days a week, debuts on CBS Radio.

Joan Baez and John Lee Hooker are among the performers at the second annual Newport Folk Festival, in Newport, Rhode Island.

The Silver Beatles and Gerry and the Pacemakers perform at the Grosvenor Ballroom, Wallasey, England.

Above Beach party films, including scenes like this, were all the rage in the early sixties.

July

The Ventures' "Walk, Don't Run" enters the US charts, introducing the instrumental 'surf sound' – invented by guitarist Dick Dale – to America.

August

Ike and Tina Turner's first single, "A Fool in Love" enters the US charts.

Chubby Checker's cover of Hank Ballard's "The Twist" enters the US charts.

"Itsy Bitsy Teenie Weenie Yellow Polka Dot Bikini" by Bryan Hyland is Number 1 in the United States.

The Beatles, no longer 'Silver', perform their first gig at the Indra Club in Hamburg, Germany. The next day they sign a contract with Bruno Koschmeider, the owner of the club.

September

Instrumental group the Piltdown Men have their first UK chart success with "Brontosaurus Stomp".

Bill Black Combo's version of 'Don't Be Cruel' enters the American charts.

October

Aretha Franklin, 18, makes her New York stage debut, singing at a Greenwich Village club called the Village Vanguard.

Ben E King, former lead singer with the Drifters, records his first solo record, "Spanish Harlem"/"Stand by Me". "Spanish Harlem" is produced by Jerry Leiber and Mike Stoller, with Phil Spector assisting.

The Indra Club in Hamburg is closed by police and the Beatles are transferred to the Kaiserkeller, where Rory Storm and the Hurricanes are also performing.

Roy Orbison's "Only the Lonely" reaches Number 1 in the UK charts and Number 2 in America.

November

Kim Wilde born 18 November, in London.

Ray Charles has his first Number 1 hit with "Georgia On My Mind".

Elvis Presley enters the US charts with "Are You Lonesome Tonight?"; it will become his third Number 1 hit of 1960.

December

Mary Wells debuts in the R&B charts with "Bye Bye Baby". The record is her first, and one of Motown Records' first releases.

The Beatles return to Liverpool after four months in Hamburg.

Tamla Motown has its first big chart hit: the Miracles' "Shop Around" reaches Number 2.

Spector of Things to Come

1961

Two of the first three chart toppers of 1961 were by Bert Kaempfert and the indomitable Lawrence Welk, and the uncommitted observer could have been forgiven the assumption that rock'n'roll had never really happened. Yet there was life in the infant music, much of it concentrated in the nascent soul scene. In Detroit, Berry Gordy was establishing the basis for his Tamla Motown empire. The trump card in his pack, then as later, was Smokey Robinson, a songwriter as prolific as any within the Brill Building, who found time to lead his own group, the Miracles, and provide material for a variety of other fledgling Motown stars. The Miracles had their first hit early in 1961 with "Shop Around", the first in a string of hits that stretched to the end of the decade. Other Motown hits that year were by Mary Wells and the Marvelettes.

Move on up

Meanwhile, in Chicago, another great black vocal group was about to make its mark. Two young friends, Curtis Mayfield and Jerry Butler, came together to form the Impressions in 1958 and they scored a hit almost immediately with "For Your Precious Love". Butler left the group soon afterwards, when subsequent releases failed to click, but he continued to work with Mayfield and the result was "He Will Break Your Heart", a co-written hit for Butler. Mayfield continued with the Impressions and they attacked the charts in 1961 with "Gypsy Woman".

Runaway boys

Back in the pop camp, 1961 saw the rise to fame of a number of new talents. Del Shannon made the top of both the US and UK charts with "Runaway". Gene Pitney emerged as performer of some merit with a series of nasal, emotion-choked ballads. It was a good year, too, for Dion Di Mucci, who had embarked on a solo career after leaving his backing band the Belmonts. He had two big hits in the shape of "The Wanderer" and "Runaround Sue"; the latter topped the charts.

Left Del Shannon, a former carpet salesman, combined his piercing falsetto with a squawking organ on "Runaway" (1961) – a hit formula was discovered. *Below* Marvin Gaye, whose sweet soul vocal style was born of church Gospel roots.

In the UK the charts were dominated by American acts, with the occasional flurry from home-grown talents such as Eden Kane, John Leyton and the jazzman Acker Bilk. The surprise newcomer was a young lady called Helen Shapiro, who sported an improbable tower of hair and reached Number 1 twice in 1961 with "You Don't Know" and "Walkin' Back to Happiness". As for the rest . . . it was as if they knew something big was about to break and were waiting for it.

PRODUCING THE GOODS

Although it might seem at first sight a little early in his career, 1961 was the year Phil Spector made his big move and it was, accordingly, the year when producers started to make the news. The logical adjunct to the Brill Building songsmith was the producer, often an independent, who gave this rich but raw material its final recorded shape. Phil Spector was the archetypal early sixties record producer because, in his own way, he was just as driven, as hungry for success as any performer. The teenage Spector made his first spectacular entry on to the scene as part of the Teddy Bears, whose "To Know Him Is to Love Him" reached the top of the charts in 1958.

Wall of sound

A period of mixed fortunes ended when Spector went to the Brill Building to work with Leiber and Stoller, co-wrote "Spanish Harlem" for Ben E King and produced his first sessions. As soon as he could afford it, Spector started his own record label – Phillies – in 'partnership' with one of his original mentors, Lester Sill. That was late in 1961. From that moment, the producer as personality became an accepted part of the rock'n'roll sound. It was a development that did not particularly please many of the established producers, who viewed Spector's flair for hustling and self-publicity with mistrust and perhaps a touch of envy. The days when Spector would take and mold a series of (mainly female) artists were only just beginning, and the famous 'wall of sound' was little more than an idea, but he had established the importance of the producer in the record industry and the public mind for all time. Why else should the Ramones have turned to him late in the seventies when their career was on the slide?

Below The Temptations' early trademark was the combined vocal power of David Ruffin and Eddie Kendricks. The raw, effortless spark of songs like "Ain't Too Proud To Beg" (1966) has never been bettered.

Diary

January

Elvis Presley signs a five-year contract with Hal Wallis; the contract requires him to star in one film a year.

Frankie Avalon signs to 20th Century-Fox to star in upcoming film *Voyage to the Bottom of the Sea*.

February

Eighty-five teenagers are arrested following an 'incident' at the First World Festival of Rock'n'Roll at the Palais des Sports in Paris. The bill includes Bobby Rydell and Emile Ford.

Pop singer Brenda Lee's mother announces to the US press that her 16-year-old daughter is 'old enough to go out alone with boys'.

Paul Anka begins a European tour.

March

Scepter Records gives each member of the Shirelles a $450 diamond wristwatch, a 'thank-you' for their success with "Will You Still Love Me Tomorrow?", which reached Number 1 in the US charts.

The Beatles make their debut performance at Liverpool's Cavern Club.

Soul singer Jackie Wilson leaves the hospital where he has been recovering from a gunshot wound inflicted by a hysterical female fan.

April

Paul Revere and the Raiders make their national chart debut with "Like, Long Hair".

Bob Dylan makes his New York City stage debut at Gerde's Folk City, a small Greenwich Village club, opening for blues singer John Lee Hooker. Two weeks later he will make his recording debut, playing harmonica on the title track of Harry Belafonte's *Midnight Special* album.

The BBC bans Craig Douglas' "A Hundred Pounds of Clay" on religious grounds.

Left The Crystals, five schoolgirls from Brooklyn, were plucked from obscurity and put in the studio by Phil Spector. Though their early hit "He Hit Me (And It Felt Like A Kiss)" caused mild outrage, their appeal was based on a wholesome innocence.

Right The appeal of the Ronettes, on the other hand, was less than wholesome and innocent. Their come-hither looks and figure-hugging attire were blatantly flirtatious; their booming hit, "Be My Baby" (1963), was Phil Spector at his best.

May

The Kingston Trio splits up.

Tony Orlando makes his chart debut with the record "Halfway to Paradise".

The Everly Brothers launch their own record label, Calliope, intending to 'develop new talent'; their own records will continue to be issued exclusively by Warner Brothers.

June

Ricky Nelson's million-seller, "Travelin' Man", reaches Number 1 in the American charts.

Elvis Presley's seventh film, *Wild in the Country*, premieres in Memphis. The film was originally released without any of Elvis' singing but it received such negative reviews, from both critics and fans, that it was re-edited with several songs being added.

In Hackensack, New Jersey, two men receive one-year sentences and a third man a suspended sentence in the first successful conviction of record bootleggers.

July

The first issue of *Mersey Beat*, the fan magazine of the Liverpool rock'n'roll scene, is published in Britain. The issue contains an article by local musician John Lennon, entitled 'Being a Short Diversion on the Dubious Origins of the Beatles'.

The Supremes' debut single, "Buttered Popcorn"/"Who's Loving You", is released on Motown Records. It will fail to enter the charts.

The Platters' musical director, Rupert Branker, is beaten to death on a Los Angeles street corner.

August

"Tossin' and Turnin'" by Bobby Lewis reaches Number 1 in the American charts. It will go on to be the year's biggest-selling single.

The Marvelettes' debut single, "Please Mr Postman", is released by Motown label Tamla Records. The all-girl quintet first came to the attention of Motown executives after winning a school talent contest at Inkster High School, in Detroit.

September

Bob Dylan begins a two-week engagement at Gerde's Folk City in New York, opening for the Greenbriar Boys.

The Dave Brubeck Quartet's jazz number "Take Five" is released; it will go on to reach Number 25 in the *Billboard* Hot 100 and to sell over a million copies.

Ray Charles co-stars with Sarah Vaughan at Broadway's Palace Theater.

October

Elvis Presley offers his services to help raise money for flood victims in Louisiana.

Bob Dylan records his first album, *Bob Dylan*, for Columbia Records.

Phil Spector's Phillies label releases its first record, the Crystals' "Oh Yeah, Maybe Baby". The label will go on to become one of the most successful and influential labels of the sixties.

November

The Everly Brothers report to Camp Pendleton, California, for induction into the US Marines.

Acker Bilk's "Stranger on the Shore" is released in Britain; it will become a surprise million-seller Number 1 on both sides of the Atlantic.

Record shop manager Brian Epstein sees a lunchtime performance by the Beatles at Liverpool's Cavern Club. After the show he introduces himself to George Harrison and Paul McCartney and within three months has convinced the Beatles that he should be their manager; a contract between them will be signed on 24 January 1962.

December

The Beach Boys' first record, "Surfin' ", is released by Candix Records. Later in the month they will make their stage debut under that name at the Ritchie Valens Memorial Concert at Long Beach, California's Municipal Auditorium.

Chubby Checker's "The Twist" has now been in the Hot 100 chart for 23 consecutive weeks – longer than any other record in the chart.

Far left Even in the relatively staid confines of the television studio, Ike and Tina Turner turned on the most electrifying of performances.
Center The tragedy in Roy Orbison's songs was to cross over into real life – in 1966 his wife Claudette died in a motorcycle accident; two years later, two of his sons perished in a house fire. He focused on the dark side of love from behind a permanent pair of sunglasses.
Left Sam Cooke who lays strong claim to the title of "Father Of Soul". His unadorned style influenced a generation of soul singers, white and black, before his tragic death – shot in a motel – in 1964.

'Times they are a-changin'

At first glance, 1962 had a familiar ring about it, even cosy. Elvis continued his domination of the charts on both sides of the Atlantic with songs like "Rock a Hula Baby" and "Good Luck Charm", while Chubby Checker was still twisting through his fifteen minutes of fame. Even Acker Bilk took his emotion-laden instrumental "Strangers on the Shore" to the top of the US charts, a feat that was beyond the range of the Shadows at the height of their fame. Yet beneath the apparent unchanging serenity there lurked new musical forms which would change the face of pop forever and would end the careers of many existing stars.

The Mersey sound

The northern town of Liverpool seemed, at first sight, an unlikely place for a new music explosion. London was the center of such teen excitement as existed, and any new developments would have been expected to emanate from there. Yet Liverpool was a port and, therefore, open to a variety of cultural and social influences as a consequence of international trade. One such influence was the American R&B records brought over by sailors, and the excitement generated by these was at the root of a new rock'n'roll scene – Merseybeat.

Liverpool also maintained unofficial trading links with Hamburg, and a steady stream of groups went to Germany in order to satisfy a voracious appetite for loud, beat-heavy music as an accompaniment to the drinking and fighting that went on in the seedier clubs. New bands had a chance to prove themselves in front of a difficult and demanding audience so that when, and if, they made the big time, they were ready for it.

Far right The very picture of a sensitive modern troubadour, Bob Dylan arrived on the scene via acoustic performances in smoky Manhattan bars. It was not until he turned his back on the traditional folk music of America, on which he had been brought up, and began launching vitriolic and bitter attacks on the state of the world to fierce electrical accompaniments, that his genius emerged.

Right The Ventures shot to fame in 1960 with the instrumental hits "Walk Don't Run" and "Perfidia" – million sellers both. And while other groups to emerge during the instrumental boom of the early sixties sank without a trace once the Beatles had arrived, the Ventures kept afloat by dint of their uncanny ability to turn musical trends to their own advantage. LPs like *Ventures Go Country*, *Psychedelic Guitars* and many more kept the bank manager smiling.

Let me take you down...

One of these groups was the Beatles. By the end of 1962 they had a dynamic live act of cover versions and originals – and a recording contract. Their first release, "Love Me Do", only reached Number 17 in the singles chart, but those who had ears could hear the sound of the times changing.

All the way from Memphis

Meanwhile, in America, several new faces were making their moves. From Memphis came Booker T & the MGs, a multi-racial instrumental R&B group, whose tastefully refined yet swinging style (particularly that of guitarist Steve Cropper) was widely admired and imitated. "Green Onions" gave them their first hit.

Berry Gordy was enlarging his stable of talent in Detroit. His most significant new artist of the year was Marvin Gaye who entered the charts with "Hitch Hike". Phil Spector was entering the phase of manic creativity that would keep him in the public eye for the next three years, and towards the end of the year the Crystals went to Number 1 with "He's a Rebel", written by Gene Pitney.

On the West Coast the Beach Boys were formed, and songwriter Brian Wilson, relying on some factual help from his sporting brother Dennis, penned the first of a series of surfing anthems that were to be the band's early stock in trade – "Surfin' Safari". Down in the small clubs of Greenwich Village, where the sun never shone, a young folk singer called Bob Dylan was injecting wit and vinegar into a staid musical form – his self-named debut LP was released early in 1962.

Left The Tornados. Masterminded by opportunist record producer/composer Joe Meek, "Telstar" (1962) was the biggest-selling instrumental hit of all time.

Below They were just four working-class lads from Liverpool playing no more than competent versions of American pop and rock'n'roll standards. They became worldwide representatives of a British pop explosion, symbols of Britain's new-found self-confidence, and pioneers of new ways of making music. They were, of course, the Beatles.

SOUNDS INSTRUMENTAL

The early sixties were the heyday of the instrumental. The period after rock'n'roll's first flourish was filled by the teen idols, peddling a cleaned-up version of the original wild sounds, but one area where the untamed spirit survived was in the vocal-less number, often played by bar bands and, as a consequence, fiercely regional. The better of these groups sometimes made the jump to national fame, making the charts ring with their wild energy – for example, Johnny and the Hurricanes, whose run of frenetic hits started in 1959. An altogether smoother outfit were the Ventures, from Seattle, whose style was polished and understated but whose music packed a deceptive punch. Their two most famous hits arrived in 1960 – "Walk, Don't Run" and "Perfidia" – but they continued to find a large international audience well into the seventies. The West Coast surf music boom also threw up a host of instrumental combos. Two who achieved national fame were the Chantays and the Surfaris.

Winds of change

Instrumental rock in the UK was an altogether more sedate affair. The Shadows had their moments of wild abandon but were too firmly rooted in the old showbiz traditions to really let it rock. The Tornados whirled into view in 1962 with a tune called "Telstar", in honor of a recently launched satellite. Written and produced by Joe Meek, the attractively modish song was a Number 1 on both sides of the Atlantic. It was a performance that the group were unable to repeat, although they scored a top five hit in the UK with "Globetrotter" and also charted in 1963 with songs "Robot" and "The Ice Cream Man".

The advent of the Beatles spelled doom for the instrumental as a fashionable form: a record without vocals was no record at all. Even so, scarcely a year goes by without a representative of the genre successfully gracing the charts.

Below Surf instrumental giants the Surfaris, once described by singer Tim Hardin as "the only true poets of modern America". From left: Jim Fuller, Jim Pash, Ron Wilson, Pat Connolly and Bob Berryhill.

1962 Diary

January

Dick Clark's *American Bandstand* dedicates its entire program to Elvis on his 27th birthday – 18 January.

The Beatles have their first big audition, for London's Decca Records. The same day, Brian Poole and the Tremeloes are also being auditioned; Decca's Mike Smith decides to sign only the Tremeloes.

Folk group the Weavers are banned from NBC-TV's *The Jack Parr Show* because of their refusal to sign a US loyalty oath.

February

Don Everly marries film star Venetia Stevenson in San Diego, California.

Bobby Darin is signed to star with James Cagney in *The Last Westerner*.

March

The Beatles make their television debut, appearing on BBC's *Teenager's Turn*, to play Roy Orbison's song "Dream Baby".

Ray Charles starts his own record label, Tangerine.

Alexis Korner's Blues Incorporated, with Charlie Watts on drums, play their first gig, at London's Ealing Club.

April

Stuart Sutcliffe, an original member of the Beatles, dies at 22 of cerebral paralysis caused by a brain hemorrhage, in Hamburg, Germany.

Just four days after the death by drowning of his son Steve Allen, Jerry Lee Lewis returns to England for the first time in four years. He receives an enthusiastic welcome at his first concert, in Newcastle.

Mick Jagger and Keith Richards meet Brian Jones for the first time at the Ealing Club in London.

Below When the Beach Boys harmonized about sun, sand and surf, it was, as they put it in their 1964 hit song, "Fun, Fun, Fun". Soon, however, the smiles gave way to bizarre musical experiments and spiritual excursions.

May

The Freewheelin' Bob Dylan, his second album, is released by Columbia Records. Initial sales are four times higher than for his first album.

Bobby Rydell makes his screen debut in *Bye Bye Birdie*.

Billboard reports that the most-played jukebox disc in 1961 was "Big Bad John" by country star Jimmy Dean.

June

Dimension, a new label formed by publishing team Al Nevins and Don Kirshner, releases its first record – Little Eva's "The Locomotion".

British vocal group the Springfields, which includes Dusty Springfield, release their debut single, "Silver Threads and Golden Needles".

The Beatles audition for EMI producer George Martin.

Below Early Motown act the Contours whose stunningly raucous "Do You Love Me?" reached Number 1 in America in 1962. The song was the group's only major hit but was included in the repertoires of many a Liverpool beat group — including the Beatles.
Below right Beatles manager Brian Epstein.

July

The Platters refuse to play a concert in Atlanta, Georgia, unless they can perform before an integrated audience.

The Rolling Stones make their stage debut at London club The Marquee.

Bob Dylan makes his radio debut, performing on New York station WRVR-FM's hootenanny special.

August

Ringo Starr, former drummer for Rory Storm and the Hurricanes, makes his first appearance as a member of the Beatles at Liverpool's Cavern Club. He replaces the original drummer, Pete Best, whom manager Brian Epstein asked to leave two days before, at the urging of producer George Martin.

John Lennon marries Cynthia Powell at the Mount Pleasant Registry Office in Liverpool.

The Four Seasons' "Sherry" enters the Hot 100, at Number 91.

September

The Beatles record Lennon and McCartney compositions "Love Me Do" and "PS I Love You" at EMI's London studios, with George Martin producing.

Brian Epstein arranges for the Beatles to be interviewed by journalist Peter Jones for London newspaper the *Daily Mirror*. Jones concludes that they are 'a nothing group'.

The Foreign Press Association in Hollywood names Bobby Darin as best actor of the year for his role in *Pressure Point*, co-starring Sidney Poitier.

October

Bobby 'Boris' Pickett's American hit, "Monster Mash", is banned by the BBC under a regulation that prohibits the broadcasting of anything deemed 'offensive'.

The Beatles' first single, "Love Me Do"/"PS I Love You" is released in the UK on the Parlaphone label; it will peak at Number 17 in December.

In Washington, DC, Motown Records launches its two-month package tour of the United States. The bill features the Miracles, Mary Wells, Marvin Gaye, the Supremes and Little Stevie Wonder.

November

The Crystals' "He's a Rebel", released on Phil Spector's Phillies label, reaches Number 1 in the Hot 100.

New releases this month: the Miracles' "You've Really Got a Hold on Me" on Motown Records, and the Four Seasons' "Big Girls Don't Cry" on Vee Jay Records.

The Beatles begin a two-week engagement at their old haunt, the Star Club, in Hamburg, West Germany.

December

The Tornadoes instrumental hit "Telstar" becomes the first record by a British group to top the US charts.

Pop singer Brenda Lee is slightly injured when she runs into her burning Nashville home to rescue her poodle, CeeCee. Unfortunately, the dog who toured the world with Lee dies of smoke inhalation.

Elvis Presley's "Return to Sender" reaches Number 1 in the UK charts.

Right The searing falsetto of Frankie Valli was the secret weapon of the Four Seasons. They notched up a staggering 25 Top Forty hits in America in the six years from 1962 to 1967 — or 26 hits if you include "Don't Think Twice" (1965) which the group released as "Wonder Who."

Main picture The polished harmonies and groomed appearance of the Hollies showed British beat at its most presentable and polite.

Insets Although newspapers announced that the Beatles (*right*) had been toppled by the Dave Clark Five, the Fab Four proved them completely wrong.

Mersey Mania

In the American charts of 1963, it was possible to see that a change was on the way. For a start, Elvis Presley failed to record a Number 1 and there was a general lack of the old familiar faces at the top. Important newcomers included the Four Seasons, featuring the sweet high-pitched tones of Frankie Valli, who hit the top with "Walk Like a Man". Tamla Motown unveiled one of its greatest discoveries in the shape of Little Stevie Wonder, a 13-year-old musical prodigy whose third single, "Fingertips Part Two", went to Number 1 and heralded the beginning of a long and fine career. Other occupants of the Number 1 slot were not destined for such longevity. For the likes of Kyu Sakamoto, Jimmy Gilmer and the Fireballs and the Singing Nun, it was a case of enjoying the moment while it lasted.

Walk on, walk on...

Meanwhile, in the UK, Mersey mania swept the country with a force that consigned large sections of the pop hierarchy to oblivion. The Beatles racked up three monumental top sellers in "From Me to You", "She Loves You" and "I Want to Hold Your Hand", but they were not the first Mersey group to scale those heights. Gerry and the Pacemakers were much more lightweight than the Beatles in every sense, not even writing their own material, but they entered the record books as the first act to start their career with three consecutive Number 1 hits (a feat only equaled in the eighties by fellow Liverpudlians Frankie Goes To Hollywood).

The third big act in the stable of manager Brian Epstein was Billy J Kramer, a hulking crooner of the old school, who achieved his early breakthrough with Lennon/McCartney material. Billy and his backing group the Dakotas eventually went to the top of the charts with "Bad to Me". Another Liverpool group to make their recording debut in 1963 were the Searchers. "Sweets for My Sweet" and "Sugar and Spice" marked the start of two years' chart success for them.

Manchester sounds

Although Liverpool was regarded as the source of all that was best on the bright new pop scene, other cities had their own home-grown heroes. The Hollies, from Manchester, were one of the very best of the new beat groups. Their initial impact was not as spectacular as that of some of their contemporaries, but they developed into a solid unit, capable of writing tuneful and interesting songs. Also from Manchester were Freddie and the Dreamers, a comedy cabaret act who happened to be in the right place at the right time.

Brian Poole and the Tremeloes from Essex were one of the raunchiest of the new bands, being heavily influenced by American R&B. Their first two hits were both cover versions of earlier US successes – the Isley Brothers' "Twist and Shout" (also recorded by the Beatles) and the Contours' "Do You Love Me?", a Number 1 hit for the Trems. Brian Poole eventually went solo, with little success, and the Tremeloes eclipsed their former front man by recording a string of tuneful hits throughout the sixties.

Ready to roll

London's main representatives in the first wave of the beat boom were the Dave Clark Five. Their sound was firmly based on the somewhat rudimentary but undeniably effective drumming of Dave Clark and the pleasantly throaty vocals of organist Mike Smith. "Glad All Over" and "Bits and Pieces" are their best remembered hits. Another London group appeared first in 1963, although they did not experience national success until the following year. This new group, the Rolling Stones, had to be content with a local reputation. For the time being.

Far left William 'Smokey' Robinson possessed a voice that could win the heart of the most stony-souled listener. Not content with this God-given talent, Smokey also composed some of the most exquisite musical cameos of all time. Songs like "Tracks Of My Tears" (1965) and "I Second That Emotion" (1967) are pop at its simplest, most moving and most poetic.
Center The Swinging Blue Jeans, one of thousands of British beat groups to emerge in the wake of the Beatles, are chiefly remembered for their 1963 hit "Hippy Hippy Shake" and their trick of playing their guitars behind their heads.
Left Little Stevie Wonder, initially an oddity, quickly matured into one of rock's geniuses.

SURFING SAFARIS

While America had yet to fall under the spell of the Beatles, it became besotted with a home-grown phenomenon that in a way was equally alien. The surfing craze reached its height in 1963, mainly through the efforts of the Beach Boys and Jan and Dean, and even established stars were having a go (as had been the case with the Twist). Yet it was strange that an activity that was only available to a small proportion of the American population should so fire the public imagination that endless records could be sold off its back.

On the beach

Of course, it was the imagery that was the appealing factor. A surf record, even, it seemed, an *instrumental* surf record, conjured up a vision of sun and sand, of endless big waves ridden in by bronzed and healthy figures performing feats of nonchalant grace and balance. This was the only exercise required, for the rest of the time was spent soaking up the sun and flirting with the outrageously attractive 'California girls' who shared the beach.

A natural extension of surf music was hot rod music, usually cranked out by the same artists. The element of competition was fiercer here than on the beach – not only your honor but your life was at stake, as in Jan and Dean's "Dead Man's Curve". At the other extreme, the whole cycle of 'beach party' movies and records that revolved around the talents of Annette Funicello presented a completely mindless image of love and jolly japes on some magical beach where the greatest danger was getting a spot of tar on the bikini.

Where the boys are

The first national surfing hit is credited to the Marketts with "Surfin' Stomp" in 1962. The greatest exponents, however, were the Beach Boys, who filled their first three LPs with surf songs. And the surf music that has survived perhaps best of all are instrumentals like "Pipeline" by the Chantays and "Wipe Out" by the Surfaris.

Above left Brian Poole and the Tremeloes hit the top with "Do You Love Me?" in 1963. But success was shortlived. By 1966, Poole was working in his father's butcher's shop while his group was forging a new career as teenybop idols.
Below left The sport that spawned the sound of surf.

Above Mick Jagger and Keith Richard in 1964. The Rolling Stones, with their shaggy hair and impolite utterances, brought 'outrage' back to music.

1963 Diary

January

The Beatles begin a five-day tour of Scotland to promote their single "Love Me Do".

Gary 'US' Bonds files a $100 000 suit against Chubby Checker, charging that Checker 'stole' Bonds' "Quarter to Three" and turned it into "Dancing Party". The case will eventually be settled out of court.

Los Angeles' first rock club, the Whiskey-A-Go-Go, opens on Sunset Boulevard.

Bob Dylan records a radio play, *Madhouse on Castle Street*, for the BBC, in London. In it he takes the role of a hobo and sings his composition, "Blowin' in the Wind".

"Please Please Me"/"Ask Me Why", the Beatles' second single, is released in England.

February

Helen Shapiro begins a UK tour, with support group the Beatles.

The Chiffons' "He's So Fine" enters the American charts.

Vee Jay Records release the first Beatles record in the United States – "Please Please Me"/"Ask Me Why". Though a hit in its native England, it goes virtually unnoticed in America, not helped by its incorrect credit – 'The Beattles'.

March

Country singers Patsy Cline, Cowboy Copas and Hawkshaw Hawkins are killed when their single-engine plane crashes in Tennessee. They had been returning from St Louis, where they had performed at a benefit concert for the widow of DJ Cactus Jack Call, recently killed in a car crash.

Joan Baez is one of 50 folk artists who meet at New York City club the Village Gate to plan a protest against ABC-TV, which has blacklisted folk singer Pete Seeger because of his left-wing politics.

Otis Redding makes his R&B chart debut with "These Arms of Mine".

April

Martha and the Vandellas make their first chart entry with "Come and Get These Memories". The all-girl Motown trio, led by Martha Reeves, first recorded as back-up singers for Marvin Gaye; their group name is derived from 'vandal' because they were said to have stolen the limelight from Gaye.

ABC-TV premieres folk music show *Hootenanny*, despite a program boycott by most of America's most popular lead singers, a result of the network's ban on left-wing folkie Pete Seeger.

"From Me To You"/"Thank You Girl", the Beatles' third single, is released in Britain.

Bob Dylan plays his first major solo concert, at New York City Town Hall.

Cliff Richard and the Shadows perform their Number 1 UK hit "Summer Holiday" on *The Ed Sullivan Show*.

A 19-year-old music-business publicist, Andrew Loog Oldham, sees the Rolling Stones' gig at London's Crawdaddy Club; the next day he convinces them to sign him as manager.

Above Billy J Kramer and the Dakotas, second stringers in Brian Epstein's Merseybeat stable, stumbled into the public eye with a couple of John Lennon and Paul McCartney's less spectacular tunes — "Do You Want To Know A Secret?" (1963) and "Bad To Me" (1963).

May

Bob Dylan walks out of dress rehearsals and refuses to appear on *The Ed Sullivan Show* when network censors forbid him to perform his "Talkin' John Birch Society Blues", a song about the nationalistic and racist US organization, the John Birch Society.

The Rolling Stones, with a sixth member, pianist Ian Stewart, record their first single "Come On"/"I Want to Be Loved".

Joan Baez, Bob Dylan, and Peter, Paul and Mary are among the performers featured at the first Monterey Folk Festival.

Little Stevie Wonder, just 13 years old, records his first hit, "Fingertips".

June

The Searchers' debut single, a cover of the Drifters' "Sweets for My Sweet", is released.

The Rolling Stones make their TV debut performing "Come On" on *Thank Your Lucky Stars*.

July

The New York Mets baseball team hire several rock'n'roll acts, including Chubby Checker, to perform before their game with the Pittsburgh Pirates; the game is won by the Pirates.

Motown Records releases the Miracles' new record "Mickey's Monkey".

Bob Dylan, Joan Baez, Phil Ochs and Tom Paxton perform at Rhode Island's Newport Folk Festival.

Gerry and the Pacemakers, managed, again, by Brian Epstein, was the first of the Liverpool groups to reach Number 1 in the UK. Their hit, "How Do You Do It?" (1963), had, ironically, been turned down by the Beatles as a follow-up to "Love Me Do".

August

The Beatles play their last gig at the Cavern Club in Liverpool.

The original beach movie, *Beach Party*, starring Frankie Avalon and ex-mousketeer Annette Funicello is released.

The BBC broadcasts its pop show *Ready Steady Go!* for the first time.

September

The Beatles' single "She Loves You" reaches Number 1 in the British charts.

Cilla Black's first single, "Love of the Loved", written for her by John Lennon and Paul McCartney, is released.

The Rolling Stones share the bill with the Everly Brothers and Bo Diddley at the New Victoria Theatre in London.

October

Foremost among the latest teen fad of hot-rodding songs is the Beach Boys' "Little Deuce Coupe", which reaches Number 15 in the US charts.

The Beatles appear on BBC-TV's *Sunday Night at the London Palladium*. Thousands of fans jam the streets surrounding the theater, and hundreds battle with police, trying to gain admittance to the rehearsal.

Liverpool group Gerry and the Pacemakers have their third British Number 1 of the year with "You'll Never Walk Alone", the group's third release.

November

Dion walks off the stage during a live taping of the British TV show *Ready Steady Go!* after complaining, to no avail, that the on-stage go-go dancers were distracting him.

The British press reports that 'the Royal Box was stomping', the morning after the Beatles perform at *The Royal Command Performance* in London.

The Rolling Stones enter the UK charts with their version of the Lennon and McCartney song "I Wanna Be Your Man".

December

"Dominique", by The Singing Nun, is a surprise Number 1 in the US charts.

In a *New York Times* interview, John Lennon remarks: 'I'd hate to be old. Just imagine it. Who'd want to listen to an 80-year-old Beatle?'

Capitol Records release the Beatles' "I Want to Hold Your Hand"/"I Saw Her Standing There". Within five weeks it reached Number 1 in the US charts.

Invasion of the US

Without doubt, 1964 was the year of the Beatles. The four lovable but razor-sharp mop tops had experienced a good 1963 at home, but "Love Me Do" was not even considered worthy of release by Capitol, the Beatles' official record company in America, and was off-loaded on to a minor label. It reached Number 110 in the charts, considerably worse than an insipid Del Shannon version of the song. Yet in January 1964 Capitol released "I Want to Hold Your Hand" and within a month it was firmly ensconced at the top of the charts, only to be replaced by "She Loves You", which was in turn knocked off the perch by "Can't Buy Me Love". By April, the Beatles were holding the first five places in the Top Ten and their extraordinary domination was complete.

With a little help from their friends

The next British act to crack the American market in a big way was Peter and Gordon. They had a secret weapon in that Paul McCartney was going out with Peter's sister, Jane Asher. In no time at all, a Lennon/McCartney song was made available to the lucky twosome – and "World Without Love" was a worldwide smash.

Other British acts to make the top of the charts in 1964 were the Animals with Alan Price's dazzling re-arrangement of "House Of The Rising Sun" and Manfred Mann with a song bearing a title straight out of the annals of rockabilly gibberish, "Do Wah Diddy Diddy". Through the wide open door poured a flood of British groups, including Gerry and the Pacemakers, Herman's Hermits, the Searchers, the Dave Clark Five, Billy J Kramer and the Dakotas, the Kinks, the Zombies and the Moody Blues. Although the music was not always of the high standards set by the Beatles, these invaders scored heavily with their hairstyles, their clothes, their general deportment and, if all else failed, with their cute British accents.

Left Dusty Springfield lapping up much deserved adulation following "I Only Want To Be With You" (1963).
Above The tremulous taffeta tones of the Supremes clothed the charts in feminine mystery throughout the sixties. The departure of lead singer Diana Ross in 1970 proved to be the group's undoing.
Right The Four Tops first reached the charts in 1964 with "Baby I Need Your Loving".

Girls go solo

While the boys were away conquering America, the girls finally came out of the shadows in the UK to grab their share of the chart action. Cilla Black was another Brian Epstein protégée, who had attained impeccable credentials working as a cloakroom girl in Liverpool's legendary Cavern Club under her real name of Priscilla White. She possessed a very odd nasal whine that endeared itself to the record-buying public via such songs as "Anyone Who Had a Heart" and "You're My World". Sandie Shaw also possessed a peculiar voice, but her success was ensured by her gimmick of never wearing shoes when she performed chart toppers like "There's Always Something There to Remind Me".

Easily the most accomplished female vocalist of this bunch was Dusty Springfield, formerly of the Springfields, who possessed a genuinely soulful voice without any trace of tense screechings. Her first solo hit was "I Only Want to Be With You", and she continued as a force in the pop world for the rest of the decade before fading from public view, the great voice unimpaired.

Establishing supremacy

The female element was also strong in America. The Shangri-Las scored spectacular successes with "Remember (Walkin' in the Sand)" and "Leader of the Pack", whose over-the-top melodrama was created by producer George 'Shadow' Morton. A more durable proposition was the Supremes on Tamla Motown, whose immaculate Holland/Dozier/Holland-penned hits included "Where Did Our Love Go?" and "Baby Love". Also on Tamla Motown, the Four Tops turned out a stream of classics from the same writing partnership – starting with "I Can't Help Myself".

Outside the black music scene, interesting new developments were at a premium. It was a good year for crooner Bobby Vinton, who racked up a pair of Number 1s with "There I've Said It Again" and "Mr Lonely". It was also a good year for P J Proby, who mounted a one-man US invasion of the UK armed with his dinstinctively passionate style of balladry. He quickly scored three Top Ten hits with "Hold Me", "Together" and "Somewhere". His career was abruptly halted when the tight trousers that were his trademark gave way during a couple of performances. It proved to be Proby's undoing.

One of the more intriguing representatives of the Liverpool sound, Cilla Black — real name Priscilla White and another Brian Epstein protégée — made the transition from cloakroom attendant at the Cavern Club to mink-coated dolly-bird almost overnight.

BEAT FROM BRITAIN

The British invasion of the United States was the most extraordinary thing that had yet happened during the short but volatile life of rock'n'roll. Prior to the emergence of the Beatles and the rest, the traffic in musical terms had been all one way. Suddenly, the flow was reversed as the better British groups assimilated the spirit of American R&B, added a dash of the contemporary, and sold it back to its place of origin. Of course, the average American teenager didn't see it like that at all – the Beatles and their cohorts were a phenomenon and had arrived from nowhere, fully formed.

Dreamers' drivel?

Much of the music produced in this golden era of British beat does not stand up too well to modern scrutiny. There is no doubt that around 1964 there was a market for anything British as long as it was a part of this wonderful scene. Thus the US market was prepared to put up with the musical drivel of

Right Ex-convent school girl Marianne Faithfull first appeared in the charts singing the Mick Jagger and Keith Richards ballad "As Tears Go By" in 1964. With her straight blond locks and fragile voice, she seemed the picture of feminine innocence – but her torrid, well-documented affair with Jagger later in the decade, and her appearance in the erotic film *Girl On A Motorcycle* changed all that.
Below Jagger, meanwhile, continued his bacchanalian romp through the pop world with devil-may-care-panache. By the late seventies, the snarling scruff who had spat out rock and R&B with such venom a decade before, had become a media figure.

Freddie and the Dreamers, but not the talented work of a band like the Zombies (after their one big hit "She's Not There") because they quickly slipped out of musical bounds and ceased to conform to the requirements of 'the scene'. In the course of time, those with talent prevailed, but in 1964 the American record-buying public was in the grip of a mania that concerned itself more with acquiring locks of hair and the state of Ringo's tonsils than it did with any notions of quality. In the long term, it was lucky for them that quality was present in such surprising quantities.

1964 Diary

January

BBC-TV broadcast the first *Top of the Pops*, featuring leading British and American chart bands.

Meet the Beatles, their US debut album, is released by Capitol Records.

The Rolling Stones appear on British TV show *Juke Box Jury*, and cause a bit of controversy with their impolite behaviour.

February

The first demonstration of American 'Beatlemania' occurs at New York's Kennedy Airport: the Beatles, arriving for their debut appearance on *The Ed Sullivan Show*, are greeted by thousands of screaming fans.

Indiana governor Matthew Welsh announces that the song "Louie Louie", by the Kingsmen (at the time Number 6 in the charts), is pornographic and tries, unsuccessfully, to have it banned on Indiana radio.

New releases include the album *Beatlemania in the USA* by the Liverpools, and singles "The Boy With the Beatle Hair" by the Swans, and "My Boyfriend Got a Beatle Haircut" by Donna Lynn.

March

Britain's first pirate (unlicensed) radio station, Radio Caroline, begins broadcasting from five miles off the East Anglian coast.

A great demand arises for Cassius Clay's album *I Am The Greatest* after Clay's defeat of Sonny Liston on 25 February. It sells over half a million copies. Boasts Clay, 'I'm better and prettier than Chubby Checker.'

For the first time in UK chart history, all the Top Ten acts are British.

Ex-Beatles drummer Pete Best appears on American TV show *I've Got a Secret*.

April

The Beatles receive $140 000 in royalties from US sales of 'Beatles Chewing Gum' for the first quarter of 1964.

Bob Dylan makes his first entry in the UK charts with "The Times They Are a-Changin'".

Mary Wells' "My Guy", written and produced by Miracle Smokey Robinson, enters the US Hot 100.

The Rolling Stones, debut album by the group of that name, is released in the UK.

Peter and Gordon's "World Without Love", written by Paul McCartney, reaches Number 1 in the UK charts.

The top five positions in the American charts are all occupied by Beatles songs.

May

One week after its release, *The Beatles' Second Album* reaches Number 1 in the American LP charts.

Millie Small's "My Boy Lollipop", already a big hit in Britain, enters the US charts. It is the first 'ska'-based (Jamaican pre-reggae sound) song to become popular in America.

The Dave Clark Five perform on stage at New York's Carnegie Hall, the day before they appear on *The Ed Sullivan Show*.

June

The Rolling Stones make their American TV debut on *The Hollywood Palace*, hosted by Dean Martin.

"Liza Jane", debut record by David Jones and the Kingbees, is released. David (not to be confused with future Monkee Davy Jones) will become world-famous in the seventies as David Bowie.

July

The Beatles' first film, *A Hard Day's Night*, premieres at London's Pavillion Theatre. Princess Margaret and the Earl of Snowdon are among those attending the $42-a-ticket charity event. The Beatles themselves do not see the finished film until the next week.

To promote the Animals' debut single, "The House of the Rising Sun", in the United States – already Number 1 in the UK – MGM Records send disc jockeys boxes containing animal crackers, wrapped in special promotional material.

Country and western singing star Jim Reeves dies at 41 when his single-engine plane crashes in fog.

In Belfast, Northern Ireland, a Rolling Stones concert is stopped after 12 minutes when over-excited fans start to cause a riot.

August

Marianne Faithfull enters the UK charts with "As Tears Go By", written for her by Mick Jagger and Keith Richard.

The headline of *Time* magazine's *A Hard Day's Night* review reads: 'Beatles Blow It'. The article cautions readers to 'avoid this film at all costs'. Other reviews of the film are, for the most part, complimentary.

MGM signs the Dave Clark Five to a film contract. They are to star in John Boorman's *Having a Wild Weekend* (released as *Catch Us If You Can*).

Liberty Records report sales exceeding 25 000 a day for the album *The Chipmunks Sing the Beatles*.

September

Pop music show *Shindig!* premieres on ABC-TV. The program features both British and American acts, as well as its own cast of go-go dancers and a house band, the Shindogs.

The Beatles' manager Brian Epstein turns down an offer of £3 500 000 from a group of American businessmen to buy out the Beatles' management.

President Lyndon B Johnson invites the Four Seasons to perform at the forthcoming Democratic National Convention.

October

The Beatles, Sandie Shaw and Cilla Black appear in an episode of *Shindig!*, taped on location in London.

Flamboyant British pop star Screaming Lord Sutch places himself on the ballot for election to Parliament.

The Rolling Stones cancel a Christmas tour of South Africa following talks with the Musicians' Union, which is opposed to the country's racial policy of apartheid.

November

When the Dave Clark Five appear on *The Ed Sullivan Show*, their host compares them favorably to the Rolling Stones, saying that, unlike the Stones, they are 'nice, neat boys'.

"Leader of the Pack" by the Shangri-Las reaches Number 1 in the US charts.

The Rolling Stones are banned by the BBC after they arrive late for radio shows *Top Gear* and *Saturday Club*.

December

Sam Cooke is fatally shot while reportedly trying to molest a young female singer. When funeral services are held a few days later, distraught fans in Chicago break down the doors of the AR Leek Funeral Home, where Cooke's body is displayed in a glass coffin.

"Downtown" by British singer Petula Clark enters the US charts.

At a Beatles Christmas concert in London, Patti Boyd, girlfriend of George Harrison, is attacked by jealous female Beatles fans.

Far left **The Kinks soared to Number 1 in 1964 with "You Really Got Me", an exuberant slice of British R&B.**
Left **Peter and Gordon's short-lived success came courtesy of John Lennon and Paul McCartney's "A World Without Love" (1964), though they never rivaled the Beatle's success *(below).***

Stones Satisfaction

1965

The second wave of the British invasion hit America in 1965, spear-headed by the Rolling Stones. The Stones registered two chart-toppers – "Satisfaction" and "Get Off of My Cloud" – and along with Herman's Hermits, who also went to the top twice, appeared to be the only possible rivals to the Beatles' domination. Other UK successes came from Wayne Fontana and the Mindbenders ("Game of Love") and Petula Clark ("Downtown"), one of the new crop of girl singers who appeared to have bypassed her teens altogether.

Below James Brown, the self-styled "Soul Brother Number One". This was no empty boast – as powerful hits like "It's A Man's Man's Man's World" (1966) proved.

Who's generation

Back in England, the Mod scene, comprised of a group of sharply-dressed young folk who took their entertainment and life style very seriously indeed, was taking shape in London. The Mods' first love was black American R&B (in contrast to their rivals, the rockers, who swore allegiance only to greaseball rock'n'roll), but a group of bands soon sprang up to satisfy their pilled-up needs with more localized fare. Foremost among them was the Who, whose anthems for disaffected youth (in particular, "My Generation") were to become enormously influential, although they made little impact in the United States yet. The Small Faces also surfaced at this time, riding high on singer Steve Marriott's soulful vocals and a string of adventurously quirky singles ("Itchycoo Park", "Sha La La La Leee", "All or Nothing"). Although the group never scaled the heights in America, the individual members all went on to bigger, if not greater, things.

The Yardbirds were a strict blues outfit from the London area whose early failure with traditional work-outs like "Good Morning Little Schoolgirl" persuaded them to try on the mantle of pop with much greater success in, for example, "For Your Love". The group also proved a veritable breeding ground for guitarists, with Eric Clapton, Jeff Beck and Jimmy Page all passing through the ranks. Constant touring in the United States gleaned a useful following for their virtuoso, guitar-led music, which was later capitalized on by both Clapton (with Cream) and Page (with Led Zeppelin).

Best of the rest

Other groups that came to prominence in 1965 and also contained future superstars within their ranks were Them and the Spencer Davis Group. Them, from Belfast, had only two hits in a mercurial and strife-torn career – "Baby Please Don't Go" and "Here Comes the Night" – although the B-side of the first single, "Gloria", is also well known. Yet the smoldering presence of frontman Van Morrison was striking from the start, and he went on to carve out an extraordinary solo career in America. The Spencer Davis Group also featured a future star in the shape of teenager Steve Winwood. After

leading the group through a series of R&B belters – notably "Gimme Some Loving" and "Keep On Running" – Winwood left to form Traffic and later settled for a reclusive solo career. Away from the burgeoning beat scene, the art of the big ballad was alive and well in the hands of Tom Jones, the Walker Brothers and Ken Dodd.

Soul brothers and sisters

In America, black music and a new strain called folk-rock were the major areas of interest. Wilson 'Wicked' Pickett recorded one of the great soul singles of all time with "In the Midnight Hour", a record that launched his colorful career. At Tamla Motown, the hits kept coming, seemingly regardless of what was happening elsewhere. The Temptations and Junior Walker and the All-Stars joined the Supremes and the Four Tops in establishing a permanent Motown presence in the higher reaches of the charts. Phil Spector turned his attention from girls to boys, and *white* boys at that, when he launched the Righteous Brothers in the direction of Number 1 with his superb production of "You've Lost That Loving Feeling", a true slice of pop catharsis. The Beach Boys by this time had left the surf well behind with songs of the class of "Help Me Rhonda".

The folk-rock movement was born out of the twin influences of the Beatles and Bob Dylan. The first major practitioners of the form were the Byrds, who turned Dylan's "Mr Tambourine Man" into a gorgeous mid-paced romp, driven along by chiming guitars and soaring vocals. Also from the West Coast, the Turtles took the same route to the top with their version of another Dylan song, "It Ain't Me Babe". To the general dismay of bearded folkies everywhere, Bob Dylan joined in the fun by embracing the dreaded electric guitar and storming the charts with a number of amped-up melodies, the most influential of which was "Like a Rolling Stone", which destroyed the three-minute pop barrier. In an altogether less abrasive vein, the Lovin' Spoonful, led by John Sebastian, specialized in the smoother side of folk-rock, typified by "Do You Believe in Magic?".

Left Along with his contemporaries Eric Clapton and Jeff Beck, Jimmy Page was the archetypal "guitar hero" of the late sixties and early seventies. All three had been members of the Yardbirds, and when that group fell apart in 1968, Page formed the New Yardbirds – who soon changed their name to Led Zeppelin.

FOLK HEROES

The year 1965 was the year of folk-rock, despite the claims of the second generation British new wave and the extraordinary run of classic recordings by Wilson Pickett and Otis Redding at the Stax studios in Memphis. Folk-rock claims the prize because it burned intensely but briefly, whereas the others had other days.

Timeless flight

As previously noted, the Byrds brought the somewhat unlikely fusion to the notice of the general public in 1965 and left it about a year later, at which point it slid into decline, except in the UK where an anglicized version continued to flourish

into the seventies. The idea behind folk-rock was sound enough: a marriage of the timeless melodies and sentiments of folk music with the crackling contemporary fire of Beatles-type rock. In practice, it did not always work out like that. A hybrid of two such distinctive musical forms was always likely to sound like a hybrid and so it proved. Nevertheless, the genre's finest moments – courtesy of the Byrds, the Lovin' Spoonful and, later, the Mamas and the Papas – achieved a kind of melancholy grandeur that extended the range of popular music. And if anyone wanted something less serious, there was always a court jester in the waistcoated shape of Sonny Bono who, with Cher, performed the immortal "I Got You Babe".

Below Petula Clark, child actress turned singer. With a string of booming ballads — "Downtown" (1964), "This Is My Song", "Don't Sleep In The Subway" (1967) and many more — Pet, as she was affectionately known to the British public, represented pop at its most inoffensive. *Right* Jeff Beck.

Left The Rolling Stones perform for the TV cameras in 1966 when the band was still considered to be the bad boys of pop.

Right Van Morrison in 1967. The previous year, Morrison had disbanded his R&B group Them and was now on the brink of a hugely successful solo career.

1965 Diary

January

Hullabaloo, NBC-TV's answer to *Shindig!*, premieres. The first show features a segment from London in which Brian Epstein presents the Zombies and Gerry and the Pacemakers.

Disc jockey and rock'n'roll pioneer Alan Freed dies of uremia at 43.

British singer Donovan makes his TV debut on *Ready Steady Go!*

PJ Proby splits his trousers for the first time, at a dance hall in Croydon, England.

February

George Harrison has his tonsils out.

PJ Proby is banned by ABC-TV and the BBC because of his trouser-splitting incident. Meanwhile, his latest single, "I Apologize", enters the UK charts.

"I Can't Explain" by London band the Who enters the UK charts.

March

In London, Mick Jagger, Keith Richard and Bill Wyman are arrested for 'insulting behavior' – urinating on a garage wall – after being refused permission to use a men's room.

Eric Clapton leaves the Yardbirds, claiming the group has become too commercial; he will be replaced by guitarist Jeff Beck.

PJ Proby is ordered off the stage at Watford Town Hall, in England, for his allegedly obscene trouser-splitting stage act.

April

The Sir Douglas Quintet make their American chart debut with "She's About a Mover".

Grammy Award winners for 1964 are announced: Record of the Year is "The Girl From Ipañema" by Stan Getz and Astrid Gilberto.

Freddie and the Dreamers hit Number 1 in the US charts with "I'm Telling You Now".

Above right The Who: (from left) John Entwistle, Keith Moon (drums), Roger Daltrey and Pete Townshend.
Right A group of mods on their scooters.
Far right The original line-up of the Small Faces: (from left) Kenny Jones, Stevie Marriott, Ronnie "Plonk" Lane and Jimmy Winston. Winston was sacked from the group in 1965 as he was too tall! (His fellow members were all under 5′6″).

May

Bob Dylan concludes his European tour with two concerts at London's Albert Hall. In the audience the first night are the Beatles and Donovan, who spend the evening with Dylan after the show.

The Byrds make their first chart entry with an electric version of Bob Dylan's "Mr Tambourine Man".

Blues legend Sonny Boy Williamson dies of natural causes in his home in Arkansas.

The Kinks cancel the remainder of their UK tour after guitarist Dave Davies is knocked unconscious when he collides with drummer Mick Avery's cymbals during a London concert.

June

It is announced in London that all four members of the Beatles will receive MBE awards (Member Of the Most Excellent Order of the British Empire). Several previous MBE recipients turn in their medals in protest.

The Rolling Stones' "Satisfaction" enters the US charts, despite being banned by many radio stations because of its suggestive lyrics.

Joan Baez and Bob Dylan take part in a protest march in London against the Vietnam War.

July

Sonny and Cher make their US chart debut with "I Got You Babe". The couple met at a Ronettes recording session, at which Sonny Bono was production assistant and Cher La Pier was singing backing vocals. They were married in 1964.

At the Newport Folk Festival, Bob Dylan performs his new 'electric' single "Like a Rolling Stone", and is booed off the stage by the crowd of angry folk purists.

The Beatles' second movie, *Help!*, premieres at London's Pavillion Theatre.

August

The Beatles visit Elvis Presley at his Beverly Hills home.

The Jefferson Airplane (pre-Grace Slick) make their stage debut at San Francisco's Matrix Club.

The Beatles perform to a screaming crowd of 56 000 fans at the Shea Stadium in New York.

The Dave Clark Five organist Mike Smith breaks two ribs when fans drag him from the stage of the Avalon Theater, Chicago.

September

The Who have their equipment van stolen from outside the Battersea Dog's Home in London while they are inside buying a guard dog.

The Beatles, a Saturday morning cartoon show, premieres on ABC-TV. It features genuine Beatles songs but not the group's real voices.

Shindig! guests this month the Yardbirds, Booker T and the MGs, the Pretty Things, the Turtles, and Racquel Welch (singing "Dancing in the Street").

October

The Who make their American TV debut on *Shindig!*. Other guests this month include the Kingsmen performing "Louie Louie".

Bill Black, former bass player with Elvis Presley and leader of his own instrumental combo, dies while undergoing surgery for cancer, in Tennessee.

The Supremes make their first appearance on *The Ed Sullivan Show*.

November

Decca release the Who's "My Generation". The song will peak at Number 74 in the US charts.

Entrepreneur Bill Graham produces his first rock concert at San Francisco's Fillmore Auditorium, featuring Jefferson Airplane and the Grateful Dead.

Writer Ken Kesey and his Merry Pranksters hold their first public 'acid test' in San Francisco. The 'event' features music by the Grateful Dead.

Bob Dylan marries Sara Lowndes in New York City. Four days later he begins a world tour.

December

The Beatles' new album, *Rubber Soul*, goes gold, two-and-a-half weeks after its release.

New American chart entries this month include the Kinks' "A Well Respected Man", Ray Charles' "Crying Time", the Young Rascals' "I Ain't Gonna Eat My Heart Out Anymore", and the Rolling Stones' "As Tears Go By". At Number 1 is the Dave Clark Five's "Over and Over".

Above left One year after marrying, Bob Dylan released his classic double album *Blonde On Blonde*.

Gasoline Alley

As if to emphasize the uncertain nature of the pop scene in 1966, the year was marked by a series of faintly odd newcomers, who lined up at the top with more established artists. Barry Sadler had a one-shot hit with the appallingly jingoistic "Ballad of the Green Berets", while the Sinatra family, in the persons of Frank and Nancy, experienced US and UK Number 1s with "Strangers in the Night" and "These Boots Are Made for Walkin'".

The year was also notable for what didn't happen and what ceased to happen. Phil Spector, previously considered infallible, sunk an unprecedented amount of effort into his first release with Ike and Tina Turner and created a breathtaking vortex of sound on "River Deep Mountain High". The American public refused to be sucked in and the single failed to reach the Top Fifty, although it was a huge hit in the UK. Spector was overwhelmed by this totally unexpected reverse and promptly retired hurt. The Beatles,

meanwhile, were plagued by too much success and in August announced their retirement from live gigs so that they could concentrate on recording and preserve their health.

Gently does it
Simon and Garfunkel recorded their first big hit with "Sounds of Silence" and Donovan, the diminutive Scottish proto-hippy, equalled the feat with "Sunshine Superman". It was also a good year for new groups in America. The Mamas and the Papas embarked on a sequence of fine singles with "Monday Monday" and the Young Rascals from New York started a similar process with "Good Lovin'". Also from New York, the Left Banke scored with "Walk Away Renee", which was later covered with great success by the Four Tops. Tommy James and the Shondells represented a new strain of tough pop that found national favor with "Hanky Panky". "Kicks" turned the same trick for Paul Revere and the Raiders, before Paul devoted the rest of his career to devising a complex series of personnel changes within the group. Sweet harmony work characterized the West Coast's Association, who achieved hits with "Along Comes Mary" and "Cherish".

Opposite page above **Looking scruffier and sounding rawer than the Stones, the Pretty Things were just too harsh for widespread appeal, though their early discs, "Rosalyn" (1964), "Don't Bring Me Down" (1964) and "Honey I Need" (1965), were examples of white R&B at its exuberant best.**

Far right **with hits like "Sunshine Superman" (1967), Paul Simon's gift for composing within the folk idiom and Art Garfunkel's sweet and perfectly-pitched voice made the duo popular with all ages.**

Right **Donovan. Scottish troubador Donovan Leitch was spotted by talent scouts from the British TV pop show *Ready Steady Go!* in 1965 and became the program's first resident performer. With his cap, curly hair, acoustic guitar, harmonica holder and gentle songs of protest, he appeared to be little more than a Scots version of Bob Dylan, right down to the slogan emblazoned on his guitar, 'this machine kills', borrowed from Woody Guthrie's guitar motto, 'this machine kills fascists'. In time, however, Donovan would mature into an original, reflecting the flower power optimism of post-'swinging London'.**

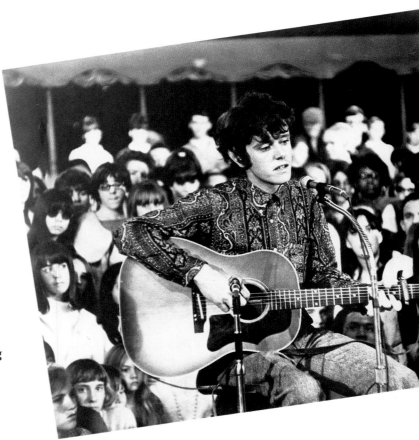

Don Kirshner turned his agile pop brain to the task of coming up with an American Beatles. The result was the Monkees, an identikit pop group groomed for visual appeal via a television series and denied the chance to play on their own singles. They were, however, provided with some excellent material, such as the first two hits – "Last Train to Clarksville" and "I'm a Believer" – the second of which was written by Neil Diamond, who also began a solo career that year. Perhaps the two greatest singles of the year were "When a Man Loves a Woman", a soul smash for Percy Sledge, and "Good Vibrations" from the Beach Boys, which set new standards in studio sound complexity and vision.

GARAGE BANDS

It probably started with the Kingsmen's version of "Louie Louie" in 1964. It was firmly based on the power of electricity to transcend talent. It fueled a new rock revolution ten years after its heyday. It was called garage band music, because that was often where it was 'rehearsed' and because, as often as not, it never got any further. In 1966, yet another watershed year in the history of popular music, it even managed to sneak a Number 1 hit in the shape of "96 Tears" by ? and the Mysterians.

All the young punks

The garage bands were based on the premise that anyone could get out there and do it, given some cheap gear, the right spirit and the correct proportions of stimulants and depressants. There were garage bands all across America (and one in England – the Troggs who also went to the top of the charts with "Wild Thing"), and although the various garage arenas were separated by thousands of miles with little or no communication between them, the sound that evolved was remarkably similar from place to place. Fuzztone and electric 12-string guitars, tinny organ and powerfully murky rhythm sections were the order of the day, topped by vocals that took demented as the norm and built from there.

The great garage groups included the Standells ("Dirty Water", "Good Guys Don't Wear White"), the Thirteenth Floor Elevators ("You're Gonna Miss Me"), the Seeds ("Pushin' Too Hard") and the Count Five ("Psychotic Reaction"). And the Electric Prunes ("I Had Too Much to Dream Last Night"). The list is endless. The story of the garage bands is the story of ingenuity with a few basic chords.

Below The Mamas and the Papas: (from left) Michelle Phillips, John Phillips (the leader and guiding light of the group), Dennis Doherty and Cass Elliot.

1966 Diary

January

The final episode of ABC-TV's *Shindig!* is broadcast. The farewell show features British acts the Kinks and the Who.

Parlaphone Records release the single "Can't Help Thinking About Me", sung by David Bowie and the Lower Third.

George Harrison marries his girlfriend Patti Boyd.

At Number 1 in the US charts is "The Sounds of Silence" by Simon and Garfunkel.

February

The first issue of rock-culture magazine *Crawdaddy* is published in New York.

Nat 'King' Cole dies at 46 following surgery for lung cancer in California.

New chart entries feature the Marketts' "Batman Theme", the Barbarians' "Moulty", and Nancy Sinatra's "These Boots Are Made For Walkin'".

March

In Liverpool, England, over 100 teenagers barricade themselves inside the Cavern Club, to protest at its recent closing.

London newspaper the *Evening Standard* publishes an interview with John Lennon that contains his controversial remark 'we're more popular than Jesus Christ now'.

The Kinks enter the US charts with the single "Dedicated Follower of Fashion".

April

Pye Records release David Bowie's first solo single, "Do Anything You Say".

Folk singer and future Monkee Peter Tork, formerly with the Phoenix Singers, opens a solo engagement at Hollywood folk club the Troubador.

Richard Farina, author and folk singer/songwriter, dies in a motorcycle accident in Venice, California, following a party to celebrate the publication of his novel *Been Down So Long It Looks Like Up To Me*.

Dusty Springfield tops the UK charts for the first time with "You Don't Have to Say You Love Me".

May

Sixteen-year-old Bruce Springsteen and his first band, the Castles, record their only disc, "That's What You Get". The single will never be released.

New chart entries in the US this month include Simon and Garfunkel's "I Am a Rock", the Kingsmen's (re-released) "Louie Louie", Ike and Tina Turner's "River Deep Mountain High", and the Temptations' "Ain't Too Proud to Beg".

June

The Beatles' LP *Yesterday and Today* is released by Capitol in its controversial 'butcher' sleeve, which shows a photo of the Beatles surrounded by bloodied, decapitated baby dolls. It is quickly withdrawn from circulation and replaced by a more conventional jacket photo, much to the relief of the 'horrified and outraged' segment of the population.

A few days after Who singer/guitarist Pete Townshend suffers minor injuries in a car accident, several European radio stations mistakenly report that the band's lead singer, Roger Daltrey, is dead.

Before beginning their US tour, the Rolling Stones initiate legal proceedings against 14 New York hotels that have banned the group from entering.

Right The Troggs. Guided by their outspoken and single-minded lead singer Reg Presley, the group bounced into view with a blatantly 'sexy' rendition of "Wild Thing" (1966).

July

Bobby Fuller, the leader of Texas rock band the Bobby Fuller Four, is found dead in his car in Los Angeles; no conclusive cause of death will be established.

Bob Dylan crashes his Triumph 55 motorcycle near Woodstock, New York. Rushed to the Middletown Hospital, he remains in a serious condition for a week.

Percy Sledge's first hit, "When a Man Loves a Woman", goes gold.

August

The South African government bans all Beatles records from radio or TV broadcast in response to John Lennon's statement about the band being 'more popular than Jesus Christ'.

While performing at the National Jazz and Blues Festival in Windsor, England, the Who create a sensation by their ritual on-stage destruction of their equipment, causing thousands of pounds worth of damage. Some members of the audience responded by smashing chairs and damaging canvas screens.

While the Beatles kick off their American tour in Chicago, most of the country's radio stations are banning their records (because of John Lennon's controversial remark . . .). When they perform in Memphis, the audience bombards them with firecrackers, rotten fruit and other assorted rubbish.

September

The Monkees TV show premieres on NBC.

George Harrison visits spiritual guru Maharishi Mahesh Yogi for the first time, in India.

New chart entries: "Reach Out I'll Be There" by the Four Tops, "Summer in the City" by the Lovin' Spoonful, and "96 Tears" by ? and the Mysterians.

October

Early British rocker Johnny Kidd is killed in a car accident in Lancashire, England.

The US Government officially declares LSD to be an illegal substance.

Grace Slick makes her first appearance with Jefferson Airplane, at San Francisco's Fillmore West.

The Jimi Hendrix Experience play their debut concert, at the Olympia Theatre in Paris, opening for French pop star Johnny Halliday.

November

Elvis Presley's twenty-second film, *Spinout*, premieres in Los Angeles.

Tom Jones' first and only UK Number 1, "The Green, Green Grass of Home" enters the charts, where it will remain for 22 weeks.

New chart entries are the Supremes' "You Keep Me Hanging On", the Yardbirds' "Happenings Ten Years Time Ago", and Wilson Pickett's "Mustang Sally".

December

The BBC broadcasts pop music TV show *Ready Steady Go!* for the last time.

Pink Floyd perform at the opening of a new London club, the UFO.

In Boston, Ray Charles is fined $10 and given a five-year suspended sentence for possession of heroin and marijuana.

The Monkees' "I'm a Believer" enters the US charts. It will go on to become their second Number 1 hit.

New releases include the Jimi Hendrix Experience's debut single "Hey Joe"/"Stoned Free" and Tommy James and the Shondells' "I Think We're Alone Now".

Below **The Monkees visit Britain in 1967. The group was fabricated by US TV moguls in an attempt to emulate the success of the Beatles** *(right).*

Acid Rockers

1967

In 1967, the focus of attention in the rock world returned to the United States, specifically to San Francisco, where a whole new plethora of groups sprang up. The catalyst for this sudden change was the drug LSD which scrambled the user's mind for some hours, inducing hallucinations, visions of global unity and profound theories on the structure of the universe. It also occasionally led people to eat vast quantities of breakfast cereals or make tragically short flights from high windows. It became essential for rock musicians to use LSD (or at least pretend) to stimulate their lyrics and musical structures and from LSD's nickname was derived the generic term for this style of music: acid rock.

Day trippers

The length of much of the material performed by this new generation of bands, not to mention its often anarchic lyrical content, meant that a great emphasis was placed on LPs and these, for the first time in history, began to outstrip singles in terms of sales. Although the West Coast, and specifically San Francisco, was the breeding ground for acid rock, it was the Beatles who again led the way. *Sergeant Pepper's Lonely Hearts Club Band* was released in June of the so-called 'summer of love' and it was quite apparent from the album's title and sleeve, let alone the music, that the Beatles had been dabbling with mind-expanding potions.

Although the Beatles provided the first great acid artefact, several other bands in and around San Francisco were warming to the task of turning on this new breed of cosmic child, the hippie. The Grateful Dead were early heroes, having already paid their psychedelic dues as house band for Ken Kesey's infamous 'acid tests'. The Dead's rambling structures, which tended towards marathon length, did not transfer all that well to record, far greater success being achieved by Jefferson

Right Pink Floyd. Formed in late 1965, the band began to pick up a cult following amongst London's 'underground' set the following year with a series of concerts at "Spontaneous Underground" (held at the Marquee Club), London Free School Sound/Light Workshop and at the legendary UFO Club. Their blend of blues, beat and R&B filtered through eerie acid space-rock sounds and backed up with a liquid light show was experimental and innovative, leaving few who witnessed their performances unmoved.
Center right The Doors: (left to right) Jim Morrison, John Densmore, Ray Manzarek and Robby Krieger.
Far right Aretha Franklin, the 'Queen Of Soul', mixed a gospel singing style with pop melodies to perfect effect.

Airplane during 1967 with two albums, *Surrealistic Pillow* and *After Bathing at Baxters*, and even two singles, "Somebody to Love" and "White Rabbit", riding high in the charts. Other notable LPs were produced by Country Joe and the Fish (*Electric Music for Mind and Body*) and the underrated Moby Grape (*Moby Grape*). Big Brother and the Holding Company was a great live draw, featuring as it did the untamed vocals of Janis Joplin, as were the Doors.

If Grace Slick of Jefferson Airplane was a focus for male attention, then Jim Morrison of the Doors gave the girls something to look at. His persona mixed the doomed poet with the leather-clad outlaw to dramatic effect and it received national exposure (as it were) when "Light My Fire" carried the Doors to the top of the singles charts. An even more volatile outfit was Love, a laughably ironic name considering the members' feelings for one another. The group managed to hold it all together for long enough to make probably the best of all the acid rock LPs, *Forever Changes*, released in 1967.

Outside the acid swirl, Buffalo Springfield, featuring the maturing talent of Neil Young, Richie Furay and Steven Stills, began its troubled and brief existence. The group left its calling card in the shape of songs like "For What It's Worth", "Mr Soul" and "Broken Arrow". From out of Memphis exploded the Box Tops with "The Letter", the first of a short run of great singles driven along by the impassioned vocals of Alex Chilton. Aretha Franklin finally arrived in 1967, after a number of false starts, with a Number 1 cover version of Otis Redding's "Respect".

In the pink

Meanwhile in the UK a parallel music explosion was taking place. Pink Floyd were widely regarded as the stars of this new 'underground', employing a dizzying light show to simulate the psychedelic experience. Their early inspiration was Syd Barrett, a madcap performer who also penned the group's early singles successes, "Arnold Layne" and "See Emily Play".

Cream mixed psychedelic rock with straight pop to good effect, before conquering America with a live set made up of long and deafening blues improvisations. The most exciting new talent on either side of the Atlantic was Jimi Hendrix, a gifted, black guitarist from Seattle, who made his name in England. He scored four Top Twenty hits in 1967, among them the definitive aural acid blitz of "Purple Haze". His style was inimitable.

ALL YOU NEED IS LOVE

This was the first year of the serious music, when it was first stated that music could change the world and make it a better place to live in. Music was no longer seen in a vacuum, but as a touchstone to a new lifestyle based on peace, love and understanding. It appeared to work for one short summer in San Francisco and a few long nights at the Roundhouse in London, but it had certainly broken down by the following year. Yet it was an important stage in the development of music because it gave rise directly to an expansion of rock's narrow lyric concerns into wider fields of social comment and protest. The price that had to be paid was the proliferation of the most ghastly fashions the world has yet had to contend with.

The high point of the year, in every sense, was the Monterey Festival. It was smaller than the mega-festivals that were to follow and happened away from the full glare of the media. The line-up was catholic, mixing the wild antics of the Who and Jimi Hendrix, the contrasting vocal styles of Janis Joplin and Otis Redding (who broke through to a white audience overnight), and even the epic ragas of Ravi Shankar, in a heady brew that proved difficult to recapture.

Far left Jimi Hendrix played the electric guitar like no-one before or since and still has a legion of devoted admirers years after his death in London in 1970 at the age of 27.

Left Janis Joplin established herself at the Monterey Pop Festival in 1967 as a remarkable blues and white soul singer. Just three years later, she would be dead, a victim of drugs.

1967 Diary

January

Boston's first rock venue, The Tea Party, opens. It is the second largest rock ballroom in the country, after San Francisco's Avalon.

The first Human Be-In, at San Francisco's Golden Gate Park, kicks off with Gary Snyder blowing a conch shell while Timothy Leary, sporting yellow flowers in his hair, chants 'Turn on, tune in, drop out'.

John Sinclair, leader of the White Panther Party and manager of rock band MC5, is arrested at his Artists' and Writers' Workshop in Detroit. He, along with the 57 others present, is charged with the possession of two marijuana cigarettes; he will eventually be convicted and sentenced to a term in prison.

Below By 1967, the Beatles had changed from wise-cracking, working-class innocents into spokesmen of the hippie generation. They grew their hair, sprouted moustaches, dabbled in drugs and mysticism and grew ever more experimental in the recording studio.

February

Record producer Joe Meek shoots himself dead outside his North London apartment.

The Bee Gees return to their native Britain after nine years in Australia, where they are already pop stars with their own weekly TV show. In just three months they will enter the UK Top Ten with "New York Mining Disaster 1941".

British group the Move turn down an offer to appear on a BBC-TV show to be broadcast from Birmingham Cathedral, England, after the group's request to burn an effigy of the Devil during their performance has been refused.

March

In Ottawa, Ontario, Canada, British band the Animals refuse to play a scheduled concert unless they are paid in advance; the irate audience starts to riot, and causes $5000 worth of damage.

The Spencer Davis Group's manager, Chris Blackwell, announces that Steve Winwood and his brother Muff will leave the band in April. Eighteen-year-old Stevie, who has been with the band for four years, will go on to form Traffic.

The Walker Brothers, Cat Stevens, Engelbert Humperdinck and the Jimi Hendrix Experience appear at London's Finsbury Park Astoria. Hendrix sustains a burned hand after setting fire to his guitar.

April

DJ Tom 'Big Daddy' Donahue initiates 'progressive FM radio' on San Francisco station KMPX as an alternative to the frantic chatter and bubblegum approach of AM Top Forty radio.

When the Rolling Stones play their first concert behind the Iron Curtain, at Warsaw's Palace of Culture, police armed with batons and tear gas bombs are required to subdue nearly 2000 fans hoping to get into the sold-out concert.

Catch My Soul, a modern version of Shakespeare's *Othello*, ends a successful New York run. Jerry Lee Lewis, portraying the villain Iago, plays the role straight until act five, when he ad-libs: 'Great balls of fire! My Friend Roderigo!'

The Greyhound Bus Company starts running sightseeing trips through San Francisco's hippie area, Haight Ashbury.

May

Elvis Presley marries Priscilla Beaulieu in Las Vegas.

Beachboy Carl Wilson appears before a Los Angeles court on draft evasion charges.

The Grateful Dead's self-titled debut album enters the American album charts.

Don't Look Back, DA Pennebaker's documentary of Bob Dylan's 1965 UK tour, premieres in San Francisco. Dylan will later denounce the film and file a court injunction to bar its being shown.

June

During the course of an interview, Paul McCartney admits to having taken LSD.

Jimi Hendrix is refused admission to Kew Gardens in England because, according to a spokesman, 'people in fancy dress costumes aren't allowed'.

Fifty thousand people gather for the three-day Monterey Pop Festival. The bill includes Jefferson Airplane, the Doors, Buffalo Springfield, Simon and Garfunkel, the Jimi Hendrix Experience, the Byrds and Smokey Robinson.

Procol Harum's single "A Whiter Shade of Pale" tops the UK charts.

July

The Monkees begin a US tour with the Jimi Hendrix Experience as support. The Daughters of the American Revolution protest at the inclusion of Hendrix on the bill, claiming his stage act is 'too erotic'.

The Who open as the backing group for Herman's Hermits at a San Diego concert.

London's *The Times* carries an advertisement by various rock groups, including the Beatles, petitioning the British government to legalize marijuana.

The Doors top the US charts with "Light My Fire".

Below left Flower power. The Beach Boys *(below)* were just one of a thousand groups to espouse the cause.

August

Pink Floyd's first album, *The Piper at the Gates of Dawn*, is released.

At the Sunbury Jazz Festival in England, the audience becomes so over-excited by Jerry Lee Lewis' performance that festival officials stop the show and ask Lewis to leave the stage.

The Beatles, accompanied by Mick Jagger and Marianne Faithfull, attend a lecture given by Maharishi Mahesh Yogi at University College in Bangor, North Wales. John Lennon's wife, Cynthia, does not accompany them because police, mistaking her for one of the hordes of fans at the railway station, prevent her from boarding the train.

At a press conference the Beatles announce that they have offered themselves as disciples to the Maharishi Mahesh Yogi.

The day after the Beatles' press conference announcing their conversion, the group's manager, Brian Epstein, is found dead in his London apartment. The coroner's report reveals that his death was caused by an overdose of sleeping pills.

September

The Doors perform their Number 1 hit "Light My Fire" on *The Ed Sullivan Show*. Before the show, Sullivan asks lead singer Jim Morrison to omit the line 'Girl we couldn't get much higher'. Morrison agrees, but then sings it anyway.

The Beatles' psychedelic Magical Mystery Tour bus begins traveling around England, carrying the band and others involved in the making of the film of the same name.

The Move's "Flowers in the Rain" is the first song to air on the BBC's new pop station, Radio One.

Below Otis Redding, the 'King Of Soul'.
Right Mick Jagger and Keith Richard, the self-styled 'Glimmer Twins'.

October

Folk singer Woody Guthrie dies at 52 of Huntington's chorea in a New York hospital. Both his political commitment and his 'talkin' blues' musical style were decisive influences on Bob Dylan, who was a frequent visitor during the long, slow illness that preceded Guthrie's death.

The rock musical *Hair* opens in New York.

Disc jockey Murrey the K is fired from New York City's WOR-FM because of his 'inability to live with direction'.

Joan Baez, along with 123 anti-draft demonstrators, is arrested for blocking the entrance to the Army Induction Center in Oakland, California. Baez and the other demo organizers are jailed for ten days.

Ravi Shankar admits in a *New York Times* interview that he is disturbed by the adulation he receives from hippy fans.

November

The first issue of *Rolling Stone* magazine, which includes a free 'roach clip' (drug-taking paraphernalia), is published in San Francisco.

After a two-year absence, Gene Clark returns to the Byrds, replacing ousted David Crosby, who will go on to form Crosby, Stills and Nash the following year.

Monkee Davy Jones opens a boutique, Zilch In, in New York's Greenwich Village.

December

Elvis Presley's 25th film, *Clambake*, is released.

Otis Redding is killed when his plane crashes into a frozen lake in Wisconsin.

Jimi Hendrix appears as Santa Claus at a children's party at London's Roundhouse Theatre.

The Beatles film *Magical Mystery Tour*, directed by themselves, premieres on BBC-TV. It is a complete flop with both the critics and the public.

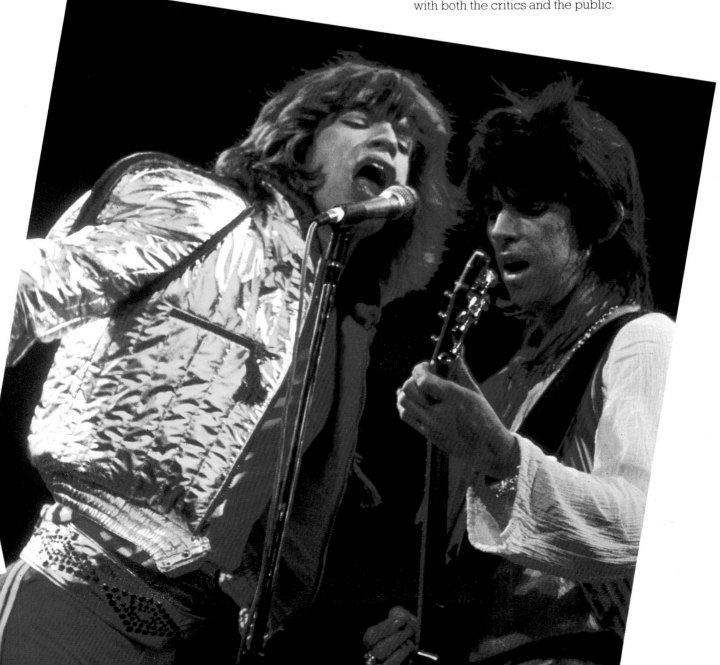

Bubblegum and Blues

1968

The inevitable reaction to the summer of love was a return to conservatism. While the area round Haight Ashbury descended into a squalid hell of beggars, bad drugs and psychos, the rest of America sent a stream of pop pap to the top of the charts, featuring artists like Bobby Goldsboro, Herb Alpert and Paul Mauriat. It was left to the unlikely figure of Jeannie C Riley to strike a blow for progressives everywhere with her uncompromising attack on small town hypocrisy in the memorable "Harper Valley PTA".

In the UK, there was a blues rock boom that unearthed a number of groups who would go on to greater things. Midlands blues boogie band Ten Years After released their second LP, *Undead*, which highlighted the fast, effects-free playing of leader Alvin Lee. After their appearance at Woodstock the following year, Lee led the group on a series of triumphant American tours. Destined to be almost as big, and without an appearance at Woodstock, were Savoy Brown, an altogether less showy combo. A third group who started out in blues territory, but quickly abandoned it, was Jethro Tull. Blues-based guitarist Mick Abrahams barely lasted through the first LP before being ousted as Tull, led by singer/flautist Ian Anderson, changed musical course and set themselves up for huge interntional success in the seventies.

Zeppelin over the USA

The biggest new act of the year was Led Zeppelin, the brainchild of guitarist Jimmy Page. Their early sound was distinctively blues-based and an astonishingly powerful first LP (*Led Zeppelin*), together with constant touring, saw them break through in the United States with great rapidity. American response to these new UK bands such as Cream and Led Zeppelin came in the shape of Blue Cheer and Iron Butterfly. The former tended to substitute stacks of speakers for talent, while the latter endlessly recycled their one well-known song, "In-A-Gadda-Da-Vida". Far more interesting were Spirit, whose personnel were adept at a variety of musical styles. From their first, self-named LP in 1968 "Fresh Garbage" emerged as one of the great forgotten singles.

Sugar and Spice

Away from all the blues rock and near heavy metal of the expanding group scene, the most interesting development in the charts was the rise of what was labeled 'bubblegum music'. In sharp distinction to the amped-up onslaughts of the live gigs and albums of these new decibel aristocrats, bubblegum was around three minutes of mindless fun and strictly no guitar overload.

Sweet things

The masterminds behind bubblegum were two producers called Jerry Kasenetz and Jeff Katz, who worked for Buddah records. The formula for bubblegum was simple: a set of meaningless lyrics, which could therefore mean anything; a solid 4/4 beat; a seemingly innocent tune carrying a hook so sharp it would penetrate the brain instantly and stay there. Groups had separate names, but it was generally a case of experienced session men whipping up these little confections, under the strict control of the producers. This was, in effect, pure music with absolutely no artist image to tempt record buyers: the groups were faceless, so people bought records for the songs.

And what songs! Some of the greatest moments of bubblegum included "Yummy Yummy Yummy" and "Chewy Chewy" by the Ohio Express, "Simon Says" and "123 Red Light" by the 1910 Fruitgum Co, "Gimme Gimme Good Lovin'" by Crazy Elephant and, perhaps bubblegum's finest three minutes, "Quick Joey Small (Run Joey Run)" from Kasenetz-Katz Singing Orchestral Circus. The only bubblegum Number 1 was achieved by a group of comic characters, in the literal sense, created by Monkee maestro Don Kirshner. They were called the Archies and the hit was "Sugar Sugar".

When the music in the charts is a bit grim and the live groups are taking liberties with one's patience, then is the time to listen for the sound of Captain Groovy and his Bubblegum Army.

Iron Butterfly on stage: (left to right) Doug Ingle, Erik Braunn, Ron Bushy and Lee Dorman. In 1968 their second album, "In-A-Gadda-Da-Vida", featuring the 17-minute sprawl of the title track, sold some three million copies. Iron Butterfly have been described by more than one critic as founding fathers of heavy metal.

1968 Diary

January

Dick Clark premieres his latest TV series called *Happening 68*.

Bob Dylan performs at New York's Carnegie Hall in a benefit concert commemorating the late Woody Guthrie. Also featured are Pete Seeger, Judy Collins, Arlo Guthrie, the Band and Richie Havens.

The Bee Gees make their US live debut with two concerts in Anaheim, California, after which they return immediately to England, without stopping anywhere else in America.

February

Priscilla Presley gives birth to Elvis' only child, Lisa Marie, in Memphis.

The Beatles close Beatles USA, their American fan club and business office, severing all American business connections.

Guitarist Dave Gilmour replaces Pink Floyd's founding member, Syd Barrett, who checks himself into a psychiatric hospital.

Frankie Lymon, who had a Number 1 hit with the Teenagers' "Why Do Fools Fall in Love?" when he was 13 years old, is found dead at 25 of a heroin overdose at his mother's New York City apartment.

The Beatles are joined by Mia Farrow and Donovan when they fly to India for two months of transcendental meditation study with Maharishi Mahesh Yogi. Weeks later, at a New York press conference, the Maharishi announces his upcoming tour with the Beach Boys.

Blues harmonica blower Little Walter is killed in a knife fight in Chicago.

March

Sales of "Simon Says" by the 1910 Fruitgum Company pass the million mark.

The Diocese of Rome announces that it disapproves of, but will not prohibit, rock'n'roll masses.

English pop group Grapefruit, managed by John Lennon, make their stage debut at London's Royal Albert Hall; after the concert, the group rapidly returns to obscurity.

Israeli duo Esther and Abi Ofarim top the UK singles charts with "Cinderella Rockefella".

April

The Beatles' new record company, Apple Corps Ltd, opens at 95 Wigmore Street, London.

Deep Purple make their concert debut in Trastrup, Denmark.

The Beatles refuse to perform for the Queen at a British Olympic Appeal Fund Show. Explains Ringo Starr: 'It's nothing personal. We just don't do benefits.'

May

Singer Mary Hopkin appears on British talent-scouting TV show *Opportunity Knocks*, where she is spotted by super-model Twiggy, who recommends her to Paul McCartney.

In Italy, at the Rome Pop Festival, 150 riot police storm the stage when the Move set off explosives as part of their act. No damage is done.

In Santa Clara, California, 24 people are hospitalized after taking mysterious pills at the Northern California Folk Rock Festival. The pills had been given out by people calling themselves 'Hog Man' and 'Hog Woman', who, at one point, leapt on stage and shouted 'We're all on Hog!' into the mike.

June

"Yummy Yummy Yummy" by the Ohio Express goes gold.

The Jeff Beck group makes its US stage debut at New York's Fillmore East. Lead singer Rod Stewart, overcome by stage fright, hides behind the speaker cabinets at the back of the stage throughout the first song.

Pink Floyd stage the first free rock concert in London's Hyde Park.

Below Led Zeppelin in flight.

July

Eric Clapton announces the break-up of Cream, due to the group's 'loss of direction'. This occurs three days after Clapton's former band, the Yardbirds, split up.

At London's Royal Albert Hall, British rock band Nice stomp on and burn an American flag during their performance of "First Amendment", a song based on "America", from the Broadway musical *West Side Story*.

The American release of new Rollings Stones album, *Beggar's Banquet*, is delayed when the group's US label, London Records, refuses to distribute the record with its cover photograph of a grafitti-covered lavatory wall.

Gram Parsons, guitarist and singer with the Byrds, refuses to accompany the band on their tour of South Africa, whose apartheid policy he opposes. Later, having left the Byrds, he will go on to form the Flying Burrito Brothers, with Sneeky Pete Kleinow, Chris Etheridge and others.

August

New releases this month include the Doors LP *Waiting for the Sun*, and The Band's debut album *Music From Big Pink*; Apple Corps Ltd releases the Beatles single "Hey Jude"/"Revolution".

Returning from a vacation to find Yoko Ono living in their London home, Cynthia Lennon sues husband John for divorce.

September

The latest Rolling Stones single, "Street Fighting Man", is banned in Chicago and other US cities because of fears that the song will incite riots and public disorder.

CBS-TV premieres *The Archies Show*, a Saturday-morning cartoon program about a high-school rock band, based on the Archie comic books.

In Washington, DC, overseas officials of the US Information Agency are required to attend a Blood, Sweat and Tears concert as part of the agency's program to acquaint overseas staff with US cultural developments.

Below Ian Anderson, founder of progressive rock legend Jethro Tull.

October

John Lennon and Yoko Ono are arrested for possession of marijuana during a raid on Ringo Starr's London home, where the couple are staying.

A US Army captain tells *Rolling Stone* magazine that 'rock'n'roll music contributes to both the usage of drugs and the high VD rate among enlisted men'.

During the Supremes' appearance at the Royal Command Variety Performance in London, singer Diana Ross interrupts the show with a plea for inter-racial understanding, and is applauded for two minutes by the audience.

November

Joe Cocker tops the UK charts with his version of the Beatles' "With a Little Help From My Friends", while the Beatles themselves are Number 1 in the American charts with "Hey Jude".

Cream play their farewell concert, at London's Royal Albert Hall.

December

NBC airs TV special *Elvis*, which includes clips from a recent live performance, Presley's first since 1961, at NBC's Burbank, California, studios.

Nixon aides send out 66 000 letters, signed by the president-elect, to potential administrative office holders. Among the recipients is Elvis Presley.

Crawling around inside a large white bag, John Lennon and Yoko Ono 'perform' onstage at the Underground Club in London – the beginning of what Yoko terms 'baggism'.

Below Alvin Lee of Ten Years After — "the fastest fingers in rock".

Woodstock Goes Pop

The Band play on

An example to all the above were the Band, who had originally backed Ronnie Hawkins and then Bob Dylan. Working in seclusion, with a settled line-up of gifted and complementary musicians, the group's first two LPs – *Music From The Big Pink* and *The Band* – were perfect examples of contemporary material rooted in traditional forms, played with a rock'n'roll sensibility. Another group working in the same rich field was Creedence Clearwater Revival, who in 1969 produced their first two LPs and a string of fine singles – including "Bad Moon Rising", a Number 1 UK. hit. Two outfits specializing in more raucous rock released debut LPs that year: Iggy and the Stooges and the MC5, both of whom would exert a greater influence than could be measured through album sales. Equally loud, though less influential, were Grand Funk Railroad, whose first LP also appeared in 1969, signaling the start of a career that made a lot of noise and even more money with undemanding (musically, at least) heavy metal.

This was the year of the supergroup. Serious musicians now populated the rock scene in ever-increasing numbers, due to the public's adulation of technical virtuosity, often for its own sake. Bands were increasingly prone to fall apart through ego-related problems (often euphemistically described as 'musical differences') and the big names tended to gravitate towards one another in the belief that this would result in better bands with bigger audiences. It was not always the case. Blind Faith were the first big British supergroup, comprised of Eric Clapton and Ginger Baker from Cream, Steve Winwood from Traffic and Rick Grech from Family. After one LP, an outdoor appearance in London's Hyde Park and a US tour, the group began to fall apart.

In America, Crosby, Stills, Nash and Young teamed up for the first time, bringing together refugees from the Byrds, Buffalo Springfield and the Hollies. Theirs was a more lasting success (particularly the second LP *Déjà Vu*), but the group were constantly involved in internal squabbles that saw them break up and reform on several occasions, thus losing creative consistency. Humble Pie suffered a similar fate when the two principals, Steve Marriott (ex-Small Faces) and Peter Frampton (ex-Herd), exchanged differences of musical opinion, and Frampton left the group.

Right Crosby, Stills, Nash and Young in performance. In 1968 ex-Byrd David Crosby (second from left), ex-Hollie Graham Nash (second from right) and ex-Buffalo Springfield Stephen Stills (right) came together to form a super group dependent on soft-rock compositions and close harmony singing. Another ex-Buffalo Springfield member Neil Young (left) joined in 1970, bringing a more acerbic edge to the music.
Far right Steve Marriott with Humble Pie, the group he formed after the disbandment of the Small Faces.

Future legends?

In London, the skinhead cult was at its height and this triggered off a boom in bluebeat/ska music from the West Indies, which was the preferred soundtrack for the shaved head and big boot tribal dances. Desmond Dekker, with "The Israelites" and "It Mek", and the Upsetters ("Return of Django") were among the artists to benefit.

Space travel and future prophecy proved fertile topics for hit singles. Zager and Evans took "In the Year 2525" to the top of the charts on both sides of the Atlantic and then promptly disappeared into a time warp. Seemingly destined for the same fate was David Bowie, who had what seemed a typical one-shot hit with "Space Oddity". He, however, was destined to go on to greater things, not the least of which was a Number 1 with exactly the same song six years later. In the UK, Jane Birkin and Serge Gainsbourg scored the first pornographic chart topper with a heavy breathing epic called "Je T'Aime (Moi Non Plus)", which anticipated Donna Summer by half a decade.

THE WOODSTOCK NATION

In the year of the festival, Woodstock towered over the rest. It was not originally meant to be a free event, but sheer force of numbers (400 000) forced the issue. Held on farmland in upstate New York, the Woodstock festival came to be regarded as the high point of the sixties' dream of peace, love and good music. An international cast of artists and bands were present, as were the film cameras and mobile recorders who would immortalize the event on celluloid and vinyl, thus rather denting the carefully nurtured 'spontaneous' feel.

Yet Woodstock was remarkably well-organized and lacked the tensions and violence that were to mar similar events later the same year. More importantly, it set a trend for large groups of people to congregate outdoors and listen to live music. It also taught these people to relish inclement weather, terrible acoustics, invisible performers, primeval sanitation and disgusting

food at cordon bleu prices. The craving for this type of entertainment, albeit in a more highly organized form, has shown no signs of diminishing.

Woodstock had more particular effects, in that it launched the careers of several artists, in the way Monterey had promised to do for Otis Redding. The beneficial influence of the event on Ten Years After has already been noted. Other grateful recipients of Woodstock kudos included Santana, blending Latin rhythms and rock on "Soul Sacrifice", Sha Na Na, rock'n'roll revivalists with eye-catching gymnastics; Sly and the Family Stone, mixing soul fire and rock flash to electrifying effect; and Richie Havens, all thumbs, no teeth and a voice of gravel. The Who, on the other hand, did not enjoy it. The events and spirit of the festival were summarized in music by Joni Mitchell (who featured neither as performer nor spectator at the actual event) in "Woodstock", which was recorded to great commercial effect by Crosby, Stills, Nash and Young (who were there) and Matthews Southern Comfort (who weren't).

Other important outdoor events that same year featured John Lennon and his Plastic Ono Band (with Eric Clapton) in Toronto, a bad-tempered Isle of Wight festival with Bob Dylan topping the bill, and – the most infamous of them all – the Rolling Stones' misconceived gesture at Altamont, which ended in mayhem and murder. It did nothing to discourage festival organizers or festival goers. Where there is mud, there you will find, as often as not, a festival in progress.

Left Creedence Clearwater Revival: (left to right) Stu Cook, Tom Fogerty, Doug Clifford and John Fogerty. Their Bayou country pop lit up the charts from 1968 to the group's break up in 1972.
Below Iggy Pop, rock's prime anarchist.

1969 Diary

January

To illustrate an article entitled 'Jimi Hendrix Socks it to the White Cats', *LOOK* magazine publishes a photo of the guitarist surrounded by bikini-clad white women.

In their final public appearance as a group, the Beatles perform on the roof of Apple Studios, Savile Row, London. After a couple of songs they are stopped by police, at the request of neighbors who dislike the noise.

"Maybe Tomorrow" by Apple band the Iveys is released in America where it goes on to reach Number 67 in the Hot 100. The Iveys subsequently become Badfinger.

February

English pop stars Lulu and Maurice Gibb, of the Bee Gees, are wed at St James Church in Buckinghamshire, England. Three thousand uninvited guests turn up for the celebrations.

Opening for Tyrannosaurus Rex on their UK tour is David Bowie – performing a silent mime act that tells the story of a young Tibetan monk.

Ringo Starr takes his first non-Beatle role in the film *Candy*, which opens this month. The movie also stars Marlon Brando and Walter Matthau, with music provided by Steppenwolf and the Byrds.

March

Tommy Roe's single "Dizzy" goes gold.

Paul McCartney marries American photographer Linda Eastman at London's Marylebone Registry Office.

In the Dickenson suite of the Amsterdam Hilton, newly-weds John Lennon and Yoko Ono begin their first 'bed-in for peace'.

At Miami's Dinner Key Auditorium, Jim Morrison of the Doors is arrested for allegedly exposing himself during their act on stage.

April

Philadelphia's biggest rock ballroom, the Electric Factory, is closed by a local judge on the grounds that it 'provides a gathering point for dealers in illicit drugs'. The American Civil Liberties Union joins the Philadelphia press and TV stations in protest at the closure.

At the Los Angeles Free Festival, a riot breaks out after a youth is arrested on the beach. There are several injuries and 117 people are arrested. None of the scheduled bands perform.

Baltimore's Rally for Decency erupts into a race riot when the guest star promised by rally organizers, James Brown, fails to show up.

John Lennon and Yoko Ono's film *Rape* is screened at the Montreux Film Festival.

Below John Lennon performs with the Plastic Ono Band soon after the 1970 split of the Beatles.
Right David Bowie as Ziggy Stardust.

May

Arrests this month include Jimi Hendrix, for narcotics possession, in Toronto; Jefferson Airplane bassist Jack Casady, for marijuana possession, in New Orleans; Who guitarist Pete Townshend, for assault (having mistaken a policeman for a fan and kicked him off the stage), in New York; and Mick Jagger and Marianne Faithfull, for marijuana possession, in London.

John Lennon's standing visa is revoked by the US Embassy on the basis of his drug conviction in England in November 1968.

Frank Zappa becomes a lecturer on the college circuit, speaking on such topics as 'Pigs, Ponies and Rock'n'Roll'. Zappa is paid $1500 per appearance.

Frank Sinatra's "My Way" enters the UK charts, where it will remain for an unprecedented 122 weeks.

June

Feast of Friends, a documentary on the Doors made by the band and their chums, premieres in Los Angeles, along with Andy Warhol's *I, a Man*, in a benefit in aid of Norman Mailer's bid to become mayor of New York City.

Brian Jones announces his departure from the Rolling Stones; he will be replaced by guitarist Mick Taylor.

American soul singer Shorty Long dies at 29 in a boating accident.

July

Brian Jones is found dead in the swimming pool of his home in Hartfield, Surrey, England. The official coroner's report attributes his death to 'misadventure'. Two days after Jones' death the Rolling Stones give a free concert in London's Hyde Park; Mick Jagger reads from Shelley's *Adonais*, in tribute to the late guitarist.

The Beatles' single "The Ballad of John and Yoko" is banned by about half of all US radio stations because of the line 'Christ, you know it ain't easy', which is considered to be sacrilegious.

Neil Young makes his first appearance with Crosby, Stills and Nash, at the Fillmore East in New York City.

Right Joe Cocker established himself in 1968 with his raw version of the Beatles' "With A Little Help From My Friends" and the most raucous soul voice since his hero Ray Charles.

August

At the Hibbing, Minnesota, High School Class of '59 reunion, Bob Dylan makes an unexpected appearance with his wife Sara, but leaves after an hour when a drunk ex-classmate tries to pick a fight with him.

When 400 000 people, mostly without tickets, show up for the three-day Woodstock Music and Arts Fair in Bethel, New York, the concert organizers declare the festival open and free.

Beach Boy Carl Wilson is arrested in Los Angeles for failure to report for civilian duty in lieu of two years' army service.

September

John Lennon and Yoko's Plastic Ono Band makes a surprise live debut at Toronto's Rock'n'Roll Revival concert; the band also includes Eric Clapton on guitar and Klaus Voorman on bass.

Ed Sullivan releases a rock'n'roll record, "The Sulli-Gulli". The eternal TV host is backed on the single by the Ed Sullivan Orchestra.

The Flamin' Groovies are among the featured acts when San Francisco's original Fillmore Auditorium reopens as a rock dance hall.

October

Paul McCartney officially denies rumors of his death.

The Beatles' single "Something"/"Come Together" is released, making it the first George Harrison song ever to make the A side of a 45.

Elvis Presley tops the American charts with his new single "Suspicious Minds".

Below The Band, Bob Dylan's one-time backing group, became legends in their own right with superbly crafted albums like *Music From Big Pink* (1968) and *Stage Fright* (1970).

Right Keith Emerson. With his bands the Nice (formed in 1967) and Emerson, Lake and Palmer (formed 1970), Emerson brought keyboards to the fore of rock.

November

Jim Morrison is arrested for drunkenness and 'interfering with the flight of an intercontinental aircraft', when, en route to Phoenix from Los Angeles to see a Rolling Stones concert, he pesters a flight attendant. All charges will later be dropped when the attendant withdraws her testimony.

Janis Joplin is arrested in Tampa, Florida, for using 'vulgar and obscene language' at her concert.

John Lennon returns his MBE, citing British involvement in the Nigeria-Biafra war, political support of the US position in Vietnam, and the poor reception of his single "Cold Turkey" as his reasons for denouncing the award.

"Sugar Sugar" by the Archies, a summertime Number 1 in America, tops the UK charts.

December

President Nixon and Vice-President Agnew are among a group of politicians attempting to discover the causes of the 'generation gap' in America by 'viewing films of simulated acid trips and listening to anti-establishment rock music'.

John and Yoko's 'War Is Over!/If You Want It' billboards go up in 12 major cities around the world.

The Trouble With Girls (And How to Get Into It), Elvis Presley's thirtieth film, is released.

Beatles Break Up

1970

In the same way that 1960 had proved to be a transitional phase following the first hot flush of rock'n'roll, so, in retrospect, 1970 was the year that the fizzing energies of the sixties gave out, to be replaced by a somewhat forced jollity. The charts, particularly in the UK, reflected a paucity of new talent, with the likes of Dana, Lee Marvin, Rolf Harris and England's World Cup Squad all hitting the top of the charts. Jimi Hendrix cheered things up later in the year with his first Number 1, "Voodoo Chile", but it was to be his only one, for he had already succumbed to a sad fate.

Hello, goodbye

It was also the year when it was formally announced that the Beatles were no more, a fact that had been self-evident for some time. They left behind a patchy last LP, *Let It Be* (with a production credited in part to Phil Spector), and a film of the same name that detailed the bickerings and flickerings of irretrievably sundered personalities.

Another influential group to go under in 1970 was the Velvet Underground. Although the name survived for some time after, Lou Reed's departure signaled the end of the road musically, and it was ironic that the release of *Loaded* that year provided the purveyors par excellence of the urban nightmare with their first commercial hit.

Below Rod Stewart (left), Ronnie Lane (center) and Ron Wood of the Faces. Formed in 1969, the group did not share the serious stance of many of their contemporaries.

Reasons to believe

Nevertheless, there were encouraging newcomers. Rod Stewart, who had spent a long apprenticeship with the likes of Jeff Beck and Long John Baldry, formed the Faces with Ronnie Wood and the remnants of the Small Faces, but more importantly launched a concurrent solo career with the release of his first two LPs – *An Old Raincoat* and *Gasoline Alley*. Free broke into the big time with their single "All Right Now", which precipitated a brief but turbulent career at the top. Another supergroup, Emerson, Lake and Palmer, produced their first LP in 1970. ELP were led by Keith Emerson, who had first come to prominence with Nice in the sixties as a flamboyant keyboards player. The members were all considered virtuosos (bass player Greg Lake required a special carpet on stage) and their grand classical/rock concerts brought them a huge audience during the seventies. A fusion of heavy rock and classical music was also favored by Deep Purple in 1970, although their *Concerto for Group and Orchestra* fared rather less well than the same year's *Deep Purple in Rock*, which presented a less ambitious decibel barrage.

The hottest new act in America was the Jackson Five. The five brothers had no less than four Number 1s in the year – "I Want You Back", "ABC", "The Love You Save", "I'll Be There" – all distinguished by the clear soprano voice of littlest brother Michael, who was not yet in his teens. Sweet-voiced vocalizing was also the speciality of three other newcomers – Three Dog Night, Bread and the Carpenters – who all topped the charts.

Center **Glitter showers down upon Rod Stewart while on stage with the Faces.**

Below **Rod Stewart presenting a smoother image for the publicity photographers.**

BEDSITTER BLUES

The pendulum swung after Woodstock. It was no longer 450 000 people in a field, but one person in a room with a record player. The fervent gregariousness of the sixties gave way to some serious introspection in the early seventies, and the ideal accompaniment for this activity was the output of the singer/songwriters.

The ideal raw material for a singer/songwriter was a person whose own private life was, or had been, in a shambles and who was able to communicate this directly, but delicately, to the listener and thereby provide solace. A prime example was James Taylor, whose *Sweet Baby James* LP, released in 1970, was ecstatically received. Taylor made no bones about the fact that he had been a drug addict, indeed it was the fact that he had overcome this weakness that formed the basis of his appeal. It was also the lyric basis of one of his biggest singles – "Fire and Rain". Taylor went on to marry Carly Simon, a singer/songwriter in her own right, who had a big hit in 1972 with the witty "You're So Vain".

Left Ringo *(top),* John *(center),* George *(bottom)* and Paul *(below).* The film *Let It Be* (1970) proved to be the Beatles' epitaph.

Never too late

The great female success of the genre was Carole King, whose 1971 LP *Tapestry* was an all-time bestseller. King had spent most of the sixties inside the Brill Building churning out songs for others. Now she lavished her undeniably commercial songwriting talents on herself, and very effectively. There were no dramatic revelations from Carole, just pretty sentiments prettily expressed, for example in the single hit "It's Too Late". A more traumatic vicarious experience was to be found on the albums of Laura Nyro, notably on 1970's *Christmas and the Beads of Sweat*. Laura went through hell with her men and was quite prepared to share, even magnify, the experience. Joni Mitchell was altogether more sophisticated, both musically and emotionally. Her love life among the stars was well documented in the press, and her ups and downs formed the content of her songs – everywoman's emotional X-rays blown up to huge size.

Below In the sixties, Carole King had been one of pop's most prolific composer, writing the music (husband Gerry Goffin supplied the words) for numerous hits. In the seventies, she was to forge a new career as a leading singer-songwriter, beginning with her highly successful LP *Tapestry* (1971).

Strong and silent?

Apart from James Taylor, men were not particularly well represented in the category, because of their reluctance to communicate directly. It would be hard, for instance, to imagine any listener leaning (metaphorically) on Randy Newman's shoulder. Leonard Cohen brought a certain gloom and guilt to the male camp, but the full effects were deflected by an overtly poetic sensibility. Perhaps the most interesting exponent of the form was Jackson Browne, who actually completed an unreleased LP in 1967 before his debut proper in 1972. His best work mixed reticence and charm with forthright expression and he developed into one of the most challenging artists of the seventies via a series of LPs.

One of the least challenging artists of the seventies was John Denver, another offshoot of the genre. He was direct in the way of a vegetarian party bore who abhors offal and has had his brains replaced by muesli. And wants to tell you about it.

Diary

January

Max Yasgur, on whose New York farm the Woodstock Festival was held, is sued by neighboring farmers for $35 000 in property damages.

At a London art gallery, John Lennon's exhibit of erotic lithographs, 'Bag One', is confiscated as evidence of pornography by Scotland Yard detectives.

Bobby Sherman's LP *Bobby Sherman* goes gold.

February

Arlo Guthrie attends the British premiere of his film *Alice's Restaurant* at the London Pavilion.

Black Sabbath's debut album is released; although the group is still relatively unknown, the LP will go on to be a chart success on both sides of the Atlantic, selling over a million copies.

Simon and Garfunkel top the US charts with "Bridge Over Troubled Water".

March

Charles Manson, on trial for the murder of actress Sharon Tate and others, releases an LP, *Lie*, to finance his legal defense.

Tammi Terrell dies at New York's Graduate Hospital after undergoing her sixth operation for brain tumors in 18 months. She was 24.

Peter Yarrow, of Peter, Paul and Mary, whose song "Puff the Magic Dragon" won a Grammy award for Best Children's Record, pleads guilty to 'taking immoral liberties' with a 14-year-old girl, in Washington, DC.

April

Washington news: Johnny Cash performs at the White House, at President Nixon's invitation. One week later, First Daughter Tricia invites Grace Slick to a White House tea party for alumni of Finch College. Slick arrives with escort Abbie Hoffman, currently on trial for conspiring to riot at the 1968 Democratic National Convention. When Hoffman is turned away at the gate, Slick leaves with him, without meeting the President's young offspring.

Blues piano legend Otis Spann dies of cancer in Chicago at the age of 40.

McCartney, the first solo album by Paul McCartney, is released. He simultaneously mentions in a press release that the Beatles no longer exist.

Below The Jackson Five whose phenomenal reign of success kicked off in 1970 with "I Want You Back". **Right** Canadian chanteuse Joni Mitchell.

May

Woodstock, a triple LP set recorded at the 1969 festival, is released. It will sell over a million copies within four months, in spite of being the most expensive rock album ever.

In the week that Fleetwood Mac's single "The Green Manalishi" enters the UK charts, Peter Green announces that he is leaving the group.

June

Chubby Checker and three others are arrested at Niagara Falls after marijuana, hashish, and unidentified drug capsules are found in the singer's car.

Bob Dylan receives an honorary doctorate of music from ivy-league Princeton University.

Derek and the Dominoes, featuring Eric Clapton, make their debut at London's Lyceum.

July

American Top Forty, Casey Casem's syndicated radio show, debuts in several US cities.

A New Haven, Connecticut, district court rules that the Powder Ridge Rock Festival, to which over 18 000 tickets have been sold at $20 apiece, would create a public nuisance and cannot be held. Although police barricade all roads to the festival site, and all utilities there are cut off, over 30 000 people show up and stay to groove at the (non-musical) festival.

August

The Medicine Ball Caravan, featuring the Grateful Dead, leaves from San Francisco on a cross-country trip, pulling seven tie-dyed teepees along with it. The moving rock festival will eventually reach the UK.

At the Isle of Wight Pop Festival in England, Joni Mitchell bursts into tears when, during her set, a man jumps onstage, grabs the mike, and shouts: 'This is just a hippie concentration camp.'

Lou Reed performs with the Velvet Underground for the last time, at Max's Kansas City Club in New York.

September

Canned Heat singer/guitarist Al Wilson is found dead, beside an empty bottle of barbiturates, at his Los Angeles home. He was 27.

Jimi Hendrix is found dead in his London apartment.

Josie and the Pussycats, a Saturday-morning cartoon series about an all-girl rock trio, debuts on CBS-TV.

October

Janis Joplin is found dead at 27 of a heroin overdose in her room at Hollywood's Landmark Hotel.

In Johannesburg, South Africa, a rock festival is raided by 200 students from Pretoria who assault members of the audience. They claim to be acting in protest at the festival's being held on President Kruger Day.

President Nixon, speaking at a radio broadcasters' conference, appeals for the screening of rock music lyrics, with those advocating drug use to be banned.

November

Connie Francis and the Cowsills are among 18 acts dropped by MGM Records for 'exploiting and promoting hard drugs through music' (though Eric Burdon and the Animals are retained). Next month, Mike Curb, MGM chairman, will be officially commended by Richard Nixon. Curb goes on to become Lieutenant Governor of California.

Bob Dylan's book *Tarantula* is published by Bantam Books.

Avant-garde jazz saxophonist Albert Ayler is found drowned in New York's Hudson River. He was 34. Rumors that he was discovered tied to a jukebox remain unconfirmed.

December

The Beach Boys play a command performance for Princess Margaret at London's Royal Albert Hall.

Osmonditis

1971

Anyone spending the middle ten weeks of the year in the UK would have been in for a nasty surprise. Consecutive chart toppers by Dawn ("Knock Three Times") and Middle of the Road ("Chirpy Chirpy Cheep Cheep") might have been regarded as proof that the nation had lost its collective musical marbles. The presence of 'grandad'-actor Clive Dunn and comedian Benny Hill in the Number 1 slot at the beginning and end of the year only made it worse. However, there were compensations. Dave Edmunds, a veteran of Love Sculpture who had a one-shot hit in 1968 with "Sabre Dance", had retired to his studio in Wales from where he issued a stream of well-crafted rock'n'roll tunes. One of them, "I Hear You Knocking", hit the top at the beginning of the year. Less exalted fare was provided by Slade, whose yobbo-rock hit the top in the shape of "Coz I Luv You", and Sweet, who affected the look of bricklayers in drag and got to Number 2 with "Co-Co".

Solo Beatles

Various individuals who had been Beatles were active during the year. Paul McCartney and his wife Linda had a Number 1 in America with the double A-side, "Uncle Albert"/"Admiral Halsey". John Lennon penetrated the UK Top Ten with "Power to the People", as did Ringo Starr with "It Don't Come Easy". Pick of the bunch was George Harrison's "My Sweet Lord", which outsold the rest handsomely. Unfortunately it was later decided that the tune leaned a bit heavily on the Chiffons' 1963 hit "He's So Fine".

The biggest new act in the United States was the relentless Osmond family who scored hits in various combinations. One had to look hard for inspiration, but the year saw the first LPs from a pair of groups who would make the early seventies more palatable: Little Feat and Crazy Horse.

Above Paul McCartney was the first member of the Beatles to release a solo album following the band's demise. *Ram* (1970) provided further proof that his gift lay in the writing of pop melodies, with the single "Maybe I'm Amazed" being the LP's best example. Throughout the seventies and into the eighties, McCartney's muse stuck with him and, though at times his songs have been over-sweet and bordered on the cloying, his career has never faltered.

Right Mick Jagger. For The Rolling Stones, the seventies opened with the live album *Get Yer Ya-Ya's Out!* on which a stage announcer introduced them as 'the greatest rock'n'roll band in the world!' There was little arguing with that.

POMP AND CIRCUMSTANCE

Two of the most successful and long-lasting bands to emerge during the year were Yes and Genesis. Both groups had released their debut albums in 1969 and both were products of a UK underground scene from which it was hard to escape. Both *The Yes Album* and *Nursery Cryme* were third LPs for the two groups and introduced them to wider audiences. Neither group was much interested in singles, concentrating instead on albums and live performances that became ever more elaborate. They were extensions of the 'progressive rock' school of thought that was concerned with pushing back the boundaries within which rock musicians were traditionally wont to work.

The hallmarks of such groups were long pieces of music, rather than songs, often containing several changes of mood and time and sometimes making use of forms of music outside the rock mainstream. Yes and Genesis were thus the latest additions to an exclusive school led by Pink Floyd (with LPs such as *Atom Heart Mother* and *Meddle*) and ELP (*Tarkus* and *Pictures at an Exhibition*).

Doing the light fantastic

This form of music (dubbed variously art rock, symphonic rock and pomp rock) exerted enormous appeal throughout the first half of the seventies. It brought with it certain benefits, such as improvements in sound quality at concerts and a broadening of musical outlook in its adherents. It brought other things of a more dubious nature, like the omnipresent light and special effects extravaganzas, which could be stunning, but were more often tired excuses for a lack of onstage dynamism. Nevertheless, most of the groups came through the excesses to deliver worthwhile records and concerts, notably Pink Floyd with *Dark Side of the Moon* and Yes with *Going for the One*. Genesis was the launch pad for the interesting solo careers of Peter Gabriel and Phil Collins. Without any of the above, Mike Oldfield's *Tubular Bells* may never have happened.

Below Genesis gained an enormous following in the mid-seventies with songs that were strong on complexity and drama.

1971 Diary

January

Aretha Franklin volunteers to stand bail of up to $250 000 for black activist Angela Davis, who is in a California prison awaiting trial for supplying guns used in a robbery.

At the Midam Festival in the south of France, Eric Burdon and War play for over an hour, although they have been allotted only 15 minutes. Elton John, due to follow them, departs in a rage.

Bob Dylan makes a rare public appearance, accompanying country star Earl Scruggs on a public TV documentary.

February

Rock critic Bill Hilton comments in the Santa Barbara *News Press:* 'Led Zeppelin has a rhythm that is unbeatable – plus one of the best girl singers in the business.'

The Osmonds reach Number 1 in the US charts with their first single, "One Bad Apple".

March

The Partridge Family's "Doesn't Somebody Want to Be Wanted?" receives a gold disc.

"Power to the People", by John Lennon and the Elephant's Memory Band, is released.

Harold McNair, flautist with Ginger Baker's Airforce and Donovan, dies of lung cancer.

April

Argent guitarist Russ Ballard is rushed to hospital in Frankfurt, Germany, after being electrocuted by a live mike while performing at the Zoom Club. He survives.

In Minneapolis, the audience at the Café Extraordinaire initiate a riot when they arrive at the club to find an imposter in the place of the advertised drummer, Buddy Miles. Total damages exceed $50 000.

New York City's New School For Social Research becomes the first institution in the country to offer a course on rock'n'roll music.

Below The Osmonds: (from left) Donny, Alan, Wayne, Jay, Merrill. The singing brothers from Ogden, Utah – committed Mormons all – were the white answer to the Jackson Five. Their enormous pop chart success during the years 1972 to 1975 was based firmly on the teen appeal of young brother Donny *(left)*.

May

"The Battle Hymn of Lieutenant Calley" by Company C peaks at Number 37 in the US charts. The record, a song in praise of the American army officer recently convicted for the pre-meditated murder of 22 Vietnamese at My Lai, goes gold the following April.

Mick Jagger marries Nicaraguan Bianca Perez Morena de Marias in St Tropez.

Bob Dylan celebrates his thirtieth birthday at Jerusalem's Wailing Wall.

June

Elvis Presley's birthplace, a two-room house in Tupelo, Mississippi, is opened to the public.

Clyde McPhatter, ex-lead singer with the Drifters, dies of heart and liver disease, in the Bronx, New York City.

Paul Revere and the Raiders' "Indian Reservation", their only American chart-topper, goes gold.

July

Doors singer Jim Morrison is found dead in a bathtub by his wife Pamela while on vacation in Paris.

Jazzman Louis Armstrong dies in New Orleans, at the age of 71.

T Rex's "Get It On" reaches Number 1 in the UK charts.

August

The Concert for Bangladesh, organized by George Harrison, is held at New York's Madison Square Garden. Performers include Harrison, Ravi Shankar, Billy Preston, Eric Clapton, Leon Russell, Ringo Starr, Badfinger and Bob Dylan.

Saxophone player King Curtis is stabbed to death in New York City.

Above James Taylor. The phenomenal success of his LP *Sweet Baby James* (1970) prompted *Time* magazine to put Taylor on the cover and describe his popularity as a sign of a new maturity in rock music.
Right Progressive rock supremos Yes.

September

Donny Osmond's "Go Away Little Girl" hits Number 1 in the US charts.

Guitarist and singer Peter Frampton announces his departure from Humble Pie.

The Old Grey Whistle Test, devoted to 'serious' rock music, debuts on BBC-TV. The show will survive the seventies and become even more popular in the eighties when, having shortened its name to *The Whistle Test*, it stars Paul McCartney lookalike Mark Ellen.

October

Rock'n'roll legend Gene Vincent dies at the age of 36 in Los Angeles.

The Allman Brothers' guitarist, Duane Allman, is killed in a motorcycle accident near his home in Macon, Georgia.

At a rock'n'roll revival at New York's Madison Square Garden, Ricky Nelson is booed for performing new material. The experience will be recounted in Nelson's 1972 hit, "Garden Party".

November

The Frank Zappa film *200 Motels* is premiered at the London Pavilion.

Bob Dylan records protest song "George Jackson".

Blues singer and harpist Herman 'Little Junior' Parker dies while undergoing brain surgery in Chicago.

December

Frank Zappa falls from the stage and breaks a leg at London's Rainbow Theatre after being attacked by a fan's jealous husband.

John and Yoko appear at a benefit concert for John Sinclair in Anne Arbor, Michigan. Sinclair, former manager of left-wing rock group MC5 and leader of the radical White Panther Party, is serving a prison sentence for possession of two marijuana cigarettes.

English comedian Benny Hill's hit single "Ernie (the Fastest Milkman in the West)", reaches Number 1 in the UK charts.

Below **Genesis on stage in the early seventies with singer Peter Gabriel striking a typically theatrical pose. When Gabriel left the band in 1975, Phil Collins took over as lead singer at the mike.**

Soul and Glitter

1972

The soul music scene in the United States was particularly active during 1972. The immaculate, swooping voice of Al Green was heard to great effect on "Let's Stay Together", the first big hit for him in a career that spanned the seventies, until he turned to God and gospel music. Roberta Flack stormed to Number 1 with the emotion-soaked ballad, "The First Time Ever I Saw Your Face", a feat she repeated the next year with "Killing Me Softly With His Song". Bill Withers, who had been plucked from his job fitting toilets into airliners, also reached the top with "Lean On Me". Tamla Motown had its usual productive year as the Temptations cruised to Number 1 with the deliriously funky "Papa Was a Rolling Stone" and Michael Jackson kicked his promising solo career into overdrive with his spooky ballad to a rat, "Ben".

The new sound was from Philadelphia and was masterminded by producers Kenny Gamble and Leon Huff. It was a controlled and sophisticated music, which at its best was deeply affecting and highly danceable to at the same time. The best of the year's crop included "Back Stabbers" by the O'Jays, "If You Don't Know Me By Now" by Harold Melvin and the Blue Notes, and the chart-topping "Me and Mrs Jones" by Billy Paul.

Rock'n'roll outlaws

New groups included the Eagles, whose self-named debut LP appeared in 1972. Despite its sun-kissed West Coast sound, the album was actually recorded in London. The Doobie Brothers also made a certain impact by virtue of their single "Listen to the Music".

The most interesting newcomers of the year were Steely Dan, who touched a nerve with their very first LP, *Can't Buy a Thrill*, which spawned two hit singles in "Do It Again" and "Reeling in the Years". Steely Dan were an uncompromising unit, both musically and lyrically, and never pandered to an audience (least of all a live audience, as they retired from touring early in their career). Although they experienced a commercial decline after this, they persevered, and were rewarded by a huge following by the end of the seventies with big-selling albums such as *Aja*.

Below Image-conscious and imaginative, David Bowie brought elements of theater to the world of rock.

All that glitters

After the euphoria of the late sixties and the subsequent return to more conservative musical modes, it was inevitable that there would be a return to extrovert rock. This duly happened in the early seventies with the glam-rock explosion, a particularly contemporary display of hard, metallic colors, future games, androgyny and harsh noise.

One of the most important figures in the movement was Marc Bolan, who neatly spanned the gap between the late-sixties flower children as the leader of Tyrannosaurus Rex and the brash glitter children of the early seventies as the leader of T Rex. Whereas the former band specialized in cross-legged acoustic noodlings of a wispy and mystical bent, the latter were a hot pop combo. T Rex strongly featured Bolan's elementary but instinctive electric guitar thrashings and lyric concerns altogether more worldly. "Ride a White Swan" was Bolan's first big effort of the seventies and while its title betrayed a lingering hippie perfume, the music conformed to the rhythms of the new pop. Successive hits completed the transformation: "Hot Love"; "Get It On" (also a hit in America); "Metal Guru"; "Telegram Sam". Bolan also transformed himself from elfin pixie to a pouting and suggestive rock'n'roll prophet.

Left Marc Bolan who, at the start of the seventies, transformed himself from uncompromising hippie into teen idol. In 1968 Tyrannosaurus Rex was making LPs with titles like *My People Were Fair And Had Sky In Their Hair, But Now They're Content To Wear Stars On Their Brows*, but changed style and became T. Rex in 1970, singing songs like "Hot Love".

WHEN ZIGGY PLAYS GUITAR...

If Bolan was the prophet, then David Bowie was the messiah. After his 1969 single hit with "Space Oddity", he had disappeared to an arts lab in South London, completely rethought his act and then launched himself on an unsuspecting world with the albums *Hunky Dory* and *The Rise and Fall of Ziggy Stardust and the Spiders From Mars*. The second of these was the masterstroke, with Bowie in futuristic garb and a space helmet of hair fronting a genuine power trio, featuring Mick Ronson's slabs of dense guitar. The image, the stage show, the LP were all perfectly realized and put a huge firecracker under the lethargy of the early seventies.

Below Neil Diamond had been a successful pop writer in the sixties, and in the seventies he became a successful performer in his own right, signing for Columbia records in 1973 for a staggering $5 million.

An even more calculated attack was launched during 1972 by the only genuine newcomers, Roxy Music, who appeared from nowhere with a stunning debut LP and a top five single, "Virginia Plain". Whereas Bowie was an instinctive performer, whose act derived from his innate theatricality, Roxy Music worked from the outside, encasing themselves within a style that was an artful combination of art deco fleapit and future shock. Their stage shows were minutely choreographed around the mock-classic vibrato crooning of Bryan Ferry – with visual assistance from the colorful figure of synthesizer-player Brian Eno. The music combined a timeless melodic flair with thoroughly modern arrangements to achieve a sensational – and highly successful – effect.

Toiling away in the boiler room of UK glam-rock was Gary Glitter, an old trouper who had already been through one incarnation, as Paul Raven, in the sixties. Although widely regarded as the joker in the pack, an aging fowl trussed up in silver foil, Glitter's music was solidly based in a sub-Spector wall-of-guitar sound (courtesy of producer Mike Leander). The primitive vocal style was undeniably effective and, in a movement that took itself seriously, refreshingly tongue-in-cheek.

Below Alice Cooper's real name was Vincent Furnier. His onstage antics — jiving with real live snakes, decapitating dolls and the like — was designed to shock.

Plastic Dolls

In America, meanwhile, glitter-rock was taking some peculiar forms. The New York Dolls had built up a stage show based firmly on excess as the only response to the conditions of life. They dressed outrageously and emphasized their strikingly cadaverous features with garish make-up. A combination of high heels and high spirits made them a volatile, not to say unstable, live act. Their LPs (all two of them) never quite captured the band's ferocious charm, but they were later widely acknowledged as progenitors of the punk movement.

Alice Cooper, on the other hand, based his act on the old traditions of Gothic melodrama, complete with all the props required to simulate death on stage. To this, Cooper added the requisite amount of gender confusion and an enthusiastic rock'n'thrash. His 1972 smash "School's Out" was fairly typical of his output — mildly anarchic lyrics set to a traditional rock anthem.

Below Bryan Ferry, suave, cool singer of Roxy Music who shot to notoriety in 1972 with the hit single "Virginia Plain".

1972 Diary

January

David Seville, creator of the Chipmunks, dies at 52.

George Harrison and co's album *The Concert for Bangladesh*, a three-record set, goes gold, one month after its release.

Jazz singer 'Big Maybelle' Smith dies at 47 in Cleveland.

British pop group the New Seekers receive a gold record for their hit single "I'd Like To Teach the World to Sing", a song based on the music for the advertisement of a well-known carbonated beverage.

Gospel singer Mahalia Jackson dies in Chicago aged 64.

February

David Bowie, whose *Hunky Dory* LP was released in January, tells the press: 'I'm going to be huge – it's quite frightening.'

The BBC ban Paul McCartney and Wings' debut single, "Give Ireland Back to the Irish", on political grounds.

John Lennon and Yoko Ono are guest hosts for one week on an afternoon chat program, *The Mike Douglas Show*. The week's guests include Black Panther Bobby Seale and rock'n'roller Chuck Berry.

Below Inspired by the Byrds and the Flying Burrito Brothers, the Eagles formed in Los Angeles in 1971. Right During their brief existence (1971-74), the New York Dolls, with their thrashing guitars, high heels and snarls, were treated as a joke. Their influence on the punk movement to follow, however, was enormous.

March

Trevor Howell, the jealous husband who attacked Frank Zappa at London's Rainbow Theatre the previous December, is given a one-year prison sentence.

Los Angeles radio station KHJ is raided by the police, who have been receiving calls from frantic listeners who feared that the station was under siege when disc jockey Robert Morgan played Donny Osmond's single "Puppy Love" non-stop from 6.00 to 7.30am. No arrests are made.

Carole King, James Taylor and Barbra Streisand are among the featured acts at a benefit show for Democratic presidential contender George McGovern at the Los Angeles Forum.

April

Sly Stone fails to appear on stage for a performance with the Family Stone at New York's Apollo Theater, preferring to remain in his dressing room watching TV.

The management of London's Royal Albert Hall ban all future rock concerts because of a 'growing hooligan element'.

New York City's Mayor John Lindsay asks the federal government to halt deportation proceedings against John Lennon and Yoko Ono, citing the couple's 'unique contributions in the fields of music and art'.

May

Les Harvey, guitarist for Stone the Crows, is fatally electrocuted on stage at a concert in Swansea, Wales.

Gospel and blues guitarist Reverend Gary Davies dies at the age of 70 in New Jersey.

Paul McCartney and Wings' single, "Mary Had a Little Lamb", is released. The BBC do not ban it.

June

Blues singer 'Mississippi' Fred McDowell dies at the age of 68.

Rock'n'roll musical *Grease* opens at Broadway theater the Broadhurst, after a four-month run off-Broadway.

The Tallahatchie Bridge, immortalized in Bobbie Gentry's hit "Ode to Billy Joe", collapses.

July

Bobby Ramirez, drummer of Edgar White's White Trash, is fatally stabbed outside a Chicago nightclub.

Emerson, Lake and Palmer are mobbed by hysterical fans at Tokyo Airport.

After 1729 performances, Broadway rock musical *Hair* closes.

A bomb, placed under the loading ramp of the Montreal Forum, blows out 30 speakers stored in the nearby Rolling Stones equipment truck. Montreal radio stations receive over 50 different phone calls, from persons and groups claiming to be responsible for the incident, but the culprit is never discovered.

August

Brian Cole, founder member of the Association, dies from a heroin overdose at his New York home.

Alice Cooper's "School's Out" replaces Donny Osmond's "Puppy Love" at the top of the UK charts.

Bobby Vinton opens for John Lennon and Yoko Ono at Madison Square Garden.

September

Rory Storm, lead singer of Liverpool band Rory Storm and the Hurricanes (Ringo Starr's pre-Beatles band), dies from an overdose of sleeping pills.

Francisco Carrasco, a sandwich vendor, is murdered while working at a Wishbone Ash concert in Texas.

San Antonio declares 'Cheech and Chong Day' and two representatives from the mayor's office meet the comedy duo at the airport and officially welcome them.

October

Michael Jackson reaches Number 1 in the American charts with "Ben", the title song of a film about a rat of that name.

The Who's "Join Together" is adopted as the official theme for the US Council for World Affairs.

Elton John gives a Command Performance for HM Queen Elizabeth. He is first rock star to be requested by the monarch since the Beatles' Command Performance in 1963.

November

Singer/songwriters Carly Simon and James Taylor marry in New York.

Berry Oakley, bass player for the Allman Brothers Band, dies in a motorcycle crash in Macon, Georgia, where Duane Allman had died similarly the previous year, aged 24.

The Rainbow, London's first permanent rock'n'roll theater, opens with The Who as the first act.

New York Dolls drummer Billy Murcia, 21, dies after a night of excess at the Speakeasy Club in London.

December

The BBC bans Wings' new single "Hi Hi Hi" because of its suggestive lyrics, yet Chuck Berry's "My Ding-a-Ling" tops the UK charts.

James Brown is arrested while talking to fans after a show in Knoxville, Tennessee, and charged with disorderly conduct. It is soon realized that the police acted on false reports – that the singer was trying to incite a riot – and the incident is written off as a 'misunderstanding' after Brown threatens to sue the city for $1 million.

Alexander's department store in New York City stays open especially late one night, to allow Alice Cooper to do his Christmas shopping.

Soft Rock

1973

Established stars dominated the charts in 1973. The glitter boom apart, there was no radically new movement to distract the record-buying public. Various ex-Beatles maintained a high chart profile, while the Stones and Stevie Wonder carried on as before. Diana Ross, having split from the Supremes, was embarked on a wildly successful solo career with hits like "Touch Me in the Morning". Elton John, after a long apprenticeship on the UK club scene, hit the top with a series of pleasing melodies and eye-catching piano playing that boosted him to international superstar status. The Who returned to their mod origins for the inspiration behind *Quadrophenia* (1973) a highly ambitious double-album set that was later turned into a film, as was their earlier concept set *Tommy* (1969). Country singer/songwriter Jim Croce began a run of success that was all the more extraordinary because it was largely posthumous (echoing a similar phenomenon involving another country star, Jim Reeves, in the UK in the late sixties).

Cult heroes

Late entrants in the glitter stakes were Queen, who mixed hard rock with camp posturing, and Lou Reed, whose post-Velvet Undergound doldrums came to an end when David Bowie took a hand in his career. The result was an LP, *Transformer*, and a single, "Walk on the Wild Side", that gave Reed his first taste of mass commercial acceptance. A touch of the occult was the trademark of new heavy metal band Blue Oyster Cult, who developed a menacing sound, on record and live, which would eventually bring them to the attention of a wide audience.

In the UK, Suzi Quatro, a diminutive bass-player from Detroit, hammered out several gutsy pop-rock singles – including "Can the Can" and "48 Crash" – that achieved considerable chart success. Roy Wood, talented songwriter behind the sixties success of the Move and a founder member of the Electric Light Orchestra, took his new group, Wizzard, to the top with a pair of clever, Spector-esque singles – "See My Baby Jive" and "Angel Fingers".

Below Suzi Quatro, the leather-bound glitter queen of the mid-seventies.

FAMILY FAVORITES AND ALL THAT JAZZ

There were two trends worthy of note in 1973. The first was readily apparent, particularly in the UK, and concerned the overwhelming success of clean-cut, family-orientated pop music as purveyed by the Osmonds, in all their infinite permutations, and David Cassidy, who came to prominence via the Partridge Family of TV and record fame. The accent was on wholesome good looks, hummable melodies that bordered on the banal, and a complete absence of threat. If the activities of these stars gave rise to a feeling of unease at the cold calculation involved, for this was pop pushed as merchandise like never before, then it was not a scruple shared by many.

Below **The Electric Light Orchestra were formed from the ashes of the Move by Roy Wood and Jeff Lynne in 1971. Wood soon departed, leaving Lynne to steer the assemblage to symphonic success.**

Sounds incorporated

At the other end of the scale was a more arcane movement, which nevertheless had a legion of devoted followers. Ever since Miles Davis had incorporated rock elements on his 1969 LP *Bitches Brew*, there had been a growing interest in the possibilities of fusing techniques and ideas from the worlds of rock and jazz.

Early exponents on the rock scene included the Electric Flag, Blood Sweat and Tears, and Chicago, but they tended towards simplicity, often merely adding brass sections to what were basically rock structures. More interesting were the jazz-trained musicians who strayed into the rock field. John McLaughlin, the British guitarist who made his name on *Bitches Brew*, went on to find a wider audience with his Mahavishnu Orchestra whose LPs, notably *Birds of Fire* (1973), featured an exhilarating rush of sound, led by McLaughlin's quicksilver guitar runs. Other protégés of the Miles Davis school were Jo Zawinul and Wayne Shorter, who formed Weather Report, a consistently innovative group of accomplished ensemble and solo players also operating at the boundaries of rock and jazz. More funk-orientated was Herbie Hancock, and his satisfying fusions received great popular acclaim in 1974 with the release of *Head Hunters*.

1973 Diary

January

The Osmonds' "Crazy Horses" is banned by the South African government, who suspect that the song's title refers to heroin.

Yoko Ono, on the release of her two-record set *Approximately Infinite Universe*: 'I figured if George Harrison can put out a triple album, then I can put out a double album.'

Jerry Lee Lewis makes his debut at the Grand Ole Opry, having agreed to Opry officials' conditions that he abstain from using any profanity, and that he perform only his country songs. By the end of his half-hour set, Lewis has played "Great Balls of Fire", "Whole Lotta Shakin' Goin' On", and most of his other rock'n'roll hits.

February

The film *The Harder They Come*, starring reggae singer Jimmy Cliff, opens in New York.

Max Yasgur, whose farm in New York was the site of the Woodstock Festival, dies in Florida of a heart attack at the age of 53.

NBC-TV debuts its rock concert show *Midnight Special*, hosted by Helen Reddy.

March

Grateful Dead singer and organist Ron 'Pigpen' McKern dies in Corte Madera, California, of cirrhosis of the liver.

Lou Reed is bitten on the buttock by a fan during a concert in Buffalo, New York.

Dr Hook and the Medicine Show appear on the cover of *Rolling Stone* magazine, six days before their hit record, "The Cover of the Rolling Stone", goes gold.

Above right Queen blended progressive sounds with touches of glamor with profitable results.
Below right Queen guitarist Brian May.

Below Elton John (born Reg Dwight) at the piano.

April

Rod Stewart, apologizing for the poor quality of the Faces' new album, *Ooh La La*, explains: 'We're still playing the same numbers 'cause we've got nothing else to do.'

Dawn's "Tie A Yellow Ribbon Round the Old Oak Tree" tops US and UK charts simultaneously. It will become the best-selling single of the year in both countries.

Appearing on ABC-TV's *In Concert*, the J Geils Band perform their hit song "Give it to Me", and later find they have been censored because of the lyric 'Get it up'.

May

Columbia Records fires its company president, Clive Davis, accusing him of spending $94 000 of company money on his son's Bar Mitzvah and decorating his New York apartment.

Fire and Rain's only US chart hit peaks at Number 100.

Carole King gives a free concert before an estimated 100 000 fans in New York City's Central Park.

Below By 1975 Led Zeppelin — Jimmy Page, Robert Plant, John Paul Jones, and John 'Bonzo' Bonham — had become the most popular live attraction in the world and, in the space of six years, had notched up an equal number of multi-million selling albums.

June

Soft Machine drummer Robert Wyatt is paralyzed, following an accidental fall from the fourth floor window during a party.

The film *American Graffiti*, a nostalgic look at the early sixties with a rock'n'roll soundtrack, opens in New York City.

Clarence White, guitarist with the Byrds, is hit and killed by a car in Lancaster, Ohio.

Murray Wilson, father of Beach Boys Brian, Carl and Dennis, dies of a heart attack in Whittier, California. As well as being the band's original manager/producer, he also released his own instrumental album *The Many Moods of Murray Wilson* in 1967.

July

US all-girl rock group Fanny are banned from performing at the London Palladium as the management considers their stage dress to be 'too provocative'.

Bob Dylan releases the soundtrack album to *Pat Garrett and Billy the Kid*. The feature film, which is the first that Dylan ever acted in, also stars Kris Kristofferson and Rita Coolidge.

On tour in the United States, Led Zeppelin are the victims of one of the largest cash robberies ever reported. While staying at the Drake Hotel, in New York City, $180 000 is stolen from the group's safe deposit box.

August

Stevie Wonder is rushed to hospital in a coma after a car crash in North Carolina.

Lillian Roxon, author of *Rock Encyclopedia* (1969), the first comprehensive survey of rock, dies of cancer at 41.

In Detroit, Paul Williams, one of the original Temptations, is found shot dead in his car holding a gun in his lap.

Rita Coolidge and Kris Kristofferson are married in Malibu, California, with the groom's minister-father presiding over the service.

September

Singer/songwriter Gram Parsons, formerly with the Byrds and the Flying Burrito Brothers, is found dead at the Joshua Tree Inn in California. His body is later hijacked by road manager Phil Kaufman and buried in the desert.

Singer/songwriter Jim Croce is killed when his chartered plane crashes on take-off in Louisiana.

Elton John performs a concert at the Hollywood Bowl and is introduced as 'The biggest, largest, most gigantic and fantastic man, the co-star of my next movie . . .' by the show's MC, Linda Lovelace.

Below Diana Ross's portrayal of blues singer Billie Holiday in the film *Lady Sings The Blues* (1972) gained her an Oscar nomination.

October

Elvis and Priscilla Presley are divorced.

Capital Radio, Britian's first legal commercial station, airs for the first time.

November

A Who concert in Newcastle, England, is interrupted when Pete Townshend and Keith Moon begin fighting with their sound engineers.

John Rostill, ex-bass player with the Shadows, is fatally electrocuted at his home in Hertfordshire in England.

December

Singer and film star Bobby Darin dies in Hollywood, following heart surgery.

In San Francisco, traffic is backed up for five blocks around one post office on the day that Bob Dylan fans have the first opportunity to mail in ticket requests for the singer's forthcoming tour. All the concerts – 658 000 tickets – sell out.

The Who are jailed overnight for $6000-worth of hotel destruction after playing a show at the Montreal Forum.

Rock 'n' Roll Revival

1974

This was a year of wild profusion, particularly in the American charts, where there were no less than 34 different Number 1s in the singles charts. There was the usual mixture of old faces – McCartney, Lennon, Stevie Wonder, Eric Clapton – and newcomers. Among the newcomers were Bachman Turner Overdrive, a Canadian power-pop combo who had a hit with the infectious "You Ain't Seen Nothing Yet", and Barry White, a wildly overweight soul/disco crooner.

The UK meanwhile was still deeply immersed in what had come to be called teenybop – music of a less than demanding nature made by, and for, the young teenagers who now constituted the largest part of the singles-buying public. The Osmonds and their ilk had been the first to realize the potential that was so far relatively untapped, but they were soon joined by a number of home grown artists, including the Bay City Rollers, Kenny and Mud (the last-named being far from young themselves). There was also a rock'n'roll revival spearheaded by the Rubettes and Showaddywaddy, both of whom bore a passing resemblance to earlier American revivalists such as the talented Sha-Na-Na.

Right Darryl Hall and John Oates teamed up in 1972 to record the *Whole Oates* album. Ten years and 12 LPs later, they had become the most successful duo in pop chart history.

The Company you keep

On the group scene, the most impressive newcomers were Bad Company, yet another supergroup made up of ex-members of Free, Mott the Hoople and King Crimson. Their eponymous first LP and the single from it – "Can't Get Enough of Your Love" – were instantaneous smashes, especially in America where a large market existed for exactly Bad Company's brand of raunchy hard rock.

The American heavy-rock sensation of the year was Ted Nugent, who had spent the sixties with cult band the Amboy Dukes. Under his own name, Nugent's star quickly went into ascendancy. He used a succession of tightly-run and well-drilled backing musicians and traded in a pain-threshold display of guitar pyrotechnics. He also reputedly hunted, shot and ate wild animals, which made perfect sense in the context of his music. Less outrageous but perhaps more interesting music was made by Nils Lofgren and Todd Rundgren.

SOUL LOVE

The soul scene had grown throughout the seventies into a massive and many-faceted monster. Tamla Motown had done much to popularize the form from the sixties onwards, with significant contributions from Memphis and Philadelphia. Yet it remained, strangely, a singles scene. This was partly the fault of the record companies, who had continued with the old formula of a couple of hits and ten fillers on each LP, long after rock musicians had gone over to producing music specifically designed to reward repeated listenings to an LP. However, by the middle of the seventies, the better soul artists had taken to recording albums with a flourish, and artists were reaping the rewards of wider (and whiter) audiences. Particularly worthy of note was Stevie Wonder with such hit LPs as *Talking Book*, *Innervisions* and *Fulfillingness' First Finale*, and Marvin Gaye with his magnificent documents of private passion and public venom, *Let's Get It On* and *What's Going On?*

Below Todd Rundgren, who divided his time between a successful solo career and a producer for acts as diverse as Badfinger, Hall and Oates and the New York Dolls.

Van the man
White artists had always aspired to the condition of soulfulness and some even possessed the necessary equipment. Van Morrison, who had left both Them and the UK in the sixties, had built a strong following through a series of brilliant but commercially disappointing LPs, including the all-time classic *Astral Weeks* and *Moondance*. Although the material was not overtly soulful, his voice certainly was, and by the mid seventies Morrison was performing a live act of astonishing power and soul. This was captured on a live double set – *It's Too Late to Stop Now* – which brought him to the delighted attention of a whole new audience, white and black.

Another outfit with pretensions to soul (although theirs was a cooler approach) were Hall and Oates, whose early seventies LPs (particularly *Abandoned Luncheonette*) showed an appreciation of the form, if not the fire. This new breed of white soul (or blue-eyed soul as it was often called) threw up a most unlikely representative in 1975. The Average White Band hailed from the frozen wastes of Scotland, but they set America and the UK on fire with their debut LP and the single "Pick Up the Pieces".

1974 Diary

January

Country star Tex Ritter dies in Nashville, following a heart attack.

Dino Martin, son of actor/singer Dean Martin and ex-member of pop trio Dino, Desi and Billy, is arrested for possession of firearms.

Greg Lake, of Emerson, Lake and Palmer, is arrested for nude bathing in the swimming pool at Salt Lake City's Royal Inn.

February

Seven days after being granted a legal separation from husband Sonny Bono, Cher sues him for 'conspiracy to defraud' her.

Bobby Bloom, whose "Montego Bay" was an international hit in 1970, shoots himself dead in Hollywood at the age of 28.

March

New York City band Television, featuring Richard Hell and Tom Verlaine, play their first ever gig, at the city's Townhouse Theater.

Australian nun Sister Janet Mead enters the US charts with a rock'n'roll version of the Lord's Prayer.

Ike Turner is arrested for possession of a 'blue box' – a device used to make long-distance phone calls for free.

The Ramones make their live debut at the Performance Studio in New York.

April

Swedish group Abba win the Eurovision Song Contest with "Waterloo".

Sha Na Na guitarist Vinnie Taylor dies in his room at the Charlottesville Holiday Inn of a suspected heroin overdose.

Pamela Morrison, widow of Doors singer Jim, dies of a heroin overdose.

May

Rock organist Graham Bond is killed by a subway train at London's Finsbury Park underground station.

A 14-year-old girl is killed, and over 1000 people are treated for injuries, during a David Cassidy concert at London's White City Stadium.

June

Sly Stone marries Kathy Silva on-stage at New York City's Madison Square Garden.

Geoff Britton replaces Wings drummer Denny Seiwell, who quit the band several months before.

Below In 1974 Bob Dylan reunited with the Band (guitarist Robbie Robertson, left) for a US tour that took in 21 cities and was seen by over 650,000 people.

July

Cass Elliot, one-time member of the Mamas and the Papas, dies of a heart attack after choking on a chicken sandwich in London.

Former member of the Chad Mitchell Trio John Denver receives a gold record for his all-time biggest hit, "Annie's Song".

August

Bill Chase, trumpeter with jazz-rock band Chase, dies in a plane crash in Jackson, Minnesota.

In a federal court, John Lennon testifies that the Nixon administration tried to have him deported because of his involvement in anti-war demonstrations at the 1972 Republican Convention in Miami, Florida.

September

Robbie McIntosh, drummer with the Average White Band, dies of a heroin overdose in Los Angeles.

The Place I Love, an LP by folk duo Splinter, is the first release on George Harrison's new label, Dark Horse.

Below Formed in 1969 by songwriter David Gates, Bread's laid-back, soothing pop formula yielded immediate results when their single "Make It With You" went to the top of the American charts in 1970.

October

Ted Nugent is arrested for indecent exposure when his loincloth falls off during a concert at the North Hall in Memphis, Tennessee.

Less than six months after marrying Sly Stone, on-stage at Madison Square Garden, New York, Kathy Silva Stone files for divorce.

Randy Newman performs with an 87-piece symphony orchestra at Atlanta's Symphony Hall. The orchestra's conductor is Emil Newman, Randy's uncle.

November

R&B pianist and songwriter Ivory Joe Hunter dies in Memphis, Tennessee.

Fifteen-year-old Danny Bonaduce, who plays Danny Partridge on the TV show *The Partridge Family*, is arrested for possession of marijuana.

Ted Nugent wins the National Squirrel Shooting and Archery Contest, picking off 28 squirrels with a handgun during the three-day event.

December

Ravi Shankar, suffering chest pains while on tour with George Harrison, is hospitalized in Chicago. One week later he is released and re-joins the tour in Boston.

Guitarist Mick Taylor leaves the Rolling Stones.

George Harrison meets President Gerald Ford when he accepts the invitation of the President's son Jack to lunch at the White House.

Emergence of Reggae

The year before the punk boom was not as stagnant as many commentators have suggested. A variety of new styles and artists were in evidence, some of which lasted longer than others. One that thankfully did not last was the mauling of old Ink Spots material by comedy duos – in this case Windsor Davies and Don Estelle. There were many exciting new soul/disco acts in the charts including the Ohio Players ("Fire"), Labelle ("Lady Marmalade"), Van McCoy ("The Hustle") and Earth Wind and Fire ("Shining Star"). Also getting in on the disco craze were the Bee Gees with their most successful single for some years, "Jive Talkin'". Another song with a mutant disco beat was "Fame", which took David Bowie to the top with John Lennon.

Time, gentlemen please

The disco boom swept across America, with the UK not far behind. However, the south of England was playing host to a different phenomenon: pub rock. It did not last, but it paved the way for the punk explosion by opening up many new venues where smaller bands could play for an appreciative audience – beer drinkers. The biggest act on these particular boards was Dr Feelgood, an uncompromising R&B outfit from Canvey Island, whose guitarist Wilko Johnson pioneered a staccato style of playing rooted in the style of the old Pirates' guitarist Mick Green. Graham Parker was the outstanding vocalist, and with his band the Rumour (a pub rock supergroup, no less) he made the transition from small pubs and clubs to the national charts. Supertramp, a group who had experienced an erratic early career, finally got their act together in the form of their *Crime of the Century* LP, whose success in the UK was eventually eclipsed by that in America.

Here comes the Boss

The hottest new artist in America was Bruce Springsteen. His career had been dogged early on by comparisons to Bob Dylan and two excellent LPs had died something of a death. Although he was now tagged 'the future of rock'n'roll', Springsteen released a third album, *Born to Run*, which overcame all public resistance to the hyperbole surrounding him. His tough romanticism, supported by impeccable musicianship, was a seventies tonic.

Above Bruce Springsteen arrived on the scene in 1973 with the album *Greetings From Asbury Park, N.J.* and was hailed as the new Bob Dylan.

Right Eric Clapton. During the early seventies the virtuoso tried to live down the 'guitar hero' tag he had gained with a succession of surprisingly mellow albums.

REGGAE MUSIC

The emergence of soul as a force in the LP market was only one facet of a mushrooming black music scene. The influence of West Indian ska and blue-beat has already been considered in the relatively local context of London in the late sixties, but the modern version of this music – called reggae – was now starting to make an impact. In England, Chris Blackwell's Island Records had long championed reggae (Blackwell was, in fact, a white Jamaican), even during the long periods when it virtually retreated from public sight. However, in 1975, reggae found itself a star in the person of Bob Marley, who had been active in his native Jamaica for years as part of the Wailers and whose records, if not his face, were familiar to pop audiences through cover versions by artists such as Eric Clapton ("I Shot the Sheriff") and Johnny Nash. In 1975, *Catch a Fire* was released (in a sleeve shaped like a giant zippo lighter) and Marley began his rise to stardom.

Rasta man cometh

Being a Rastafarian, his politics were hard-hitting, but Marley's knack with a tune and his unwillingness to descend to mere preaching meant that he was the first (and still the biggest) reggae artist to cross over to mainstream acceptance, via songs like "No Woman No Cry" and "Jamming" and a soul-stirring live act.

Other reggae artists who have achieved a certain prominence are Peter Tosh (an ex-Wailer), Junior Murvin, Max Romeo, Burning Spear, Black Uhuru and Dennis Brown. No less notable has been the work of various reggae producers, who early on conceived a mind-scrambling montage of echo and aural lunacy to create dub music, which has had a profound effect on subsequent mainstream rock. The Clash, the Police, the Specials and the Beat are just some of the new wave of British groups who have acknowledged their debt in this direction.

Left Leroy 'Sugar' Bonner of the Ohio Players. The Players were formed in 1959 but it was not until the mid-seventies that, with their percussive brand of funk, they began to gain public acclaim.

Below Labelle. As the Blue-Belles, they made the US Top Twenty in 1962, but it was another 13 years before they reached the Top Twenty again — having changed their image to space-queen and their sound to funk — with "Lady Marmalade" (1975).

1975 Diary

January

Barry Manilow has his first Number 1 hit in the American charts with "Mandy".

Rioting erupts at the Boston Garden among crowds waiting to buy Led Zeppelin concert tickets; Boston Mayor Kevin White cancels the concert the next day.

The Wiz, starring Diana Ross in a soul remake of *The Wizard of Oz*, opens at the Majestic Theater on Broadway.

February

R&B saxophonist Louis Jordon dies in Los Angeles. He was 66 years old.

Chad Mitchell, former leader of folk group the Chad Mitchell Trio, is sentenced to five years in prison by a San Antonio judge for possession of marijuana. Mitchell was caught by police while driving a truck carrying 600 pounds of marijuana across the Mexican border into Texas.

March

Pete Townshend's 14-year-old brother Simon releases his first record, "When I'm a Man".

Blues guitarist Aaron 'T-Bone' Walker dies of pneumonia in Los Angeles at 64.

After pulling over a car for running a red light, Los Angeles police detect the smell of marijuana, and arrest Linda McCartney for possession of six to eight ounces of the drug. Husband Paul, who is driving, is not charged.

April

Steve Miller is arrested in Mill Valley, California, for attempting to burn the clothes and jewelry of his ex-girlfriend, Bernita DiOrio.

Pete Ham, guitarist, singer and songwriter with Badfinger, hangs himself in his garage at Woking, Surrey, in England.

May

Jefferson Starship – formerly Jefferson Airplane – celebrate their tenth anniversary with a free concert at New York's Central Park.

June

Billy Preston is knocked off stage in Cleveland when a dragonhead, which arrives blowing confetti during the show's finale, falls off and hits him.

Tim Buckley dies of a heroin overdose.

Cher marries Greg Allman of the Allman Brothers; ten days later she petitions for divorce.

July

The Basement Tapes, recordings made by Bob Dylan and the Band some eight years ago in Woodstock, New York, are released as a double album.

Transvestite punk singer Wayne County's act at New Jersey nightclub Pier Nine becomes so outrageous that the club owners call the police who escort the performer out of town.

Chuck Negron, lead singer for Three Dog Night, is arrested at his Louisville, Kentucky, hotel room the first night of the band's tour and is charged with possession of cocaine. The charge is later dropped due to a legal technicality concerning how the search warrant had been obtained.

Right **Uncompromising reggae star Peter Tosh. A Rastafarian, Tosh forged a career on songs celebrating marijuana. His demand for the legalization of 'ganja' – his 1976 album was titled *Legalize It* – led to his being arrested in his recording studio in 1978.**

August

Joe Pope, lead singer of the Tams, is charged with manslaughter following the death of his wife.

Led Zeppelin vocalist Robert Plant and his family are seriously injured in a car crash on the Greek island of Rhodes. His injuries cause the band's autumn American tour to be delayed, and it will be two years before Led Zeppelin plays in the USA.

Singer/songwriter Peter Gabriel announces that he is leaving Genesis, explaining: 'As an artist, I need to absorb a wide variety of experiences.'

September

Paul McCartney and Wings begin a world tour that lasts 14 months.

Hard rock band Slade's movie *Flame* opens in St Louis. Although extremely popular in their native England, neither of the concurrent releases of *Flame* the book and *Flame* the soundtrack album earn the band much of a US following.

Soul singer Jackie Wilson suffers a heart attack while performing at New Jersey's Latin Casino and lapses into a coma.

Below Sweeping harmonies, vibrant rhythms and preaching were the fortes of Earth Wind And Fire. **Below right** Bob Marley was almost single-handedly responsible for introducing Jamaican reggae music to white audiences in Britain and the States.

October

Al Jackson, ex-drummer of Booker T and the MGs, is shot dead by an intruder in his Memphis home.

Brothers Michael and Joe Costello, disc jockeys on WRNO, New Orleans, claim to have recently interviewed Jim Morrison. They assert that the Doors singer did not die in Paris in 1971 as claimed, but instead went into hiding to escape charges of embezzlement from the Bank of America.

John Lennon wins his lengthy fight with immigration authorities to remain in America when a New York City Court of Appeals rules that his 1968 arrest in Britain for marijuana possession is invalid as a reason for banishing Lennon from America. Two days later, on his thirty-fifth birthday, his wife Yoko gives birth to their only child, Sean Ono Lennon.

Bruce Springsteen appears simultaneously on the covers of *Time* and *Newsweek*.

November

David Bowie makes his US TV debut on Cher's show.

Les McKeown of the Bay City Rollers is given a suspended sentence for assaulting photographers at the New Theatre, Oxford, England, in June.

The Sex Pistols play their first gig, at St Martin's College of Art in London.

December

Joe Walsh replaces Bernie Leadon in the Eagles.

Blues artist Theodore 'Houndog' Taylor, 59, dies in a Chicago hospital of lung cancer.

Performing at a concert in Spokane, Washington, rock star and hunter Ted Nugent finds himself at the wrong end of a gun when 25-year-old David Gelfer points a .44 Magnum at him, before being wrestled to the ground by security men and members of the audience.

Breaking New Ground

This was the year when two acts took two very different routes to international stardom. The first was Peter Frampton and he represented the traditional approach to making it to the top of the rock pile. Frampton first came to prominence as singer/guitarist/pin-up with late sixties UK outfit the Herd, who produced a string of highly acceptable pop singles. Frampton quickly tired of pop's surface glitter and went on to form Humble Pie with ex-Small Face Steve Marriott, playing guitar-dominated rock to increasingly appreciative audiences.

Once more, Frampton felt the urge to move on – this time as a solo artist. Via a series of albums and intensive tours, particularly in America, he built up a large following with his particular brand of melodic rock. All the hard work paid off in the most spectacular fashion in 1976 with the release of *Frampton Comes Alive*, a double album recorded live in concert, which became one of the biggest sellers of all time. Three top-selling singles from the record cemented his appeal and although Frampton's career subsequently declined sharply from these giddy heights, he remains the face of 1976.

The Bostonians

The second act of the year neglected to pay its dues, on the road or anywhere else. Boston was the brainchild of Tom Scholz, a technology whizz-kid who recorded an album's worth of original material at home, negotiated a record company deal and then put a band together as an afterthought. The LP *Boston* was released in August 1976 and by the end of the year had gone double platinum, boosted by the success of the single "More Than a Feeling".

Although Scholz's melodic strain of heavy metal was regarded as overly derivative in certain quarters, the LP was undeniably effective and the hit single from it remains a minor classic. Like Frampton, Boston failed to maintain this level of success and after a lackluster follow-up album in 1978, the group sunk into obscurity.

Whole lotta Zep

There was also plenty of activity among established stars. Led Zeppelin released a film, *The Song Remains the Same*, accompanied by a double album soundtrack, both of which were ecstatically received. Also active on the film front was David Bowie, who completed work on the sci-fi oddity *The Man Who Fell to Earth* before releasing one of his strongest albums ever in *Station to Station*. The Rolling Stones stirred up their usual ration of controversy with the S&M-tinged sleeve to *Black and Blue*. Notable tours were made by ZZ Top, Wings (with accompanying live triple set, *Wings Over America*) and Bob Seger, another artist for whom hard work paid off in the shape of *Live Bullet* and *Night Moves*, which did well in the LP charts.

Below left Joe Jackson, British new wave singer-songwriter for the eighties.
Below The Ramones with their leather jackets, torn jeans and chainsaw-driven pop tones were in the fore-front of the punk rock movement.

The Jackson Five left Motown, became the Jacksons and carried on churning out the hits. Stevie Wonder released *Fulfillingness' First Finale*. European disco, masterminded by Giorgio Moroder in Munich, crashed into the US singles charts via stars such as Donna Summer and Silver Convention and started the trend for extended dance-floor mixes.

The year saw the end of the road for Loggins and Messina, the Pretty Things and, most notably, the Band, who celebrated their demise with an all-star concert at San Francisco's Winterland, subsequently immortalized in the film *The Last Waltz*. Surprise of the year was Cliff Richard, who not only scored an American hit – "Devil Woman" – after 18 years of trying, but also became the first western pop star to play the USSR.

Below Johnny Thunders. As a founder member of the New York Dolls, Thunders was instrumental in shaping the alternative New York music scene of the mid-seventies. As a member of the Heartbreakers, he would keep the punk flag flying.

NEW YORK NEW WAVE

This was the year when a strange gaggle of college types and artful thugs turned their charm on a wider audience for the first time. The setting was Manhattan and the sound, in all its glorious diversity, was that of the American new wave. Since the untimely demise of the New York Dolls and the literal collapse of the Mercer Arts Center, there had been precious little to shout about in Manhattan and nowhere to shout it. Then a thin young man called Tom Verlaine talked a bar owner called Hilly Kristal into letting his band play the bar on slack nights. The band was Television and the bar was CBGBs – the initials somewhat incongruously stood for 'Country, Blue Grass and Blues'. The reverberations echoed worldwide.

Pre-punk poetess

Although Television secured the vital performance outlet, the first star of this determinedly bohemian scene was Patti Smith, a poetess-turned-songstress with a pronounced Keith Richards fixation. She released her debut album *Horses* in 1975. Apart from the fact that the LP was powerful and atmospheric in its own right, there were two additional factors that guaranteed some kind of status. The first was the presence in Smith's band of Lenny Kaye, a no-nonsense guitarist and chronicler of US garage punk of the sixties. The second was the presence as producer of John Cale, the idiosyncratic Welshman whose electric viola was central to the edgy sound of the early Velvet Underground. Between them, these two men represented the two strands that were picked up by the denizens of Lower Manhattan and woven into a modern pattern.

The early Television was very much a collaboration between Verlaine and Richard Hell, but the latter's disregard for musical niceties led to his early departure to form the Heartbreakers with two ex-New York Dolls and thence to a fitful solo career. Television, meanwhile, evolved into a twin-guitar band of sometimes epic resonance, combining elements of the Byrds and the 13th Floor Elevators to great effect. Their two studio LPs and one semi-legal live effort fueled the aspirations of many on both sides of the Atlantic.

Chainsaw massacre

Three other groups completed the hall of infamy. First, the Ramones erupted out of Queens with a common (if spurious) surname and a set of songs dealing with the more outlandish types of modern mayhem, all powered by a chainsaw guitar-driven sound of monstrous persistence. Needless to say, the first album was the best.

A counterpoint to the leather and slashed denim look of the Ramones was provided by Blondie, fronted by the deceptively frail Debbie Harry. At their best, the group delivered classic modern pop music topped off by Harry's floating vocals and occasional raunchy inflections. Blondie's first LP, self-named, was released in 1976 and remains a repository of velvet and steel.

The last and most influential of the initial big five was the Talking Heads, who pioneered a type of psychotic and angular R&B which, although much refined, continues to make the group enormously popular today. Bug-eyed leader David Byrne investigated aspects of the mundane with wit and sometimes disturbing intensity, an approach that has since found many adherents.

The ironic thing about the American new wave was that all the above acts found their first taste of wider popularity in the UK, from where they returned with reputations much enhanced. And what became of Harry Toledo and the Rockets?

Above Ann and Nancy Wilson of heavy metal outfit Heart.
Below Although she seemed to be the very antithesis of what record companies expected of female artists — she was scruffy, distinctly unglamorous and possessed of a less than sweet voice — Patti Smith signed for Arista Records in 1975 at the insistence of her friend Lou Reed, and proceeded to unleash the album *Horses*, a punk masterpiece and an aggressive statement of assertive feminism. Raw, passionate, energetic and foul-mouthed, Patti Smith went on to challenge pop music's female stereotypes and win a mass of admirers of both sexes. Her poetry was eccentric and revolutionary, her music was hard and chilling, her live performances were genuine experiences. After Ms Smith, the woman's role in rock would never be quite the same again.

1976 Diary

January

The Chillingford Chokers, alias the Stranglers, appear at London's Hope and Anchor.

Greg Allman testifies in a drug case against Allman Brothers' road manager Scooter Herring. Herring receives a 75-year prison sentence.

Chester Arthur Burnett, alias Howlin' Wolf, dies at the age of 65 in a Chicago veteran's hospital.

Mal Evans, former Beatles tour manager, is shot dead by police at his Los Angeles apartment. Called by two of Evans' friends, police arrive to find him wielding a rifle in a distressed state; when Evans ignores orders to drop his firearm, police open fire.

Kenneth Moss, former record-company executive, is sentenced to 120 days in Los Angeles County Jail and four years probation after pleading guilty to involuntary manslaughter in the 1974 drug-induced death of Average White Band drummer Robbie McIntosh.

February

American promoter Bill Sargent offers the former members of the Beatles $30 million to reform for one 'comeback' concert.

The BBC refuse to play Donna Summer's "Love To Love You Baby" because of the sounds of heavy breathing on the record.

Florence Ballard, original member of the Supremes, dies of coronary thrombosis in a Detroit hospital. She had been living on welfare for the few years preceding her death after losing an $8.7 million law suit for back royalties against Motown Records in 1971.

"More More More" by the Andrea True Connection enters the US pop charts. The disco hit, sung by ex-porno-film star Andrea True, will go on to reach Number 4 and be certified gold in September.

The peak of Kiss' American success is noted with the placing of their footprints on the pavement outside Grauman's Chinese Theater in Hollywood.

Slik play their first major concert at the Glasgow Apollo. The band, which includes future Ultravox singer Midge Ure, has already topped the UK charts two weeks earlier with its single "Forever and Ever".

March

EMI reissue all 22 Beatles singles.

Elton John is immortalized in wax at Madame Tussauds in London.

David Bowie is arrested in New York for possession of marijuana.

Rick Stevens, former lead singer of Tower of Power, is arrested in California on a charge of triple murder.

Concert dates of the Who's US tour are rescheduled following the collapse of Keith Moon on-stage at the Boston Garden ten minutes into the show.

Former Free guitarist Paul Kossoff dies of unknown causes on a London to New York plane flight.

The Sex Pistols play their first show at London's 100 Club, attracting a reported 50 people.

April

UK entrants Brotherhood of Man win the Eurovision Song Contest with "Save Your Kisses for Me".

Sixties folk-protest singer Phil Ochs hangs himself at his sister's New York home.

"Disco Lady" by Johnnie Taylor reaches Number 1 in the US charts. It goes on to become the first single to be certified platinum by the Record Industry Association of America.

The Sex Pistols play London rock club the Nashville. Also on the bill are the 101ers led by Joe Strummer.

Bruce Springsteen jumps the fence at Gracelands in an attempt to meet Elvis Presley. Security guards are unimpressed with his credentials and he is thrown off the property.

Bay City Roller Eric Faulkner almost dies after swallowing Seconal and Valium tablets at manager Tam Paton's house in Edinburgh.

David Bowie is held up for several hours on his special train by Russian-Polish border guards who, searching his possessions, find Nazi memorabilia and books.

Far left As a member of teen mod band the Herd, Peter Frampton had been heralded as 'The Face of '68' but it was as a solo artist the following decade that he found solid success; his 1975 album *Frampton Comes Alive!* was a massive worldwide seller.
Left Debbie Harry, the face and voice of Blondie.

May

Patti Smith makes her first UK appearance at the Roundhouse in London. She is supported by the UK group the Stranglers.

The Ramones' debut album, *The Ramones*, is released in the United States.

Former Yardbirds singer Keith Relf is fatally electrocuted at his home. He is found by his eight-year-old son next to a plugged-in electric guitar.

New York underground paper *Planet* publishes nude pictures of Patti Smith taken years previously.

At a Bob Dylan concert in Houston, special guest Willie Nelson is served with a subpoena for a forthcoming grand jury investigation into drug-trafficking.

The Who headline a bill at the Charlton Athletic football ground, and put their name in *The Guinness Book of Records* as the loudest rock band ever when their set measures 120 decibels.

Keith Richards is arrested in his crashed Bentley after highway police discover 'substances'. He appears in court on cocaine and LSD charges the next year.

June

Rod Stewart's "Tonight's the Night" is banned by BBC's *Top Of The Pops* for being 'too suggestive'.

Paul McCartney and Wings perform before an audience of 67 000 in Seattle – the biggest ever indoor crowd for a single act.

A 16-year-old boy is fatally stabbed outside a Yes concert at Jersey City's Roosevelt Stadium.

On a false tip-off, police search Neil Diamond's California home for drugs. The raid ends amicably and Diamond gives several officers signed copies of his latest LP, *Beautiful Noise*.

Ian Dury and the Kilburns, supported by the Stranglers, play their final show at Walthamstow Hall.

July

The Ramones play their first UK concert, opening for the revived Flamin' Groovies at the Roundhouse.

Further reggae concerts are banned from London's Hammersmith Odeon following a spate of thefts and muggings at a recent Bob Marley concert.

Brian Wilson joins the Beach Boys onstage for the first time in 12 years at a concert at Anaheim Stadium.

The Damned open for the Sex Pistols at the 100 Club in London.

Bruce Springsteen sues manager Mike Appel in Manhattan District Court for fraud and breach of trust. The lawsuit, concerning Springsteen's artistic and financial freedom, will drag on for a year, temporarily halting his music career.

Three members of Eire pop group the Miami Showband are found shot dead in a ditch by the Ulster border in Ireland.

John Lennon receives his green card, granting him permanent residency status in the United States. This follows a four-year battle with the Federal Immigration and Naturalization Service after Lennon's initial application.

August

Stiff Records issues its first release, "So It Goes"/"In the Heart of the City", by Nick Lowe.

The first European punk rock festival is held in France – the bill includes Nick Lowe, the Damned, the Vibrators and Richard Hell.

Cliff Richard begins a 20-date tour of the Soviet Union at Leningrad's Hall of the October. The crowd's enthusiasm horrifies Russian officials, who offer to errect barriers between Richard and the audience at later shows. Cliff declines the offer.

The Rolling Stones, Todd Rundgren, Lynyrd Skynyrd, Hot Tuna and 10cc play to 200 000 spectators at the annual Knebworth festival in Hertfordshire, England.

At a reunion concert of the original Spirit in Santa Monica, California, Neil Young joins in at bassist Mark Andes' request. During the encore, Randy California objects to Young's presence and tries to push him off the stage.

September

James Dempsey, MP for Airdrie and Coatbridge in Scotland, calls for a ban on the Ramones' LP after learning of a track entitled "I Wanna Sniff Some Glue".

American all-girl group the Runaways are detained by police following the theft of a hairdryer from their London hotel.

Ode Record's president Lou Adler and employee Neil Silver are kidnapped at Adler's Malibu house. They are released eight hours later after $25 000 ransom is paid. A California couple are later charged with the crime.

Stephen Ford, son of US President Gerald, invites Peter Frampton to the White House. After a lightning tour of the place, the three settle down in the First Family's living quarters for an afternoon's television viewing.

Wings play a benefit and raise $50 000 for restoration work on Venice's water-damaged St Mark's Square. However, the 25 000 people attending unwittingly do more harm than good when their combined weight loosens some paving stones and allows water to seep through into the square.

Jerry Lee Lewis, while engaged in shooting practice with his .357 Magnum, hits bass player Norman 'Butch' Owens twice in the chest. Lewis is charged with shooting a firearm within the city limits.

October

After 19 years together, Ike and Tina Turner break off their professional relationship.

The Jam play an outdoor lunchtime concert at London's Soho Market.

Steve Miller reaches Number 1 in the US charts for the first time with "Rock'n'Me".

Blues singer Victoria Spivey dies at 70 in a Brooklyn hospital. Songwriter and owner of a successful record label, she is also remembered for giving newcomer Bob Dylan one of his first New York gigs in 1961.

EMI sign up the Sex Pistols, outbidding Polydor with a £40 000 contract.

Led Zeppelin's film *The Song Remains the Same* premieres in London.

Elvis Presley records "Way Down", his last ever hit, in the studio at his Gracelands mansion.

November

The Sex Pistols' first single, "Anarchy in the UK", is released by EMI.

The Band make their farewell appearance, at San Francisco's Winterland Ballroom. The concert, which is filmed for Martin Scorsese's film *The Last Waltz*, also features Bob Dylan, Joni Mitchell, Ronnie Hawkins, Neil Young and Van Morrison.

Jerry Lee Lewis, waving a pistol and demanding to see Elvis Presley, is arrested at Gracelands.

New York City's Mayor Beame hosts a luncheon for the Bee Gees in honor of the group's decision to donate the proceeds from a forthcoming Madison Square Garden concert to the City Police Athletic League Organization. Upon being presented with a platinum record of the group's "Children of the World", Beame says, 'I look forward to taking it out of the frame and playing it.'

Richard Hell and the Voidoids make their debut at CBGB's in New York.

December

The Sex Pistols outrage Britain with their language during a television interview. By January no club or concert hall in the country will book them.

More than 3 500 000 ticket applications are received for the forthcoming Abba concert at the Royal Albert Hall in London.

Bob Marley escapes with a flesh wound when seven gunmen break into his home in Kingston, Jamaica.

Tommy Bolin, former guitarist with the James Gang and Deep Purple, dies of a drug overdose in Miami.

Gary Glitter makes a comeback at London's Theatre Royal, Drury Lane, nine months after announcing his retirement from the music business.

A 40-foot long inflatable pig being photographed for the cover of Pink Floyd's *Animals* breaks loose of its wires and takes off from Battersea Power Station. It attains a height of 18 000 feet before landing in Kent.

Three days after its release, Paul McCartney and Wings' live album, *Wings Over America*, goes gold.

Generation X play their first live show at London's Central School of Art.

Far left Television: (from left) Fred Smith, Billy Ficca, Tom Verlaine and Richard Lloyd.
Center Talking Heads: (from left) Jerry Harrison, David Byrne, Chris Frantz and Tina Weymouth.
Left Hard rock masters Boston.

Overleaf The Bee Gees, *the* pop phenomenon of 1977/8. Having tasted success in Britain in the late sixties, Barry, Maurice and Robin Gibb began to go to pieces in 1970. Flop followed flop, but in 1975 they surprised everybody by bouncing back with the disco-flavored *Main Course*. Until Michael Jackson's *Thriller* in 1983, The Bee Gees' *Saturday Night Fever* soundtrack LP (1977) was the best-selling LP of all time.

Punk Classics

1977

In terms of chart domination, there can be no doubt that 1977 belonged to Fleetwood Mac. Formed in the UK in 1967, the group went through a bewildering series of personnel changes and fluctuations in fortune (there was even a fake Fleetwood Mac on the road at one time) before surfacing in the mid seventies as a five-piece ensemble, including two original members and two new Americans. Released in 1977, their *Rumours* album surged to the top of the charts and held on to that position for more than six months. The LP also yielded four hit singles over that period, just to seal its success. It took the band nearly three years to produce a follow-up – *Tusk* – and in a sense the group fell victim to the phenomenal impact of the 1977 album.

Below Fleetwood Mac: (from left) Lindsey Buckingham, Stevie Nicks, Mick Fleetwood, Christine McVie and John McVie.

Fever pitch
Another feature of the year was the massive success enjoyed by film soundtracks. The most notable of these was the Bee Gees' score for *Saturday Night Fever*, the film which made a household name of John Travolta and his somewhat forced disco antics. The Bee Gees cut their first hits in Australia in the early sixties, before returning to their native Britain to become pop idols later in the decade. After a period of internal strife, the group moved to the United States, adopted a new style of light disco funk and easily eclipsed their former triumphs with albums such as *Main Course* and *Children of the World*.

Another act to achieve film-related success was Rose Royce, a Los Angeles group whose Norman Whitfield-directed soundtrack to the film *Car Wash* presented them with a hit album and a string of hit singles, including a platinum one for the title track. On a less elevated level, Meco scored their only hit with the "Star Wars Theme" and David Soul attempted to live up to his name with a little pop balladry, while resting between episodes of *Starsky and Hutch*. Debby Boone, daughter of Pat, recorded the top-selling single of the year in America with "You Light Up My Life", but it failed to repeat its success in Britain.

Right Stevie Nicks whose voice and melodies added another dimension to the developing sound of Fleetwood Mac.

Fleetwood Mac had been formed in London in 1967 by three one-time members of John Mayall's Bluesbreakers — guitarist Peter Green, Mick Fleetwood and John McVie. Initially a hard-core blues band, the group flirted with a variety of styles throughout the seventies — undergoing many personnel changes in the process. It was not until American guitarist Lindsey Buckingham (*below*) and singer Stevie Nicks joined the fold in 1975, that the group's fortunes began to look up.

137

Summer of love

The European influence was strongly felt on both sides of the Atlantic. Donna Summer teamed up with the Italian production team of Giorgio Moroder and Pete Bellotte at their Munich studio to crank out a stream of overtly sexy singles that filled discos and assaulted the charts: "I Feel Love" was a big hit in America and Britain. It was also a golden year for Abba, the Swedes who won the Eurovision Song Contest and lived to tell the tale. "Dancing Queen", "Knowing Me, Knowing You" and "The Name of the Game" were three of the classiest pop hits of the year.

Other notable acts included Foreigner, an Anglo-American outfit whose debut LP was an immediate success, and Kenny Rogers, who crossed over from country to pop, particularly with the single "Lucille". The most heartening success in a year that also saw the death of Elvis Presley was the mutual rehabilitation of Muddy Waters and Johnny Winter with the LP *Hard Again*.

Below In 1975, Donna Summer burst into the public eye with "Love To Love You Baby", a disco number produced by Giorgio Moroder. Although many radio stations refused to play the disc — which featured much suggestive heavy breathing — it became a huge international hit.

PRETTY VACANT

By the end of 1976, the word punk had come to be enshrined in the English language. The reason for this was the explosive appearance on London's music scene of a group called the Sex Pistols, whose name alone appeared capable of inducing widespread public outrage. The man behind this calculated insult to society was Malcolm McLaren, ex-manager of the New York Dolls and owner of a Chelsea boutique called 'Sex' which specialized in revolting articles of clothing for the chosen few.

The Sex Pistols fitted themselves out in a choice selection of ripped and torn garments held together by chains and safety pins, and they devised a set of songs fired by their loathing for seventies rock and their liking for elementary noise. Their few early fans assisted by inventing new forms of audience behavior, including spitting and a form of communal battering that passed as dancing. The whole performance appeared to be designed to alienate as many people as possible,

but the Sex Pistols' nihilistic spirit instead captured the imagination of a whole generation of fans who shared their rage and frustration.

The Sex Pistols released their first single, "Anarchy in the UK", at the end of 1976, but its progress up the charts was halted when the record was deleted by the outraged record company EMI. The group promptly signed another deal, with A&M, and were just as promptly dropped before finally releasing a string of singles and an album during 1977 on the Virgin label. "God Save the Queen", a vicious attack on the monarchy, reached Number 2 just at the time of the Jubilee celebrations in England, and the LP *Here's the Sex Pistols* topped the album charts shortly after.

Below left **Mick Jones of the Clash, the uncompromising and politically-motivated of London's early punk bands. Their first album *Clash* (1977), which contained their anarchic anthem "White Riot", was considered too 'crude' for American release.**
Below **Johnny Rotten, voice of the Sex Pistols. 'Must we throw this filth at our pop kids?' fumed headlines in Britain's national press following the Pistols' first appearance on television.**
Below right **Sid Vicious. After his suicide in New York in 1979, Vicious would be hailed as a 'martyr' of punk.**
Far right **The rise of punk rock gave birth to many a startling fashion and hairstyle.**

Clash city rockers

In the wake of the Pistols, a whole clutch of groups appeared, the best of which was the Clash. Although they lacked the Pistols' propensity for outrage, the Clash proved more musically adventurous, particularly after they got the white-hot venom of their self-named debut LP out of their systems. They ended the year with a single called "Complete Control", one of punk's finest moments. In later years the band refined their style even further and eventually crossed the Atlantic to some acclaim.

The court jesters of the punk movement were the Damned, whose vicious thrashings were often undercut by hammy theatricality. Their first album, *Damned Damned Damned* was the first punk LP to be released and the first to reach the charts. The last of the pioneering groups was the Stranglers, an older and more melodic outfit than the rest, who qualified for inclusion in the movement by virtue of their sullen and hostile world view and by being in the right place at the right time.

The significance of punk was twofold. It began to spawn a series of genuine classics that were far truer to the real spirit of rock'n'roll than much of what the seventies had previously offered. It also paved the way for a new generation of artists who would blend fire and ice and form the 'new wave'.

1977 Diary

January

Patti Smith falls off stage in Tampa, Florida, and is rushed to hospital with severe cuts to the head.

Former Fleetwood Mac guitarist Peter Green appears in court on charges of threatening behavior with a rifle and is committed to a mental hospital.

February

Folk singer Roy Harper is treated for toxopasmosis, a rare disease contracted while administering the kiss of life to one of his sheep.

Blues singer/guitarist Bukka White dies in the City of Memphis Hospital following a stroke. His age is reported variously as being between 67 and 89.

March

Bassist Glen Matlock leaves the Sex Pistols, to be replaced by Sid Vicious.

In Santa Monica, California, Bob Dylan's wife Sara files for divorce. It will be granted in June with Sara retaining custody of their five children – Maria, Jesse, Anna, Samuel and Jakob.

Margaret Trudeau, wife of the Canadian Prime Minister, attends a Rolling Stones concert at El Mocambo, a small club in Toronto. A recording of the concert will be released in September on the album *Love You Live.*

April

The Damned become the first English punk band to play in the United States when they appear at the New York club CBGBs.

The Stranglers, the Jam and Cherry Vanilla appear at London's Roundhouse Theatre.

The world's most famous discotheque, Studio 54, opens on West 54th Street in New York City.

Joan Baez and Santana, among others, play a free concert for inmates of Soledad Prison in California.

May

The Sex Pistols sign with Virgin, their third record company in two months. Their first contract, with EMI, lasted a few months and the next, with A&M, ten days.

Elvis Presley walks off stage in the middle of a concert in Baltimore – the first time in his 23-year career he has done so, except in the case of illness.

William Powell of the O'Jays dies at 35 in Canton, Ohio, of cancer.

June

UFO's lead guitarist Michael Schenker goes missing on the eve of a US tour. His fellow band members believe he may have joined a religious sect.

Johnny Rotten of the Sex Pistols is attacked and stabbed in the arm outside London's Pegasus pub. The following day, Pistols drummer Paul Cook is assaulted by a gang at Shepherd's Bush underground station.

Los Angeles mayor Tom Bradley declares 22 June to be 'Herb Alpert Day' in honor of the trumpeter's contribution to the city's culture.

Below Elvis Presley. On August 16, 1977, the King was found dead on the floor of his bathroom at Gracelands and the world went into mourning. Thousands gathered at the gates of his private mansion to pay silent tribute and radio stations across the globe dug out all the many classic (and not so classic) records to play in heavy rotation. And, inevitably, within weeks, record charts were full of tributes to the singer, such as Danny Mirror's "I Remember Elvis Presley (The King Is Dead)".

July

The Sex Pistols perform "Pretty Vacant" on video on BBC-TV's *Top Of The Pops*.

Elvis Costello plays an impromptu gig outside the London Hilton and is arrested for obstruction.

Led Zeppelin's US tour is halted when Robert Plant's son Karac dies of a respiratory ailment in London.

Below Following their victory in the Eurovision Song Contest of 1974, Abba went on to ever-bigger pop glories.
Bottom On the eve of a comeback, Marc Bolan died in a car accident in September 1977.

August

Elvis Presley is found dead at his Gracelands mansion. Within hours, thousands of fans are en route to Memphis to pay their respects.

The day after Elvis' death President Jimmy Carter issues a statement that begins 'Elvis Presley's death deprives our country of a part of life itself'.

Two days after Presley's death, funeral services are held for him at Gracelands. The 150 mourners inside (there are 75 000 outside) include Presley's manager Colonel Tom Parker attired in shirtsleeves and a baseball cap.

September

Marc Bolan, ex-fashion model and member of English glam-rock band T. Rex, is killed when his car, driven by girlfriend Gloria Jones, hits a tree in South London. He was 29.

Bing Crosby and David Bowie record a duet medley of "Little Drummer Boy"/"Peace on Earth" for Crosby's TV Christmas special.

Jazz and blues legend Ethel Waters dies in Chatsworth, California, at 81.

October

A charter plane flying Lynyrd Skynyrd to Baton Rouge, Louisiana, crashes in Mississippi killing band members Ronnie Van Zandt and Steve and Cassidy Gaines. The band's surviving members will go on to form the Rossington-Collins Band.

At the request of the Los Angeles Dodgers, Linda Ronstadt sings the national anthem at Dodgers Stadium to open the third game of the World Series. The game is won by the New York Yankees.

November

The Last Waltz, Martin Scorsese's documentary film of the Band's 1976 farewell concert, premieres in New York City.

Pat Boone's daughter Debby reaches the top of the US charts with her single "You Light Up My Life".

December

Billy Joel's fifth LP, *The Stranger*, reaches Number 2 in the American album charts.

Saturday Night Fever premieres in New York. Based on a story by Nik Cohn, the film is accompanied by a soundtrack that will be made into one of the biggest-selling albums of all time.

Two days before they are to appear on *Saturday Night Live* and to begin their first American tour, the Sex Pistols are denied visas to enter the United States. Government officials cite various sections of the US Immigration Act, including 'moral turpitude', as reasons for the refusal of the visas.

Like a Bat out of Hell

1978

Below left Guided by musicians/songwriters/producers Bernard Edwards and Nile Rodgers, Chic arrived on the scene in 1977 with their stylish brand of disco funk.
Below center Tom Petty. One of the few artists ever to emerge from the state of Florida, Petty's guitar-driven pop tunes heralded America's new wave boom.
Below right With their weird appearance and humorous art-pop approach, New Zealand band Split Enz launched their assault on the world's rock market in 1975 with the LP *Mental Notes*.

Although many artists, both old and new, staked a claim to fame in 1978, there is little doubt that the year belonged to an overweight Texan named Marvin Lee Aday. After a varied career in theater, musicals and session work, Aday sat down to write an album's worth of operatic rock with old friend Jim Steinman. Having enlisted the enthusiastic cooperation of Todd Rundgren, the pair endured a record-breaking number of rejections before finally securing a deal. *Bat Out of Hell* was finally released in 1978, with Rundgren at the controls, and the LP shot Meat Loaf (which was Aday's stage name) to fame. The record lodged in the charts until the end of the decade. The combination of hard rock, teen romance and operatic arrangements proved to be a solid gold formula which Meat Loaf has used with great success ever since.

Chic to chic

At the other end of the musical spectrum, 1978 proved to be a very satisfactory year for another set of newcomers: Chic. At the heart of the group was the writing/producing/playing partnership of Nile Rodgers and Bernard Edwards. The precise rhythm guitar of the former combined with the latter's fluid bass patterns to form the definitive disco groove of the seventies. They produced two albums in the year (*Chic* and *C'est Chic*) and finished off with a number one single in "Le Freak". As their name suggests, the group traded freely in traditional notions of the French: hedonistic but very cool. In later years, Edwards and particularly Rodgers carved out separate careers as producers to other artists, guiding the recorded output of such performers as Sister Sledge, Sheila B Devotion and Diana Ross to high chart positions.

The Rolling Stones released *Some Girls* in 1978 and the usual fuss over the cover and some of the lyrics did not conceal the fact that it was one of their best records for some time. Bruce Springsteen did not have the problem of having to live down past releases because legal problems had prevented him making any records at all for three years. Thus the release of *Darkness On the Edge of Town* was as much a relief to him as it was a joy to his fans. Kiss reached their peak in 1978 and marked it in typically excessive style. As well as two group LPs – *Alive 2* and *Double Platinum* – each of the four members found time to record a solo album. All four were released simultaneously.

Below Paul Stanley of Kiss. With their garish, comic-book make-up (without which they never ventured out in public) and simplistic heavy metal, Kiss became one of the best-selling acts of the late seventies.

Grease is the word

The film phenomenon of the year was *Grease*, which spawned hits for its stars John Travolta and Olivia Newton-John, both as a duo and individually, as well as ex-Four Season Frankie Valli, who hit the top with the title track. The most successful pop family was that of the Gibbs. The three older Gibb brothers continued to hit the top of the charts as the Bee Gees and were joined in the limelight by younger brother Andy, who topped the singles charts twice, the second time for two months with "Shadow Dancing".

LIFE AFTER PUNK

The two years prior to 1978 had seen upheavals in the music scene on both sides of the Atlantic. The arrival of US and UK punk had opened up the field. A new audience had been created that was of sufficient size to impress the record companies, whose books were groaning with overpaid stars whom nobody seemed to want to listen to any more. The flow of new talent was increased by independent labels, such as Stiff in the UK, which achieved success by astute marketing and low overheads. The Talking Heads continued to lead the field in America, but were quickly joined by a series of new groups from all over the country.

Most initially arresting were Devo from Akron, Ohio, who spouted bizarre theories and equally bizarre tunes, the most notable of which was a

Left Sting (real name Gordon Sumner), bass player, singer and songwriter of the Police.
Below left Meat Loaf (real name Marvin Lee Aday), whose operatic rock opus *Bat Out Of Hell* (1977) became a music industry legend.
Below Dylan in top hat during his 1978 world tour.

mechanized re-tread of "Satisfaction" that greatly upset fans of the Rolling Stones. While time has reduced Devo's strangeness, they still remain capable of producing quirky and often surprising pop hits.

In a more traditional vein were the Cars, who came roaring out of Boston in 1978 with an eponymously titled debut LP and a string of hit singles, including the catchy "My Best Friend's Girl". Although their sound was rooted firmly in power pop, the Cars' music was distinguished by the songs of leader Ric Ocasek, whose writing style was spare and sharp.

Tom Petty and the Heartbreakers (not to be confused with the Johnny Thunders/Richard Hell outfit) were rooted more in R&B than pop, but again approached their material in a thoroughly modern manner. Their debut LP was released in 1977, but made little impact outside the UK where the band had made a big hit supporting Television. The second set, *You're Gonna Get It*, stuck to a similar formula and was received with much more acclaim in America.

His aim was true

Meanwhile in the UK, the inspiration of the Sex Pistols was yielding a mixed crop. Outright imitation tended not to guarantee success of a lasting nature, as Sham 69 discovered. However, those who took a more original line were rewarded. Elvis Costello had released his first LP on Stiff in 1977, but it was his second set – *This Year's Model* – that brought him wide recognition. He combined the virtues of a classic songwriter with a snarling delivery delivered with great momentum. Since then, Costello has developed into an artist of major stature with a series of LPs and concerts of breathtaking range and power.

Another songwriter who came to prominence on Stiff was Ian Dury, a veteran of the UK pub rock scene that had been swept away by punk. His LP *New Boots and Panties* hit the charts at the beginning of 1978 and, although too idiosyncratically British for export, established new standards with its realistic and funny lyrics. Another very good group who failed to find much of a market outside the UK was Manchester's the Buzzcocks. They fused the angry noise of the Sex Pistols and the Ramones with pop melodies of the highest order.

This is just a sample of the artists whose way was cleared by the healthy emetic of punk. Although the stylistic range is vast, the spirit was common to all and the movement was dubbed the 'new wave'.

1978 Diary

January

Bob Dylan's ex-wife Sara pleads not guilty to charges of punching a teacher while attempting to take custody of her children.

The Sex Pistols play their last concert at San Francisco's Winterland. Johnny Rotten asks the audience: 'Ever had the feeling you've been had?'

Grace Slick of Jefferson Starship is arrested for drunken driving after appearing as a guest judge at an amateur talent contest where she pushed and swore at contestants and sang through their performances.

Terry Kath of Chicago dies after accidentally shooting himself in the head with a pistol he reportedly didn't know was loaded.

February

Bob Dylan's film *Renaldo and Clara* premieres in Los Angeles.

Sid Vicious and his girlfriend Nancy Spungen are arrested in their room at New York City's Chelsea Hotel and charged with possession of drugs.

March

Topper Headon and Paul Simenon of the Clash are charged with criminal damage after shooting six racing pigeons from the roof of a rehearsal hall.

The Rutles' *All You Need Is Cash*, a satire of the Beatles, airs on NBC-TV. Paul Simon and Mick Jagger make cameo appearances and George Harrison plays an interviewer.

Center **Elvis Costello— real name Declan McManus. With his first album, the raw and angry-sounding *My Aim Is True*, Costello revealed himself to be one of the genuine original talents of the new wave movement.**

April

Sandy Denny, ex-Fairport Convention singer, goes into a coma after falling down a flight of stairs; she dies four days later.

Bruce Springsteen, Carly Simon and Jackson Browne are among a group of over 40 rock performers petitioning President Jimmy Carter to end America's commitment to nuclear power.

May

In Leicester, England, Tubes singer Fee Waybill falls off the stage and breaks his leg.

Allan Jones, journalist with British rock paper *Melody Maker*, is punched in the mouth by Black Sabbath's Tony Iommi because of an article he wrote about the band four years previously.

June

German fans riot and set fire to the Lorelei Amphitheater after Jefferson Starship fail to appear for a scheduled concert.

Rock band Kansas are named Deputy Ambassadors of Goodwill by UNICEF.

Singer/songwriter Peter Frampton is injured in a car crash in the Bahamas.

July

Joe Strummer and Paul Simenon of the Clash are arrested at a gig at the Glasgow Apollo in Scotland after trying to stop the bouncers from manhandling members of the audience.

Prince enters the soul chart for the first time with his single "Soft and Wet", which will peak at Number 42.

Near right **The Cars on stage. Formed in Boston in 1976, the group's first album, *The Cars* (1978), sold four million copies worldwide and, in addition, spawned hit singles in "My Best Friend's Girl" and "Just What I Needed". The group's music blended adult-oriented-rock with pop and modern production values and showed that American new wave music was not a passing fad but a force to be reckoned with.**

August

Pete Meadon, original manager of the Who, dies of barbiturate poisoning.

Muddy Waters performs at a White House picnic at the request of President Jimmy Carter.

September

The Who's drummer Keith Moon is found dead in his London apartment.

Ex-Sex Pistol Johnny Rotten's new band Public Image Ltd release their first single, "Public Image".

The Grateful Dead perform a concert beneath the pyramids of Egypt.

October

French singer/songwriter Jacques Brel dies from a blood clot. He was 48.

Sid Vicious is charged with murdering his girlfriend, Nancy Spungen. The next week he slashes his wrists with a razor blade and a broken lightbulb, but survives.

Singer Steve Tyler and guitarist Joe Perry of Aerosmith are injured when a cherry bomb is thrown on stage by a member of the audience at a Philadelphia concert. The group thereafter perform behind a cyclone fence.

November

Police in the English Midlands investigate 'the sickest stunt' ever staged by a punk rock group after Birmingham band Anti-Social offer £15 000 to anyone willing to commit suicide on stage.

Queen play at New York's Madison Square Garden and try to hold the attention of the audience by having several semi-nude women cycling on stage for their hit "Fat-Bottomed Girls".

December

Sid Vicious is thrown into Ryker's Island Jail in New York after allegedly hitting Todd Smith, Patti Smith's brother, with a bottle at the rock club Hurrah.

Chris Bell, 27, a founder member of Memphis pop group Big Star, is killed in a car accident.

Soul singer Donny Hathaway dies at 34 after jumping from a fifteenth-floor hotel room in New York City.

Below Kate Bush whose quirky and novel single "Wuthering Heights" was a surprise Number 1 hit in Britain in 1978.
Below right Ian Dury's enormously successful *New Boots And Panties* LP (1977) blended old Cockney music hall traditions with modern rhythms to brilliant effect.

Headline Stoppers

1979

Two British bands made worldwide headlines in 1979. The first of these was the Police, a three-piece band formed by two rock veterans and a brand new idol for the age. Drummer Stewart Copeland (ex-Curved Air) and guitarist Andy Summers (ex-everyone else) came together with relative newcomer Sting, who sang and played bass, to take possession of the charts. With their peroxide good looks and bounding energy, the group slotted in easily with the punk scene, but their musical ambitions extended to greater horizons. The Police harnessed sophisticated pop melodies to a customized reggae rhythm, and although their early singles and first LP, *Outlandos D'Amour*, were surprisingly unsuccessful in their homeland, it took a series of grueling US tours to finally make them big. The early single "Roxanne" was a hit, and by the time of the second album, *Regatta De Blanc*, and accompanying single "Message in a Bottle", the Police had major worldwide status.

Sultans of swing

The second success story was altogether more unlikely. Dire Straits was formed in South London around a nucleus of Mark and David Knopfler and made their appearance on the scene in 1977 with a style of music altogether alien to the predominant punk sound. Mark Knopfler's songs featured melancholic tunes over a deceptively swinging rhythm section and usually showcased his own virtuoso guitar playing.

Dire Straits released their first LP in 1978 and, like the Police, it broke first in America. In 1979 the band toured America extensively to promote their second album, *Communiqué*, and were rewarded with a large hit. The final accolade came when Bob Dylan invited Mark Knopfler and drummer Pick Withers to play on his 1979 LP *Slow Train Coming*.

Other British pop phenomena failed to cross the

Atlantic so convincingly. The mod revival, spearheaded by the Jam, gained a certain momentum but its only noteworthy effect was to galvanize the original mod band – the Who – into renewed activity with drummer Kenny Jones replacing the deceased Keith Moon. Although the group put out no new records, they toured extensively and released two films – *The Kids Are Alright*, a documentary of the band, and *Quadrophenia*, a dramatization of their earlier LP.

Below David Lee Roth, wild front man of heavy metal supremos Van Halen.
Right Sting's white reggae pop songs were to help the Police become *the* top rock attraction of the early eighties – and establish the bassist/singer as an international celebrity in his own right.

Are trends eclectic?

More interesting was the emergence of the Two-Tone record label with its distinctive ska/blue beat rhythms, an early variant on the reggae form. The leading exponents were the Specials and Madness, both of which curbed their early exuberance and produced music of the highest order. Another newcomer was Gary Numan, who had paid his dues in a series of punk bands before hitting on a sub-Bowie image complete with songs about robots and cars. It took him to the top in the UK but America remained impervious to his charms.

In the United States, disco continued to exert a massive influence on the charts. Joining the likes of Chic and Sister Sledge at the top were Village People, a mind-boggling assembly of gay stereotypes. Their 1979 LP *Cruisin'* went triple platinum, while a pair of singles, "YMCA" and "In the Navy", rocked both the dance-floors and the charts. The heavy metal antidote to all this was provided by Van Halen, who had built up a considerable following through their dynamic live shows featuring the athletic presence of singer David Lee Roth and the meltdown guitar antics of Eddie Van Halen. Their second LP – *Van Halen II* – took up permanent residence in the upper reaches of the charts in 1979.

EASY RIDERS

Throughout the seventies in America, a new musical form evolved that came to be known as AOR (adult-orientated rock). It came about as the result of a demand from older rock fans, who had grown tired of the vagaries of fashion and needed a sophisticated, reliable variation on the basic theme of rock'n'roll. Sophistication was also demanded in the standards of production, because increasing affluence had led to the spread of sensitive and powerful hi-fi equipment. The AOR movement was spread across the whole country by the medium of FM radio, which eschewed the Top Forty format in favor of a diet of album tracks.

A host of bands and artists fit into the category at different times in their careers, but there are certain groups who have catered to the market from their very inception. The trademarks of an AOR band include a concern for melody, which usefully leads to the presence of a sweet-voiced singer, the use of elaborate arrangements and a willingness to experiment with new instruments to achieve different textures.

Foreigner's formula

Perhaps the archetypal AOR outfit is Foreigner, who formed in New York in 1976 around a nucleus of expatriate Englishmen: Mick Jones (ex-Spooky Tooth) and Ian McDonald (ex-King Crimson). The line-up was completed by four English and American musicians, notably Lo Gamm, a powerful vocalist. The group has been through numerous personnel changes over the years and at one time went off the scene altogether for a complete rethink. Nevertheless, the formula has remained constant – Jones' melodic ballads and rockers swathed in sympathetic arrangements and belted out by Gamm's expressive vocals. Foreigner also fulfills the other requirement for an AOR group: although their records are well known, the group members are never recognized in the street and most fans would find it hard to name one of them.

Other notable AOR groups of recent years include Toto, composed of a group of ex-session men with impeccable credentials; Journey, comprised of refugees from Santana and well-traveled British drummer Aynsley Dunbar; Kansas; and latter period Doobie Brothers.

Below Ireland's brash Boomtown Rats, led by the outspoken and articulate ex-pop journalist Bob Geldof, outlived the punk boom to become a major pop attraction. With the single "I Don't Like Mondays" (1979), which was based on the notorious Brenda Spencer snipings incident, they revealed a more sensitive side to their music.

1979 Diary

January

Jazz bassist Charles Mingus dies following a heart attack in Mexico.

The YMCA claims to be considering legal action against Village People because of the 'homosexual overtones' of the group's hit single "YMCA".

February

Sid Vicious dies of a heroin overdose in New York City.

Punk band Generation X are forced to leave the stage after 20 minutes of a concert in Birmingham, England, when the audience starts to pelt them with cans, glasses and other objects.

March

Elvis Costello is involved in a brawl at the Holiday Inn in Columbus, Ohio. While drinking in the bar with Stephen Stills and Bonnie Bramlett, Costello reportedly made racist remarks about Ray Charles and James Brown, so Bramlett hit him.

Havana Jam, the first jointly sponsored US/Cuban music event in 20 years, begins its three days of performances, which will include acts by Billy Joel, Stephen Stills and Kris Kristofferson.

Below **The Who continued to be an exciting live attraction throughout the seventies. But the death of drummer Keith Moon in 1978 left a mark on the band and, though they continued to work together for another five years, the vital spark had gone.**

April

Keith Richard plays two charity concerts for the blind, the sentence given to him by a Toronto judge after a Canadian heroin conviction in 1978.

Heavy metal band Van Halen commence their second world tour. The group carries 22 tons of sound equipment and 10 tons of lights.

The film *Rock'n'Roll High School*, featuring the Ramones, premieres in Los Angeles.

May

Wayne County is ordered to pay a 15-year-old girl £15 compensation after pleading guilty to assault during a can-throwing incident at London's Lyceum.

Tom Petty of the Heartbreakers, whose record label ABC has recently gone out of business, files for bankruptcy.

George Harrison performs with, among others, Paul McCartney, Ringo Starr, Mick Jagger and Ginger Baker at the wedding reception for his ex-wife Patti Boyd and Eric Clapton.

June

Showaddywaddy become the first Western rock'n'roll group to be televized by satellite to Cuba.

Lowell George, founder member of Little Feat, dies of a heart attack after performing a solo concert in Washington, DC.

Johnny Rotten appears with Joan Collins on the panel of the revived BBC-TV show *Juke Box Jury*.

Elvis Presley's father Vernon dies of a heart ailment in Tupelo, Mississippi. He was 63.

Below **With their rumbustious disco sound and tongue in cheek gay image, Village People had enormous success during the late seventies with numbers like "YMCA" (1978) and "In The Navy" (1979).**

July

Chuck Berry is sentenced to four months' imprisonment and 1000 hours' community service after being found guilty of income tax evasion.

Thin Lizzy fire their guitarist Gary Moore after he fails to appear for two gigs during their US tour. Ex-Slik guitarist Midge Ure is flown in as his temporary replacement.

At a revival meeting in North Richmond, California, Reverand Richard Penniman, better-known as Little Richard, warns the congregation about the evils of rock'n'roll music and declares: 'If God can save an old homosexual like me, He can save anybody.'

August

Singer/songwriter Nick Lowe marries Carlene Carter, country and western singer and daughter of Johnny Cash, in Los Angeles.

Modern jazz band leader and composer Stan Kenton dies after a long illness in Hollywood's Midway Hospital. He was 67.

Bassist Dorsey Burnett, a member with his brother Johnny of fifties rockabilly band the Rock'n'roll Trio, dies at 46 of a heart attack in Los Angeles.

September

Former Wings guitarist Jimmy McCulloch is found dead in his North London apartment.

Over 5000 people attend the first New/No/Now Wave Festival at the University of Minnesota. The dBs, the Fleshtones and Devo are among the performers.

Moments after beginning the song "Better Off Dead", Elton John collapses on-stage at Hollywood's Universal Amphitheater, suffering from exhaustion. After a brief intermission John returns to finish a concert lasting three hours.

October

The City of Los Angeles declares 10 October as 'Fleetwood Mac Day', and give the band its own star on Hollywood Boulevard's Walk of Fame.

Tom Robinson appears solo at the National March on Washington, DC, for Lesbian and Gay Rights.

November

At the opening show of his Slow Train Comin' tour at San Francisco's Warfield Theater, recently born-again Christian Bob Dylan is booed by the audience.

Marianne Faithfull is arrested for possession of marijuana at Oslo Airport.

Anita Pallenberg, common-law wife of Keith Richard, is cleared of murder charges in the shooting death of her young male companion, whose body was found in her New York home.

December

The Human League are dropped as support band on the Talking Heads' UK tour after announcing their intention to show pre-recorded tapes and slides and watch the performance from the audience.

In a rush for seats at a Who concert in Cincinnati 11 people are trampled to death.

Far left, above **Formed in London in 1977 by guitar playing brothers Mark and David Knopfler, Dire Straits were very much at odds with the prevailing trends of the time. Their music, strongly influenced by Bob Dylan and JJ Cale, depended on virtuoso guitar playing from Mark Knopfler, at a time when guitar solos of any sort were considered an anathema. But in spite of – possibly *because* of – their unfashionable approach, they soon picked up a large following, and after the success of their single "Sultans Of Swing" (1979), never looked back.**

Far left, below **Foreigner's mixture of hard rock and weeping melodies was never fashionable, but always popular with the silent majority. Just five years after their formation in 1976, they had notched up over 20 million record sales worldwide.**

Left **Madness. They arrived with the ska revival of 1979 and, with their silly costumes and chirpy approach, they stuck around. Starting with "One Step Beyond" (1977), they enjoyed a run of nine consecutive Top Ten hits in the UK. When "Cardiac Arrest" (1982) only scraped to Number 14, the bubble appeared to have burst, but the 'nutty boys' immediately bounced back with "House Of Fun" (1982), their first Number 1.**

Women At The Top

1980

A new decade brought a period of retrenchment to the world of pop music. Old favorites were once more the order of the day. Pink Floyd, who had been so inactive as to fuel a spate of rumors concerning their demise, released their first LP in three years – *The Wall* – and watched it move relentlessly to the top of the album charts, where it stayed for four months. An earlier LP by the group – *Dark Side of the Moon* – was officially declared the longest charting album of all time after 303 weeks in residence. (It beat the record held by Carole King's *Tapestry*, which had managed only 302.) Heartened by this news, Pink Floyd played a dozen of their increasingly rare dates in America with a wildly elaborate stage show.

Another recurring name was Bob Seger, whose LP *Against the Wind* was also a big seller. Seger deserved his success; he had been in the business since the middle of the sixties before he had crashed into the big time with a live double set – *Live Bullet* – in 1976.

Uptown boys

Queen, having lived down most of their cruder glam-rock associations, had a spectacularly successful year with their 1980 LP *The Game* and single "Crazy Little Thing Called Love". Billy Joel resembled Bob Seger in that his 'overnight success' took him several years of hard work to accomplish, including spells with such long forgotten outfits as the Hassles and Attila. His breakthrough came finally with an LP called *The Stranger*. By 1980, he was a regular chart topper and his contribution this year was the LP *Glass Houses*. David Bowie returned to form in 1980 with *Scary Monsters (and Super Creeps)*, an album that yielded the hit single "Ashes to Ashes", a conscious attempt to erase the memory of his old albatross, "Space Oddity". The Police consolidated their standing with *Zenyatta Mondatta*, as did Bruce Springsteen with his double set, *The River*. Most promising new group was the Pretenders, led by expatriate American Chrissie Hynde, who was another who had worked long and hard for the big break. The self-named debut LP released late in 1979 was a worldwide hit, together with its excellent single, "Brass in Pocket".

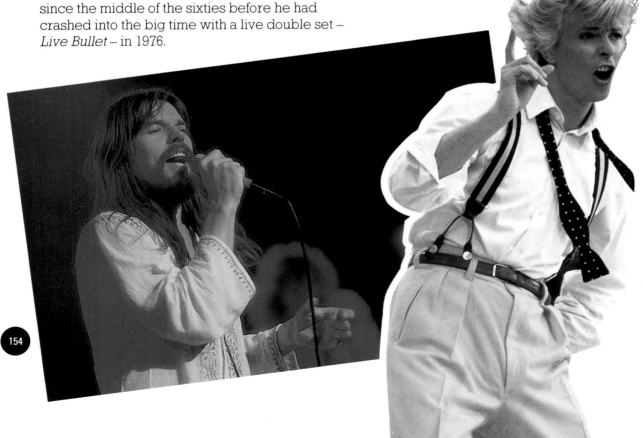

GIRLS AT THEIR BEST

This was the year when women claimed their rightful place in the scheme of musical things with a vengeance. In the early days of rock'n'roll, women performers were few and it was not until the late fifties and early sixties that girl groups and solo artistes started to make a real impression, although even then most of their material was written and produced by men. Throughout the sixties, women continued to play second fiddle, even talented songwriters like Carole King and Cynthia Weil. Aretha Franklin, the 'Queen of Soul', was dogged by uncertainty throughout her career, passing from producer to producer in an attempt to find a settled musical identity.

Iron ladies

However, by the eighties women had asserted themselves and were less prone to the kind of pressures that had seen the demise of Janis Joplin and Mama Cass. Patti Smith had played a large part in this during the latter half of the seventies with her aggressive sexuality, which met men more than half way. Grace Jones was another formidable figure who went one stage further by aping male attributes of imposing size and menace. Debbie Harrie of Blondie was quite happy to play the sexual stereotype when it suited her, but far more interesting was the way her vocals gave the band's tunes an irresistible edge. Chrissie Hynde, as already noted, led her band to international stardom by means of a melodic gift for tunes and one of the great rock'n'roll voices.

Far left Bob Seger. After years on the sidelines, Seger finally established himself in 1976 with the LPs *Live Bullet* and *Night Moves*.
Left David Bowie.
Above right Chrissie Hynde of The Pretenders. From Akron, Ohio, Hynde formed the Pretenders in London in 1978 and, from the outset, her group blended punk's aggression with the pop sensibilities of the British beat of the sixties.
Right Billy Joel. Born in the Bronx in 1948, Joel struggled for years as a member of lackluster teen beat outfits and, in the early seventies, was a singer/songwriter, before he finally succeeded in 1977 with his platinum-selling LP *The Stranger*.

1980 Diary

February

Bon Scott, the singer with Australian heavy metal act AC/DC, is found dead in the back seat of a car in south London following a night of heavy drinking.

Malcolm McLaren, ex-manager of the Sex Pistols, takes over management of the seemingly washed up punk band Adam and the Ants. McLaren's first action is to sack singer Adam – but Adam retains the group name. McLaren then brings in schoolgirl singer Annabella Lwin and turns the old Ants into Bow Wow Wow.

A thousand punks march through the center of London in honor of the first anniversary of Sid Vicious' death.

David and Angie Bowie are divorced.

Lou Reed is married to Sylvia Morales, who has a dramatic effect on revitalizing the singer's career.

January

Arriving in Japan for a tour with his group Wings, Paul McCartney is arrested at Tokyo airport when customs officers find eight ounces of marijuana among his luggage. McCartney languishes in jail for ten days and is then released.

Boogie-woogie piano legend Professor Longhair dies in New Orleans aged 62.

Cliff Richard is awarded an MBE in the British New Year's Honours List.

March

The Police hold a concert in Bombay. They're the first rock act to play there since Hawkwind appeared ten years previously.

Patti Smith marries Fred 'Sonic' Smith, former guitarist with Detroit 'activist' rockers the MC5. At the ceremony, the bride wears sneakers.

A paper napkin bearing the signature of Elvis Presley is sold for $5000 at Sotheby's auction rooms in London.

April

The first ever rock video to be made available to the British public goes on sale. It consists of footage of a 1979 Gary Numan concert in London.

Brian Johnson, ex-singer with stomping British pop band Geordie, replaces the late Bon Scott in AC/DC.

Tommy Caldwell, bass player of the Marshall Tucker Band, dies in a car crash in South Carolina.

Far left After years as a struggling country-rock performer, Linda Ronstadt struck gold in 1974 with her *Heart Like A Wheel* LP. By the end of the decade, she had become a major celebrity.
Left Grace Jones, queen of underworld disco.

May

South African authorities ban Pink Floyd's single "Another Brick in the Wall". Black schoolchildren had taken to singing the song as a protest against their school system.

Ian Curtis, singer of cult Manchester 'post-punk' band Joy Division, hangs himself from his bedroom window. According to friends, the suicide was prompted by Curtis' worsening epilepsy and relationship problems.

At a concert in Hamburg, Germany, Joe Strummer of the Clash bashes his guitar against the head of a boy in the audience. He is arrested but assault charges are subsequently dropped.

Below left Siouxsie Sioux (Susan Dallion) followed punk's do-it-yourself theme: by 1978, Siouxsie And The Banshees were in the charts with "Hong Kong Garden". *Below* Wendy O Williams of the Plasmatics.

June

Fans run amok at a Stranglers concert in Nice. Annoyed by the group's appalling sound quality, the audience smash windows and furniture, and the band are arrested for starting a riot.

The film *Roadie*, featuring Meat Loaf and Debbie Harry in acting roles, opens in the United States to dismal reviews and little business.

Pat Benatar makes a short appearance at the Philadelphia Phillies baseball stadium just before a game. She sings and dances with the Phillies' mascot – an oversized green duck.

July

Malcolm Owen, singer with London power punk band the Ruts, dies of a heroin overdose. Many of Owens' songs – including "H Eyes" – had told of the dangers and horrors of drugs.

Keith Godchaux, the Grateful Dead's keyboard player, dies in a car crash in California.

David Bowie makes his first-ever stage acting appearance in America, playing *The Elephant Man* in Denver, Colorado.

August

I, Me, Mine, George Harrison's autobiography, published in a limited edition and signed by the author, goes on sale at just $148 a copy. A snip!

Keyboard player Jools Holland leaves Squeeze. The witty south Londoner will go on to become a successful TV presenter on the rock show *The Tube*.

Cher appears on stage in New York's Central Park singing with Black Rose, the band led by her current paramour, guitarist Les Dudek.

Outrageous US punk band the Plasmatics are banned from playing in London by the Greater London Council. The group had threatened to explode a car on stage.

September

After a night of excessive drinking, Led Zeppelin drummer John 'Bonzo' Bonham collapses at Jimmy Page's Windsor mansion and subsequently dies. He is never replaced in the group and, sadly, they never perform again.

One-time rhythm section of the Jimi Hendrix Experience, drummer Mitch Mitchell and bassist Noel Redding, appear in Amsterdam at a music festival held in Hendrix's memory.

October

John Lydon, the former Johnny Rotten, is arrested in Dublin, Ireland, following a pub skirmish. Charged with assault, he is subsequently acquitted.

Bob Marley and the Wailers appear in concert in Pittsburgh. During the show Marley collapses – he never performs in public again.

John Lennon releases "(Just Like) Starting Over", his first single in six years, to mark his fortieth birthday. A sky-writer, hired by Yoko Ono, emblazons the message 'Happy Birthday John' across the New York skies.

November

Don Henley, drummer of the Eagles, is arrested at his home in Los Angeles after a naked 16-year-old girl is found there suffering from a drugs overdose. Charged with possession and contribution to the delinquency of a minor, Henley is fined $1000 and ordered to attend a two-year drug counseling course.

Sheffield electro-pop band the Human League split into two separate outfits. Martyn Ware and Ian Marsh form Heaven 17 while Phil Oakey and Adrian Wright continue as Human League who, with the help of girl singers Susanne Sulley and Joanne Catherall, soon achieve massive pop success with the best-selling single "Don't You Want Me" and LP *Dare*.

December

Mark Chapman, 25, guns down John Lennon outside the Dakota building in New York. Lennon is pronounced dead on arrival at hospital.

Larking about with friends after a gig in Belfast, Phil 'Philthy Animal' Taylor, Motorhead's drummer, falls on his head and breaks his neck.

Folk singer Tim Hardin, best known for his much-covered songs "Reason to Believe" and "If I Were a Carpenter", dies from a heroin overdose while in Los Angeles.

Within days of John Lennon's death, his recently-released single "(Just Like) Starting Over" and album *Double Fantasy* go to Number 1 in their respective charts in America.

Far left Kate Bush in one of her rare stage appearances. Discovered and encouraged by Pink Floyd's Dave Gilmour, Bush consolidated on the success of her debut single, "Wuthering Heights", with best-selling albums *The Kick Inside* (1976) and *Lionheart* (1978).
Above left Bruce Springsteen. Despite the phenomenal success of his albums, Springsteen refused to cut down on live performances.
Left John Lennon and Yoko Ono pictured in New York just days before Lennon's murder on December 8, 1980.

Heavy Metal Melodies

1981

Not unnaturally, the start of the year saw both singles and albums charts in Britain and America being dominated by John Lennon, with what had become the posthumous release of the LP *Double Fantasy*, recorded with Yoko Ono. The record showed Lennon to be in great all-round form after a relatively inactive spell during the seventies.

Long distance Moodies

After a long period of seclusion, the Moody Blues, one of the UK's most consistent hit-making outfits since their first success in 1964 with "Go Now", released an LP called *Long Distance Voyager*, which lived up to its name by traveling to the top of the US charts. The demise of Led Zeppelin and Yes brought about stories of a new supergroup for the eighties featuring Jimmy Page, Robert Plant, Chris Squire and Alan White. What actually happened was that the eighties got a new supergroup with ex-members of Yes, Buggles, ELP and Uriah Heep – it was called Asia.

Below John Wetton of Asia. Formed in 1981, the immediate success of Asia proved that there was still a market for complex, symphonic-type rock.

Two more bands earned belated but widespread recognition in 1981. REO Speedwagon had been in existence since the beginning of the seventies and had opted to make it to the top the hard way – by constant gigging around America. Their straightforward mixture of rockers and strong ballads finally found huge favor on the LP *Hi-Infidelity*. The story of Styx went back even further. Starting off as the Tradewinds in 1968, they changed their name to Styx in 1970 and started the long round of tours and moderately received albums. They broke through in the late seventies. Their 1981 effort, *Paradise Theater*, again demonstrated their flair for hard rock with splashes of melodic inspiration.

This was also a good year for women, in particular Pat Benatar (*Precious Time*), Kim Carnes (*Mistaken Identity*) and Sheena Easton (*Morning Train*).

Above right Alan Gratzer of REO Speedwagon – 30 million records sold by 1984, and growing.
Below right Styx, leaders in the field of complex hard rock since 1977.
Below Def Leppard was just one of many new heavy metal acts to spring up in Britain in the late seventies. Along with groups like Iron Maiden and Saxon, Leppard soon outstripped their 'New Wave Of British HM' contenders and by 1983, with a huge-selling LP in *Pyromania*, had established themselves in the US as well.

HEAVY MANNERS

Opinion is divided as to the origins of the music form that came to be called heavy metal. Most commentators see its roots in the early singles of the Kinks ("You Really Got Me") and the Who ("My Generation"). The nominally blues-based British bands of the late sixties certainly continued the process, in particular Cream ("Sunshine of Your Love") and Led Zeppelin ("Communication Breakdown"), whose 'songs' were often based on the sledgehammer riffing that has become a trademark of the genre. In America, the tradition is traced back through bands like Blue Cheer, Iron Butterfly and the Frost, to early practitioners of music as pain: the Velvet Underground, MC5 and Iggy and the Stooges.

The turn of the decade brought forth the true progenitors of heavy metal in the ungodly shape of Black Sabbath, whose music was a dense mass of distorted guitar, thudding bass and slugging drums that lurched around like a wounded dinosaur. The vocals carried that comparison to its logical conclusion. While other groups, from Deep Purple to Grand Funk Railroad, were exploiting the same territory, they were never as single-minded as Sabbath, who weathered several personnel changes (even the departure of oddly charismatic vocalist Ozzy Osbourne) without missing a monolithic beat. Black Sabbath were also responsible for the 'Satan and sorcery' lyrics that plagued the scene throughout the seventies, although the group itself branched out relatively quickly into more interesting areas with such singles as "War Pigs".

Metal motion

Through the seventies, heavy metal ebbed and flowed, with lean periods inevitably followed by a resurgence. Kiss and Ted Nugent kept the banner flying in America, while UK stalwarts included Thin Lizzy, Uriah Heep and Deep Purple offshoots Rainbow and Whitesnake. There was also a 12-bar boogie variant – with less distortion and more pace – the most dedicated champions of which were ZZ Top in America and Status Quo, a reformed psychedelic/pop band, in Britain.

Early in the eighties came a sudden injection of fresh blood from both sides of the Atlantic, starting in the UK with such new metal bands as Def Leppard, Tygers of Pang Tang, Saxon, UFO and Judas Priest. From America came Van Halen, who soon outgrew the narrow confines of the genre, and then a whole regiment of young turks – many of them adopting the look of the New York Dolls, complete with plentiful make-up – such as Motley Crue, Ratt, Twisted Sister, Thor and Wasp. Even Finland got into the act with Hanoi Rocks. It seems that heavy metal in one form or another is destined to be around for as long as pop itself.

Right The 'Flying V' guitar is one of the trademarks of heavy metal. This specimen is being wielded by K K Downing, lead guitarist with Judas Priest — formed in the mid-seventies in Birmingham, England.

Center right Iron Maiden make no secret of their musical aims by naming themselves after an ancient instrument of torture. The group dates back to 1977.

Left Ted Nugent has been terrorizing audiences since the sixties, when he was the star turn with Detroit garage band the Amboy Dukes. Nugent finally found fame and fortune in the mid-seventies as a solo performer, backed by an ever-changing cast of musicians. Although his albums sold in droves, it was as a stage performer that he excelled.

Above ZZ Top present their unique blend of guitars, hats and beards. Formed in 1970, some years passed before ZZ Top's brand of blues 'n' boogie reached a wide audience with such hits as "Eliminator".

163

1981 Diary

January

New American President Ronald Reagan is inaugurated in Washington, DC. At the glittering ceremony, Donny Osmond performs Chuck Berry's "Johnny B Goode", with the words changed to "Ronnie B Goode", while the 69-year-old ex-actor claps his hands.

Jerry Dammers and Terry Hall of Coventry Two-Tone band the Specials are fined $400 in Cambridge for 'inciting violence' at a concert the previous autumn.

The Recording Industry of America donates 800 albums to the Library of Congress in Washington, DC. LPs preserved for posterity include Kiss's record *Alive!*

February

Bill Haley, rock'n'roll pioneer, dies in Texas at 56.

Michael Bloomfield, former guitarist of the Paul Butterfield Blues Band and contributor to Bob Dylan's first 'electric' sessions in 1965, is found dead in his car in San Francisco of a suspected heroin overdose.

In a New York court, George Harrison is found guilty of 'subconsciously plagiarizing' the Chiffons' 1963 hit "He's So Fine" and using it as the basis for his 1970 hit "My Sweet Lord". The former Beatle is ordered to pay out some half-million dollars in back royalties.

Right Phil Lynott and Scott Gorham of Thin Lizzy. The group did not conform to any of the rigid musical genres of the seventies, having a preference for the more melodic tones of traditional music, spiced with whiplash guitar. Originally from Northern Ireland, Thin Lizzy soon turned into a truly cosmopolitan band through a series of personnel changes. A dynamic live act and LPs such as *Jailbreak* and *Live and Dangerous* kept Lizzy at the top for almost a decade.
Center right Pat Benatar conclusively proved that hard rock was not just the prerogative of the boys.

March

The Blues Project, pioneering jazz/punk/blues band of the mid-sixties, reform for a concert in their home town, New York. After squabbling, however, the group members decide not to stay together permanently.

Adam and the Ants' *Kings of the Wild Frontier* LP goes to the top of the British charts where it remains for 19 weeks – confirming the group as England's present top pop attraction.

April

Bob 'the Bear' Hite, portly singer of US rock blues legend Canned Heat, dies in California of a heart attack aged 38.

John Phillips, founder of the Mamas and the Papas, is sentenced to eight years' imprisonment in Los Angeles for possession of cocaine. He serves only 30 days of the sentence, however; the remainder is suspended.

Ringo Starr marries American actress Barbara Bach in London.

Kit Lambert, the Who's eccentric ex-manager, dies of head injuries after tumbling downstairs at his mother's house in London.

May

Bob Marley dies in Miami of a brain tumor.

Public Image Ltd perform at New York's Ritz Club. The group do not appear on stage, however, preferring to play behind a giant video screen. Members of the audience express their disgust by hurling bottles.

June

Walter Becker and Donald Fagen of Steely Dan announce that their musical partnership is at an end.

Bob Dylan plays concerts in London for the first time since his conversion to Christianity.

Bruce Springsteen, Graham Nash, Stephen Stills, Jackson Browne and other stars perform at a No Nukes rally at the Hollywood Bowl.

July

The Four Skins, a skinhead band reputed to hold racist views, play a gig at the Hambrough Tavern in Southall – a predominantly Asian area in west London. Clashes between Asians and white youths lead to large-scale rioting – and in the coming weeks there will be similar violent riots around the country.

Singer-songwriter Harry Chapin, best known for his hits "WOLD", "Taxi" and "Cat's in the Cradle", dies in a car crash on Long Island, New York.

August

Lee Hays, founder member of the US folk group the Weavers, and co-author with fellow-Weaver Pete Seeger of "If I Had a Hammer", dies in New York of heart failure aged 67.

Mark Chapman is sentenced to 20 years to life in New York for the murder of John Lennon.

September

Walter 'Furry' Lewis, one-legged blues singer and pioneer of bottleneck blues guitar playing, dies in Memphis of heart failure aged 88.

Paul Simon and Art Garfunkel reform for a concert in New York's Central Park. The audience of 400 000 fans seem delighted.

October

Koo Koo, Debbie Harry's first solo LP, goes gold in the United States.

Just weeks after the Specials have topped the British charts with "Ghost Town", singers Terry Hall, Lynval Golding and Neville Staples leave the group to form the Fun Boy Three.

November

"Under Pressure", a single by the unlikely partnership of David Bowie and Queen, goes to the top of the British singles charts.

Mick Jagger, Keith Richard and Ronnie Wood of the Rolling Stones jam with blues giants Buddy Guy and Muddy Waters in Chicago.

The British Phonographic Industry places ads in the UK music press claiming that 'home taping is killing music'. The campaign is endorsed by Cliff Richard, Elton John, Gary Numan and the Boomtown Rats, among others.

December

Michael Dempsey, former manager of the Adverts, whose 1977 disc "Gary Gilmore's Eyes" was the first punk single to make the British Top Twenty, dies in London of a punctured liver after falling off a chair while changing a light bulb.

A Rod Stewart concert in Los Angeles is televized live by satellite around the globe. A mere 35 million people are estimated to have tuned in to the show.

Below Sheena Easton broke into the music scene by means of an appearance on BBC TV's documentary *The Big Time*. She has stayed at the top through talent.

Video Madness

In terms of statistics, 1982 was a bad year for the record business, particularly in America. All the major labels instituted major cuts in the number of staff they employed amid gloomy predictions and grim talk about the whole industry being in bad shape. Yet there was plenty of action on the music front, with the usual crop of new talent (especially from the UK) and sterling new material from established stars. The main problem, in Britain at least, was claimed to be home taping, with sales of LPs falling alarmingly by approximately 20 per cent.

League of perfect love

Problems or not, the Human League had a very successful year with their LP *Dare* starting off the year at the top in the UK and one of the singles from it, "Don't You Want Me?", at the top of the US charts towards the end. Adam Ant, who had been Britain's biggest teenybop sensation for years, continued his unbroken run of success with "Goody Two Shoes" and decided life was bearable without his backing Ants, meanwhile forming plans for a solo assault on the American market. Other promising UK bands included Yazoo, who scored with singles like "Don't Go" and the album *Upstairs at Erics*. A Flock Of Seagulls and the Fixx were two groups who started to make a big impression in America, without having achieved notable results in their home market, while Culture Club hit the top in the UK first with "Do You Really Want to Hurt Me?".

Miller magic

Established figures who carried on business as usual included Steve Miller, a veteran of the late sixties West Coast underground scene, who had interspersed periods of seeming inactivity with the release of excellent records – *Sailor*, *The Joker*, *Fly Like an Eagle*. His 1982 success was *Abracadabra*. The J Geils Band, a hard-working R&B act, capped 15 years of almost making it with a chart-topping album – *Freeze Frame* – and the single "Centrefold". There were huge hits, too, for Barbra Streisand, Joan Jett (ex-Runaways), the Go-Gos and Olivia Newton-John. The Who's marathon farewell tour of America was their most profitable ever.

Successful films continued to boost records associated with them: this meant hits for Vangelis with the soundtrack to *Chariots of Fire*, and for Survivor with "Eye of the Tiger", the theme song from the latest *Rocky* smash. Everyone concerned with *Fame*, both the original film and the spin-off TV series, had reason to be thankful for the association, as it spawned a number of hit singles and an album.

Right Two of the Kids From *Fame*, the film about young singers and dancers that spawned a TV series and a number of hit singles.
Center right Steve Miller has been one of the most enduring figures on the rock scene since his appearance in the sixties, with LPs such as *The Joker*.
Far right The outrageous Adam Ant, one-time UK punk struggler who turned himself into a fantasy figure.

VIDEO EXPLOSION

Towards the end of 1981 something new came on the air. It was called MTV – a music-only cable TV station which was committed to broadcasting (via satellite) rock videos for 24 hours a day, seven days a week. MTV quickly rose to a position of great influence within the rock world as a tastemaker and selling medium. The kind of exposure which could be gained by an artist was astonishing, especially on 'heavy rotation'. For once, however, the American rock industry was slow to realize the potential of its own invention, and there was a general dearth of good videos from US bands. Other countries were much quicker to react.

In Britain, the art of video making, though relatively new, was highly advanced. A new breed of video directors sprang up, drawn from all areas of the entertainment business, who swiftly mastered the art of setting three minutes of music to suitable visuals.

Godley and Creme

A notable example was the team of Godley and Creme, who came to videos from a successful career in pop music (with UK outfit 10cc) and a less successful solo career. Their innate understanding of the form was emphasized again and again. Other groups, for example Ultravox, preferred to handle the video chores themselves: it was a democratic medium if nothing else.

Madness

When MTV got into its stride and revealed its insatiable appetite for slick videos of catchy pop songs, it was natural that it should look to the abundant product coming out of the UK. The bands and their record companies were naturally delighted, as new (to America) acts could get undreamed of exposure in the world's biggest record market, virtually overnight, and without the necessity for exhausting tours at second-rate venues, which were not any guarantee of ultimate success. Bands like Duran Duran and Madness capitalized on this approach immediately (even if the former had to tone down their *Girls on Film* video for mass US acceptance). In a sense, the British invasion was based on video.

It was not only Britain which benefited. Australian groups, relative latecomers to the world music scene, also derived lasting benefits from video in general and MTV in particular. Men At Work, the Divinyls and INXS were given a flying start by their videos. By the time that the likes of Michael Jackson and ZZ Top were offering effective competition, the Anglo-Australian invasion force had established a firm foothold in the American market.

Below Bruce Springsteen was a hero for the eighties.
Right Olivia Newton John, star of stage and screen.

1982 Diary

January

John Coghlan, the drummer of boogie kings Status Quo, leaves the group after 20 years.

Recently qualified pilot Gary Numan is forced to land on a main road in Hampshire, England, when his Cessna light aircraft runs out of juice.

R&B artist Tommy Tucker – whose song "Hi Heel Sneakers" had become a rock'n'roll standard – dies in New York of carbon tetrachloride poisoning caused by inhaling toxic fumes while stripping floorboards in his house.

Blues artist Sam 'Lightnin' Hopkins dies of cancer in Texas at 70. His talking blues style had influenced Bob Dylan, while his electric guitar style was often cited by Jimi Hendrix as a prime inspiration.

February

Scottish rock singer Alex Harvey, best remembered for his colorful and theatrical work with his Sensational Alex Harvey Band in the mid-seventies, dies of a heart attack in Belgium aged 46.

Pat Benatar marries her guitarist Neil Geraldo in Hawaii.

Veteran rock'n'roll disc jockey, Murray 'The K' Kaufman, who helped introduce the Beatles to the American public – and became known in the sixties as 'the Fifth Beatle' – dies in Los Angeles of cancer at 60.

March

Ozzy Osbourne's guitarist Randy Rhoads is killed in Florida while recklessly joyriding in a light aircraft. The plane crashes into a house, also killing the pilot and a girl passenger.

Disco star Teddy Pendergrass, one-time member of Harold Melvin and the Blue Notes, is paralyzed from the waist down after his chauffeur-driven Rolls Royce collides with a tree in Philadelphia.

David Crosby is arrested for possession of drugs and a handgun in Los Angeles. When police ask the singer why he has a pistol, he simply nods and whispers 'John Lennon, John Lennon'.

April

Lester Bangs – America's wittiest and most irreverent rock journalist – dies of a heart attack in New York.

Billy Joel is badly injured when his motorbike collides with a car on Long Island.

Joe Strummer of the Clash 'disappears', forcing the band to cancel a UK tour.

May

Adam Ant fires his backing group the Ants, deciding to pursue a solo career. Guitarist Marco Pirroni stays on as Adam's musical collaborator, however.

Tam Paton, the Scottish pop manager who steered the Bay City Rollers to teen idol success in the mid-seventies, is imprisoned for three years in Edinburgh, having been apprehended behaving in a shamelessly indecent manner.

Topper Headon, drummer of the Clash, quits the group. Five weeks later, Headon is in court charged with stealing a bus stop.

June

Pretenders bassist Pete Farndon is sacked from the band. The following day the group's guitarist James Honeyman-Scott is found dead at his London flat following a drugs overdose.

Micki Harris, member of sixties girl group the Shirelles, whose "Will You Love Me Tomorrow?" was a world-wide hit in the early sixties, dies in Los Angeles.

Bryan Ferry of Roxy Music marries Lucy Helmore in Sussex, England.

Below right The J Geils Band's Peter Wolf leads the group through yet another sizzling R&B anthem.

Above The Thompson Twins forsook experimentation to become one of the biggest UK acts of the eighties.

July

Moon Unit, 14-year-old daughter of Frank Zappa, has a surprise novelty hit in the United States with "Valley Girl", a song written by her father lampooning the extraordinary slang of the rich kids of California's San Fernando Valley area.

ABC's LP *The Lexicon of Love*, produced by Trevor Horn, tops the UK album chart.

August

Joe Tex, soul star of the sixties, dies in Texas of a heart attack aged 49.

Liverpool council renames four of the city's streets John Lennon Drive, Paul McCartney Way, George Harrison Close and Ringo Starr Drive.

Bruce Springsteen performs at the wedding of Southside Johnny Lyon in Asbury Park, New Jersey.

September

Redlands, Keith Richards' Sussex mansion, burns to the ground for the second time in nine years.

Blondie are forced to cancel a tour of Britain following pitifully poor ticket sales.

Pop duo Yazoo top the British LP charts with *Upstairs at Eric's*; for some extraordinary reason, the group's name is changed in America to Yaz.

Below Belinda Carlisle, lead singer of the Go-Gos, on stage. The group was formed in 1978 to open for the Dickies in Los Angeles.

October

Culture Club's ascent to fame and notoriety gets off the mark when "Do You Really Want to Hurt Me?" goes to Number 1 in the British singles charts.

At a Peter Frampton concert in Houston, one fan is stabbed to death, another is killed by a gunman.

Paul Weller announces that he is breaking up the Jam.

The Mayor of Worcester, Massachusetts, declares 22 October 'Van Halen Day' after receiving a petition signed by 25 000 Worcester residents.

November

British rock/soul singer Joe Cocker returns to the charts after ten years, duetting with Jennifer Warnes on "Up Where We Belong", the theme song from the box-office hit *An Officer and a Gentleman*.

Talking Heads bassist Tina Weymouth and drummer Chris Frantz – who married in 1978 – hear the patter of tiny feet when a son, Robert, is born in Nassau.

'Alternative' British TV rock show *The Tube* airs for the first time.

Joni Mitchell marries bass player Larry Klein in Malibu, California.

December

The Jam play farewell concerts in London.

A Bob Marley commemorative postage stamp is issued in Jamaica.

David Blue, the cult singer/songwriter who made an appearance in Bob Dylan's 1976 film *Renaldo and Clara*, dies of a heart attack while out jogging in New York's Washington Square.

Below A Flock Of Seagulls — early UK invaders.

Moneyspinners

This was the year when, for the first time, cassettes took a greater share of the market than LPs. There were changes afoot in the charts as well: and the second British invasion was on the way. In the forefront was the new breed of technopop/glam bands like Duran Duran (named after a character in the film *Barbarella*), the Thompson Twins (all three of them), A Flock Of Seagulls, ABC and others.

Three for the top

In a more traditional musical vein, there were hits for Culture Club fronted by Boy George (who, in August of that year had three singles in the US Top Ten), Spandau Ballet, Dexy's Midnight Runners and the Pretenders. Later in the year, these acts were joined in the first flight by the Eurythmics (with a dynamic female vocalist in Annie Lennox), Dublin's U2 and Paul Young, a tough but tender crooner. Naturally, the 'old wave' had its share of triumph with Number 1 hits for the Police ("Every Breath You Take") and David Bowie ("Let's Dance").

What all these artists had in common was teen appeal. Their effect on a somewhat dreary American music scene was electrifying. A second wave of British acts appeared during the summer

to hammer home the message. These included Eddy Grant (a veteran of the Equals), Kajagoogoo, the Human League, Madness and Billy Idol, one time singer with punk outfit Generation X who had moved to New York to start a solo career. Heavy metal was well represented by Def Leppard and Naked Eyes, Elton John and Rod Stewart joined the fun, and there was even room for a couple of real veterans who remembered the first invasion 20 years before: the Hollies and the Kinks. When Bonnie Tyler's *Total Eclipse Of The Heart* reached the top later in the year, it became clear that American defenses were well and truly down.

Left Heavy metal bands were by no means exclusively British and American. The Scorpions from Germany were formed in 1971 by Rudolph and Michael Schenker, the latter subsequently leaving to join UFO. Although the sound of the Scorpions has matured over the years, it can fairly be said that it retains a fearsome aural power which can be heard on albums such as *Lovedrive* and *Animal Magnetism* as well as in their storming stage act.

Thriller

The really big business, however, was not being achieved by any of the army of British bands. In February, Michael Jackson's *Thriller* appeared and stole swiftly to the top of the album charts. Jackson had not been exactly prolific since starting out on his solo career. His occasional singles sold well, but his only LP release before *Thriller* was 1979's disco masterpiece *Off The Wall*. The latest record eclipsed even its mega-platinum predecessor, spawning six hit singles and bouncing back to the Number 1 position whenever there was a lull in the action elsewhere. Jackson also produced a stream of beautifully choreographed videos, highlighting his own freeze-frame stick insect dance steps.

Starting late the previous year and keeping up their momentum in the early part of 1983, Men At Work (with their LP *Business As Usual*) were invaders of a different stripe: they were Australian. An unassuming, low profile outfit, Men At Work succeeded with a batch of well-crafted (if a little derivative) pop songs and some nicely self-deprecatory videos.

Altogether less unassuming were the antics of native-born, heavy metal/pop band Quiet Riot. Their particular brand of unsophisticated mayhem was well represented on the album *Mental Health*, but curiously their singles success had a British connection: their two biggest hits were both covers of old hits by UK 'yob' rock specialists Slade – "Cum On Feel The Noize" and "Mama Weer All Crazee Now". The big music movie of the year was *Flashdance* featuring an improbable story line and a lot of highly commercial sounds which duly made their mark in the charts.

A note of nostalgia was struck when a number of British bands of the sixties, including the Yardbirds, the Animals and Manfred Mann, reformed to celebrate the 25th anniversary of London's Marquee Club. A note for the future was sounded with the launch of the compact disc, offering up to an hour of music from a laser-activated five inch platter.

Left Dexy's Midnight Runners are the brainchild of Kevin Rowland. He has guided the group on an erratic but hugely entertaining course over the years.

SONS OF SOUL

The success of black artists during the sixties and seventies reached a peak in the early years of the eighties. The disco boom was fueled predominantly by black artists and out of that phenomenon grew various offshoots: rapping, scratching, breakdancing, body-popping, boystown, hip hop and many more. The 12in dance single came into vogue, and the practice of re-mixing existing tracks to enhance their dancefloor power became widespread.

Star management

Producers like Arthur Baker, Afrika Bambaata and 'Jellybean' Benitez enjoyed greater prominence than the artists they doctored. Much of the groundwork had been done in the sixties and seventies by Sly Stone (Sylvester Stewart) on albums like *There's A Riot Going On* (grinding funk with a bleak urban commentary) and *Stand* (soul/funk with a pop/rock sensibility). Sadly, by the eighties he appeared to be in artistic and commercial decline.

Another pioneer was George Clinton, the man behind such outfits as Parliament and Funkadelic, that peddled powerhouse funk with loopy cosmic mythology. During the eighties, the indefatigable Clinton took up a solo career and he continued to produce a stream of warped masterpieces, as in the dancefloor smash "Atomic Dog".

Wonder man

Stevie Wonder continued to produce hit singles at random and hit albums at rather longer intervals. Before his tragic death, Marvin Gaye had struck a rich vein of creativity with the LP *Midnight Love* and the smash single from it, "Sexual Healing". Smokey Robinson continued to produce great music, despite his full-time executive job with Tamla Motown. Lionel Richie emerged as yet another black superstar after leaving the Commodores. His album, *Can't Slow Down*, was another platinum monster from which hit singles came in a steady flow.

Michael Jackson experienced unprecedented success and then joined his brothers in the most profitable tour in the history of rock and pop. Bands like Kool & the Gang, Earth, Wind and Fire and the still potent Commodores had big hits with effortless ease. At the raunchy end of the scale, Rick James won a huge following for his X-rated rock/funk, but even his triumphs were upstaged by Prince, the face of 1984, who broke through with an LP, film and tour, all with the same name: *Purple Rain*.

Meanwhile in the ghettos of Washington DC, a new movement was forming called go-go...

Right Prince threatens to become the star of the eighties. *Purple Rain* showed him to be both talented and outrageous — traditionally, a winning combination.

Left Billy Idol used to be lead singer with punk outfit Generation X before starting a solo career.
Below Darlings of the London fashion scene, Spandau Ballet soon proved themselves as talented entertainers.

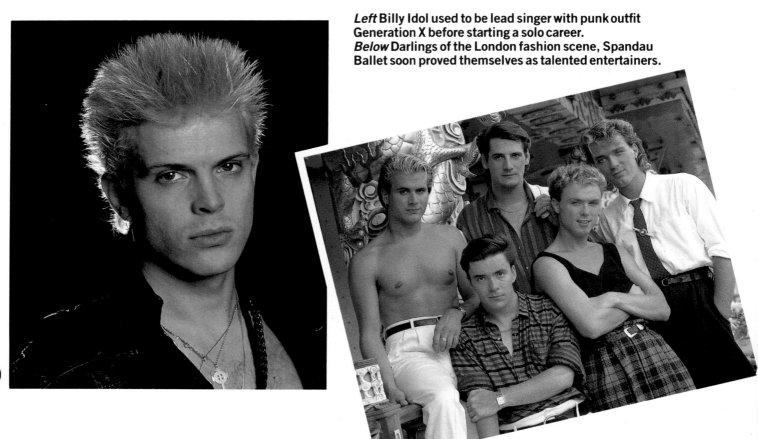

1983 Diary

January

Reebob Kwaku Baah, former Traffic percussionist, dies in Sweden from a brain hemorrhage.

Lamar Williams, one-time bass player with the Allman Brothers and Sea Level, dies in Los Angeles of cancer.

Billy Fury, British teen idol of the late fifties and early sixties, dies of a heart attack.

February

Karen Carpenter falls downstairs at her parents' home in California and dies. The coroner's report notes that the 32-year-old singer had 'heartbeat irregularities . . . associated with anorexia nervosa'.

Three people are killed and many injured in a stampede to exits at a concert by Puerto Rican popsters Menudo in Mexico.

March

Duran Duran are mobbed by screaming fans at a video store in New York.

Compact discs – a new development in digital audio systems – are launched onto the market.

Hell's Angels hold a press conference in New York to deny rumors that they are plotting to kill Mick Jagger.

April

Pete Farndon, former bass player of the Pretenders, is found dead in his bath tub in London following a drugs overdose.

Felix Pappalardi, producer of the legendary Cream and later bassist with US hard rock merchants Mountain, is shot dead in his New York apartment following a quarrel with his wife, who is subsequently charged with his murder.

Muddy Waters dies in Illinois aged 68.

Michael Fagan, who sprang to notoriety by intruding into the Queen's bedroom and asking her for a cigarette, appears at London night-club the Batcave singing with the Bollock Brothers.

President Ronald Reagan asks the Beach Boys to perform in Washington for the Fourth of July celebrations. The group decline the invitation.

Right **Bananarama were one of the UK's most successful girl groups, scoring hits with such singles as "Robert De Niro's Waiting" and "Cruel Summer". They also teamed up successfully with the Fun Boy Three.**

Below **Men At Work were one of the big hits of the eighties. The men from Australia specialized in witty videos and catchy tunes such as "Down Under".**

May

In Athens, Greece, crowds attempting to get into a Uriah Heep concert without paying attack police, badly injuring three policemen.

Meat Loaf, whose *Bat Out of Hell* (1977) has become one of the best-selling LPs ever, files for bankruptcy in New York.

June

Dexy's Midnight Runners are dropped as the support act for David Bowie at a Paris concert after Dexy's singer/leader Kevin Rowlands insults Bowie.

After ten years apart – and many bitter words – Don and Phil Everly bury the hatchet and resume their fraternal musical partnership.

Alex Van Halen, drummer of extravagant US heavy metal act Van Halen, marries Valeri Kendall in Los Angeles. The band's guitarist Eddie Van Halen is best man and Tahitian fire dancers are the highlight of a lively reception.

July

Punky Irish pop combo the Undertones play their farewell gig at London's Crystal Palace.

Fantastic, the first album by pop duo Wham!, enters the British LP charts at Number 1.

Chris Wood, sax player and founder member of Traffic, dies of liver failure at 39.

August

Jerry Lee Lewis' fifth wife Shawn is found dead at the couple's home in Mississippi, just two months after her marriage to "The Killer". An accidental overdose of prescribed medication is the suspected cause of death.

Joey Ramone, guitarist with the Ramones, is attacked by fellow musician Seth Macklin in an argument over a young lady. Ramone undergoes four hours' emergency brain surgery.

Limahl, the singer with British cutey-pie pop group Kajagoogoo, is sacked from the band.

September

Guitarist Mick Jones is fired from the Clash.

Eccentric German new wave/opera singer Klaus Nomi dies, a victim of AIDS.

Reggae dub maestro Prince Far I is murdered by gunmen in his home in Kingston, Jamaica.

After eight years at the top, Kiss decide to remove their make-up.

Scottish bubblegum idols of the mid-seventies the Bay City Rollers reform and play at a new wave festival in Leeds. They receive nothing but jeers and hurled plastic bottles from the audience and retire in disgrace.

October

Country guitar supremo Merle Travis, composer of such country and western classics as "Sixteen Tons" and "Smoke! Smoke! Smoke! (That Cigarette)", dies in Nashville of heart disease aged 65.

The Dark Side of the Moon, Pink Floyd's 1973 album, overtakes *Johnny Mathis' Greatest Hits* as America's longest-running chart LP of all time. It has been in the Top 200 for 491 weeks.

Left Tracie Ullman first came to prominence as a TV comedienne, but rapidly developed into a singing star. **Below** Men At Work formed in 1982 and hit the big time the same year with *Business As Usual*. On the left is lead singer Colin Hay.

November

Comical British punks King Kurt – famous for hurling custard and other glutinous substances about on stage – are attacked by a gang in Liverpool and are forced to cancel a UK tour.

Tom Evans, former bass player of Badfinger, and co-author with Pete Ham of Nilsson's massive 1972 hit "Without You", hangs himself at his Surrey home – seven years after Badfinger colleague Ham had hanged himself in his garage.

Michael Jackson's spooky *Thriller* video, directed by John Landis, opens to brisk business in Los Angeles cinemas.

December

Pete Townshend announces his departure from his group the Who.

Dennis Wilson, drummer of the Beach Boys, is drowned off the coast of south California while 'looking for objects on the sea bed'. Ronald Reagan grants Wilson a burial at sea – an honour usually reserved for members of the US Armed Forces.

Keith Richard marries model Patti Hansen in Mexico. Mick Jagger is best man.

Michael Jackson's *Thriller* LP reaches the top of the US album charts.

Overleaf Duran Duran named themselves after the villain in *Barbarella*, made slick videos and produced excellent singles in "The Reflex" and "Wild Boys".

Second US Invasion

![1984]

The British invasion continued throughout the year. In March, 24 of the top 50 singles in the US were by UK acts. A still more surprising manifestation of the lure of all things from across the Atlantic was the entry of seven re-released Beatles albums into the American charts, 20 years after the group's triumphant arrival. The year also saw *Thriller* instaled as the best-selling record of all time, with sales of over 30 million and rising fast.

The great Victory tour

The Jacksons' Victory tour did for tours what Michael's solo album had done for vinyl, although certain 'hard sell' techniques employed drew adverse comment. The *Victory* album by the Jacksons went double platinum before anyone realized that it was, in fact, not very good at all. Prince tried to be thought of as a twentieth century Midas, only everything he touched turned to platinum!

The music film success of the year (apart from *Purple Rain*, which did quite nicely) was *Footloose*. The soundtrack was a chart topper, as were singles from it by Kenny Loggins (the title track) and Deniece Williams.

Lauping into the limelight

Promising newcomers included Cyndi Lauper, whose album *She's So Unusual* provided the justification for a ten-year career. Huey Lewis and the News scored spectacularly with their brand of unpretentious pop/rock. Their top selling LP *Sports* contained a disproportionate number of hit singles, but there was a cloud on the seemingly untroubled horizon. Lewis sued Ray Parker Jr, who had produced the theme song for the smash hit movie *Ghostbusters*, for stealing the musical framework of the song from his own hit "I Want A New Drug".

Two bands with an openly gay contingent, Frankie Goes To Hollywood and Bronski Beat, were among the latest British acts knocking on the door in the US. Frankie Goes To Hollywood came from Liverpool, which gave them an extra boost, as did the fact that they were the first group since Gerry and the Pacemakers to see their first three singles ("Relax", "Two Tribes", "The Power Of Love") climb to Number 1 in the British charts. Other British successes were Phil Collins, taking leave of absence from the drum stool in Genesis, who managed to produce, record or collaborate in a seemingly endless stream of hit records, and the reformed Yes, who returned to the top of the charts with "Owner Of A Lonely Heart". The Wham! phenomenon, which had been plaguing the UK for the past year, reached the US.

Above **Wham! are a UK duo consisting of George Michael and Andrew Ridgeley. Their rise to fame was meteoric on both sides of the Atlantic and, in 1985, they became the first pop band to play live in China.**

LIMEY INVASION

Exactly 20 years after the first British invasion of America, a second wholesale takeover ensued. This time there was no figurehead, as there had been with the Beatles, but a general enthusiastic acceptance of all the bright new pop groups that were pouring out of Britain.

The part that video played in this has already been discussed, but a more important factor in the long term was the style of the music and the performers. The American charts in the eighties had been safe zones, not places where surprises lurked. The vast majority of songs were by AOR favorites, old and new (Australian groups like Men At Work and the Little River Band were particularly favored) and nothing which did not fit the accepted grooves tended to get a look in.

Police

When a bright legion did appear on the horizon, with new songs aimed at a youth that had been left in the cold, the results were spectacular. A certain amount of groundwork had been done by bands like the Police, the Clash and Joe Jackson, who had come to prominence during the first flush of punk rock but had shown themselves capable of producing music which went well beyond the basic three-chord thrash. The Police were the standard-bearers for these new sounds, offering a dazzling combination of mutant reggae rhythms, rock guitar colorings and Sting's matchless vocals – a satisfying synthesis which appealed to a broad spectrum of tastes.

In the early eighties, most of the interesting music on offer in America was being produced by soul/funk artists and the semi-underground rock bands (Dream Syndicate, dBs, Plimsouls), who were busy re-inventing classic, guitar-based rock'n'roll with modern trappings. This left the huge middle ground of white pop/rock in the hands of the aging AOR groups and the practitioners of lightweight, disposable pop who pandered to the flavor of the moment.

Melodic punks

Even by 1983, it was a case of, 'instead of them, the deluge'. A seemingly endless stream of (mostly) young British groups filled the market vacuum with alacrity. They derived much of their energy from the punk example, but tempered it with attention to melodic detail, often helped by synthesizers. Visually, they were a striking bunch, sporting a selection of peacock explosion hairstyles and clothes. Before too long, bright new pop was flooding the land and strange-looking young men and women were a commonplace sight on MTV speaking in the talk shows.

Below The unusual Cyndi Lauper – hits came eventually.
Below right Tina Turner, still wild in the eighties.

1984 Diary

January

Alexis Korner, founding father of British R&B, who encouraged the fledgling Rolling Stones back in 1962, dies at the age of 55.

Manchester band the Smiths team up with sixties singing star Sandie Shaw to record a new version of the group's song "Hand in Glove".

Bette Midler releases a version of the Rolling Stones' "Beast of Burden". Mick Jagger makes a short appearance in the accompanying video.

The cover of Van Halen's *1984* LP outrages health authorities in the United States. It depicts a baby puffing away on a cigarette.

US soul legend Jackie Wilson dies at 49. He had been in a coma since suffering a heart attack on stage eight years previously. The Four Tops act as pall-bearers at the funeral.

February

"Relax", the first single by Liverpool band Frankie Goes To Hollywood, is banned by the BBC for its suggestive lyrics. The resulting publicity helps the record to soar to Number 1.

Reformed group Yes top the US chart with "Owner of a Lonely Heart". The record is produced by Trevor Horn – as is the UK Number 1, "Relax".

Michael Jackson's hair catches fire during the filming of a Pepsi-Cola TV commercial.

Ozzy Osbourne's throat is injured by flying glass during the shooting of a video.

Status Quo announce their retirement from touring.

After making derogatory remarks about the Chicano population of El Paso, Def Leppard singer Joe Elliot flies from Paris to the United States to apologize in person. He donates $15 000 to Latino community organizations.

Below Chicago combined jazz funk and huge pop hits.

March

Michael Jackson sets a new record by picking up a total of eight Grammy Awards for his *Thriller* album. The same month, *Thriller* overtakes *Saturday Night Fever* as the best-selling LP of all time with 40 million sales worldwide.

Annie Lennox of the Eurythmics marries West German Hare Krishna devotee Radha Raman in a secret ceremony.

US comedian Dan Ackroyd buys Carl Perkins' original blue suede shoes in an auction.

Neil Diamond sues his record company CBS, who have refused to release his latest album because, they say, it's 'not commercial enough'.

April

Blues hero John Lee Hooker visits the set of US daytime soap opera *All My Children*. The singer says he wants to meet his heroine, actress Taylor Miller.

Marvin Gaye is shot dead on the eve of his 45th birthday by his 69-year-old father, a retired minister of the Holiness Church. The shooting occurs during an argument at Gaye's parents' home in Los Angeles.

May

The video for Queen's latest single "I Want to Break Free" features the group in drag impersonating characters from Britain's most popular soap opera *Coronation Street*.

Heavy metal heroes Deep Purple, who sold millions of records around the world before splitting up in 1975, announce they are to reform.

June

Promoter Frank J Russo sues the Jacksons for $40 million, alleging that the group reneged on an agreement for him to promote their forthcoming Victory tour.

Boy George is immortalized in wax at London's Madame Tussauds.

July

Prince's "Purple Rain" comes out in the United States. It sells 1.3 million copies on its first day of release.

At a concert in Dublin, Bob Dylan is joined on stage by U2 singer Bono and Van Morrison. The trio perform Dylan's "It's All Over Now Baby Blue".

Frankie Goes To Hollywood's second single, "Two Tribes", goes straight to Number 1, though the BBC refuse to show its video, which shows Ronald Reagan wrestling with Soviet leader Chernenko.

Left Michael Jackson left his brothers far behind with *Off The Wall* and *Thriller*.

August

Wham!'s George Michael tops the British singles charts with his first solo record, "Careless Whisper".

MC Globe and Pow Wow, two members of New York hip hop crew Afrika Bambaata and the Sonic Soul Force, are charged with armed robbery in New York.

Prince's *Purple Rain* film opens in the United States. It grosses $64 million at the box office before the end of the year.

Black artists hold six of the Top Ten slots in the US LP charts – a record. The acts are Prince, Tina Turner, the Jacksons, Lionel Ritchie, the Pointer Sisters and Ray Parker Jr.

September

African musician Fela Kuti is arrested at an airport in his native Nigeria and charged with attempting to smuggle $1600 out of the country.

October

At London's ICA, rioting breaks out in the audience when experimental group SPK leave the stage after only two numbers. The band are disgruntled because fire prevention officers have forbidden them to use welding equipment – an essential part of their act.

Ex-Japan bassist Mick Karn and ex-Bauhaus singer Peter Murphy team up to form avant-garde pop duo Dali's Car. Although Murphy claims the name for the group came to him in a dream, it is the title of a track from the Captain Beefheart LP *Troutmask Replica*.

November

Frankie Goes To Hollywood's debut album *Welcome to the Pleasuredome* sets a new record of 1.1 million advance orders in Britain. The same month the band play a concert in Washington, DC, on the night of the American elections.

Wells Kelly, drummer with Meat Loaf, chokes and dies while on tour in Britain.

December

The Bucks Fizz tour coach crashes in Yorkshire, injuring all four members of the British vocal group. Singer Mike Nolan undergoes brain surgery.

"Do They Know It's Christmas", written by Bob Geldof and Midge Ure and performed by Band Aid, tops the British singles charts. All proceeds from the sales of the record are sent to aid famine victims in Ethiopia. The cream of British pop talent is brought in to sing on the record: Boy George, Wham!, Duran Duran, Phil Collins, Bono, Bananarama, Spandau Ballet and many more.

Below left Stuart Adamson, who left the Skids to form Big Country, an immediate success on both sides of the Atlantic with a brand of power pop based on traditional Scottish music.
Below More serious was the Band Aid project. Bob Geldof and Midge Ure take a fundraising bow.
Bottom The eighties spawned many dance crazes — one of the most enduring was 'breakdancing'.

186

INDEX

Songs and Records

A

Abandoned Luncheonette 117
Abracadabra 166
After Bathing at Baxters 73
Against the Wind 154
"Ain't Too Proud to Beg" *33*, 70
Aja 106
"Alley-Oop" 31
"All or Nothing" 60
"All Right Now" 91
"All Shook Up" 12
"Along Comes Mary" 66
"Anarchy in the UK" 133, 139
"Angels Cried" 16
Animal Magnetism 173
Animals 133
"Annie's Song" 119
"Another Brick in the Wall" 157
"Anyone Who Had a Heart" 56
"Apache" 29
Approximately Infinite Universe 112
"April Love" 30
"Are You Lonesome Tonight?" 31
"Arnold Layne" 74
"Ashes to Ashes" 154
"As Tears Go By" *57*, 59, 65
Astral Weeks 117
Atom Heart Mothep" 20

B

"Baby I Need Your Loving" 55
"Baby Love" 56
"Baby Please Don't Go" 61
Bad Company 116
"Bad Moon Rising" 84
"Bad to Me" 48, *52*
Band, The 84
Basement Tapes, The 124
Bat Out of Hell 142, *145*, 177
"Beast of Burden" 184
Beatles' Second Album, The 58
"Beatnik Fly" 23
Beautiful Noise 132
"Be-Bop-a-Lula" 9, *9*, 10, 18
"Ben" 104, 109
"Big Bad John" 44
"Big Girls Don't Cry" 45
Birds of Fire 111
Bitches Brew 111
"Bits and Pieces" 49
Black and Blue 127
Black Sabbath 96
Blonde on Blonde 65
"Blowin' in the Wind" 52
"Blueberry Hill" 11
"Blue Suede Shoes" 9, 10
Bobby Sherman 96
Bob Dylan 37
Born to Run 120
Boston 126
"Brass in Pocket" 154
"Bridge Over Troubled Water" 96
Buddy Holly Story, The 25
Business As Usual 173, *179*
"Butterfly" 16
"Bye Bye Baby" 31
"Bye Bye Love" 13

C

Can't Buy a Thrill 104
"Can't Buy Me Love" 54
Can't Slow Down 174
Car Wash 136
Catch a Fire 123
Cathy's Clown 30
C'est Chic 143
Chariots of Fire 166
"Cherish" 66
Chic 143
"Children of the World" 133
Children of the World 136
"Chipmunk Song" 25
Chipmunks Sing the Beatles, The 59
"Chirpy Chirpy Cheep Cheep" 98
Christmas and the Beads of Sweat 95
Clash 139
"Class, The" 25
"C'mon Everybody" *18*
"Co-Co" 88
"Cold Turkey" 89
"Come On" 53
"Come Together" 89
Communiqué 148
Concert for Bangladesh, The 108
Concerto for Group and Orchestra 93
"Crazy Horses" 112
"Crazy Little Thing Called Love" 154
Crime of the Century 120
"Crossfire" 23
Cruisin' 150
"Crying Time" 65
"Cumberland Gap" 16
"Cum On Feel the Noize" 173

D

Damned Damned Damned 139
"Dancing in the Street" 65
Dare 159, 166
Darkness on the Edge of Town 143
Dark Side of the Moon 100, 154, 179
"Dead Man's Curve" 22, 51
"Dedicated Follower of Fashion" 70
"Dedicated to the One I Love" 26
Deep Purple in Rock 93
Déjà Vu 84
"Devil Woman" 127
"Diana" 16, *24*
"Dirty Water" 69
"Do Anything You Say" 70
"Do It Again" 104
"Dominique" 53
"Don't Be Cruel" 31
"Don't Go" 166
"Don't You Want Me" 159, 166
"Do They Know It's Christmas?" 186
Double Fantasy 159, 160
Double Live Gonzo 163
Double Platinum 143
"Do Wah Diddy Diddy" 54
"Downtown" 59, 60, *63*
"Do You Believe in Magic?" 61
"Do You Love Me?" *44*, 49, *51*
"Do You Really Want to Hurt Me?" 166, 171
"Dream Baby" 43

E

Electric Music for Mind and Body 73
"Eliminator" *165*
Elvis' Christmas Album 17
"Every Breath You Take" 172
"Eye of the Tiger" 166

F

"Fame" 120
Fantastic 177
"Fingertips" 53; "Part Two" 48
"Fire" 120
"Fire and Rain" 94
"First Time Ever I Saw Your Face, The" 104
Flame 125
"Flowers in the Rain" 78
Fly Like an Eagle 166
Footloose 182
Forever Changes 73
"For What It's Worth" 73
"For Your Love" 61
"For Your Precious Love" 32
Frampton Comes Alive! 126, *131*
Freewheelin' Bob Dylan, The 44
"Freeze Frame" 166
"Fresh Garbage" 80
"From Me to You" 48, 52
Fulfillingness' First Finale 117, 127

G

Game, The 154
"Game of Love" 60
Gasoline Alley 93
"George Jackson" 103
"Get It On" 102, 105
"Get Off of My Cloud" 60
Get Yer Ya-Ya's Out 98
"Ghostbusters" 182
"Ghost Town" 165
"Give Ireland Back to the Irish" 108
"Glad All Over" *46*, 49
Glass Houses 154
"God Save the Queen" 139
Going for the One 100
"Go Now" 160
"Good Golly Miss Molly" 9
"Good Lovin'" 66
"Good Vibrations" 67
"Goody Two Shoes" 166
"Got the Feeling" 21
"Grease" 144
"Great Balls of Fire" 17, 112
"Great Pretender, The" 14, *16*
"Green, Green Grass of Home, The" 71
"Green Onions" 41
Greetings From Asbury Park, New Jersey 120

H

"Hand in Glove" 184
"Happenings Ten Years Time Ago" 71
Hard Again 138
"Harper Valley PTA" 80
Head Hunters 111
"Heartbreak Hotel" 9, 10
Heart Like a Wheel 157
"Here Comes the Night" 61
"He's a Rebel" 41, 45
"He's So Fine" 52, 98, 164

I

"Hey Joe" 71
"Hey Jude" 83
Hi-Infidelity 160
"Hitch Hike" 41
"Hold Me" 56
Horses 128, *128*
"Hot Love" 105, *105*
"Hound Dog" 11
"House of the Rising Sun" 54, 58
"How Do You Do It?" *53*
"Hundred Pounds of Clay, A" 34
Hunky Dory 106, 108

I

"I Am a Rock" 70
I Am the Greatest 58
"I Can't Explain" 64
"I Can't Help Myself" 56
"I Don't Like Mondays" *150*
"I Feel Love" 140
"If I Had a Hammer" 165
"If I Were a Carpenter" 159
"If You Don't Know Me By Now" 106
"I Got My Mojo Workin'" 16
"I Got You Babe" 62, 65
"I Had Too Much to Dream Last Night" 69
"I Hear You Knocking" 98
"I'll Be There" 91
"I'm a Believer" 67, 71
"I'm Not a Juvenile Delinquent" 14
"In-A-Gadda-Da-Vida" 80, *81*
"I Need Your Love Tonight" 25
Innervisions 117
"In the Heart of the City" 132
"In the Midnight Hour" 61
"In the Navy" 151, *151*
"In the Year 2525" 86
"I Only Have Eyes for You" 26
"I Only Want to Be With You" *55*, 56
"I Saw Her Standing There" 53
"I Shot the Sheriff" 123
"It Ain't Me Babe" 61
"Itchycoo Park" 60
"It Doesn't Matter Anymore" 13, *15*, 25
"It Don't Come Easy" 98
"It's All Over Now, Baby Blue" 185
"It's Over" 28
It's Too Late to Stop Now 117
"Itsy Bitsy Teenie Weenie Yellow Polka Dot Bikini" 28, 31
"I Walk the Line" 9, 11
"I Wanna Be Your Man" 53
"I Want to Hold Your Hand" 48, 53, 54
"I Want You Back" 93, *96*

J

Jailbreak 164
"Jailhouse Rock" 12
"Jennie Lee" 22
"Je T'Aime (Moi Non Plus)" 86
"Jive Talkin'" 120
Johnny Mathis' Greatest Hits 179
"Join Together" 109
Joker, The 166, *166*
"(Just Like) Starting Over" 161

K

"Keep on Running" 61
Kick Inside, The 159
"Killing Me Softly With His Song" 104
Kings of the Wild Frontier 164
"Knock Three Times" 88

"Knowing Me, Knowing You" 138

L

"Lady Marmalade" 120, *123*
"Last Train to Clarksville" 67
"Leader of the Pack" 56, 59
"Lean On Me" 104
Led Zeppelin 80
Legalize It 124
Let It Be 92
Let's Get It On 117
"Let's Stay Together" 104
"Letter, The" 73
Lexicon of Love, The 171
Lie 96
"Light My Fire" 73, 77, 78
"Like a Rolling Stone" 61, 65
"Little Deuce Coupe" 53
Live Bullet 127, 154, *155*
"Living Doll" 23
"Liza Jane" 58
Loaded 92
"Locomotion, The" 44
Long Distance Voyager 160
"Louie Louie" 58, 65, 69, 70
"Love Is Strange" 11
"Love Letters in the Sand" 16, 30
"Love Me Do" 41, 45, 52, *53*, 54
"Love Me Tender" 11, 31
"Love to Love You Baby" 130, *138*
Love You Live 140
"Lucille" 138

M

"Mack the Knife" 27
Main Course 133, *136*
McCartney 96
"Me and Mrs Jones" 104
Meddle 100
Meet the Beatles 58
Mental Notes 142
"Message in a Bottle" 148
"Metal Guru" 105
Mental Health 173
"Mickey's Monkey" 53
Midnight Love 174
Midnight Special 34
Mistaken Identity 160
Moby Grape 73
"Monday Monday" 66
"Monster Mash" 45
Moondance 117
"More More More" 130
Morning Train 160
"Move It" 23
"Mr Lee" 17
"Mr Tambourine Man" 61, 64
Music From Big Pink, 83, 84, *90*
My Aim Is True 148
"My Best Friend's Girl" 145, *146*
"My Boy Lollipop" 58
"My Generation" 60, 65, 164
"My Guy" 58
"My Prayer" 14
"My Sweet Lord" 98, 164
"My Way" 90

N

"Name of the Game, The" 138
Never Mind the Bollocks ... Here's the Sex Pistols 139, 164
New Boots and Panties 145, *147*
"New York Mining Disaster, 1941" 76, *133*
Night Moves 127, *155*
1984 184

"96 Tears" 69, 71
"No Woman No Cry" 123
Nursery Cryme 100

O

Off the Wall 173, *185*
"Oh Carol" 27
Old Raincoat, An 93
"Only Sixteen" 26
"Only the Lonely" 31
"Only You" 14
Ooh La La 114
Outlandos d'Amour 148
"Over and Over" 65
"Owner of a Lonely Heart" 182, 184

P

"Papa Was a Rolling Stone" 104
Paradise Theater 160
Pat Boone's Great Hits 30
Pat Garrett and Billy the Kid 114
"Peace on Earth" 141
"Peggy Sue" 13, *15*
"Perfidia" *38*, 42
Pictures at an Exhibition 100
"Pillow Talk" 11
Piper at the Gates of Dawn, The 78
Place I Love, The 119
"Please Mr Postman" 36
"Please Please Me" 52
"Poor Me" 30
"Power to the People" 98, 101
Precious Time 160
"Pretty Vacant" 141
"PS I Love You" 45
"Public Image" 147
"Puff the Magic Dragon" 98
"Purple Haze" 74
Purple Rain 174, *174*, 185
"Pushin' Too Hard" 69

Q

Quadrophenia 110, 148
"Queen of the Hop" 18
"Quick Joey Small (Run Joey Run)" 81

R

"Rainin' in My Heart" 25
Ramones, The 132
"Rave On" 13
"Reach Out I'll Be There" 71
"Reason to Believe" 159
"Rebel Rouser" 18
"Red River Rock" 23
Regatta de Blanc 148
"Relax" 182, 186
"Remember (Walkin' in the Sand)" 56
"Respect" 73
"Return of Django" 86
"Return to Sender" 45
"Revolution" 83
"Ride a White Swan" 105
Rise and Fall of Ziggy Stardust and the Spiders From Mars, The 106
River, The 154
"River Deep Mountain High" 66, 70
"Rock a Hula Baby" 38
"Rock Around the Clock" 8, *11*
Rock Around the Clock 10
"Rockin' in the Jungle" 26
"Rock With the Caveman" 11
Rolling Stones, The 58
"Roxanne" 148

Rubber Soul 65
"Rumble" 18
Rumours 136, *136*
"Runaround Sue" 32
"Runaway" 32, *32*

S

"Sabre Dance" 98
Sailor 166
"Satisfaction" 60, 64, 147
Saturday Night Fever 133, 136, 141, 185
"Save Your Kisses for Me" 131
"Say Man" 21
Scary Monsters (and Super Creeps) 154
"School Days" 16
"School's Out" 107, 109
"Searchin'" 14
"See Emily Play" 74
"See You Later Alligator" 10, *11*
Sergeant Pepper's Lonely Hearts Club Band 72
"Sexual Healing" 174
"Shaking All Over" 29
"Sha La La La Leee" 60
"She Loves You" 48, 53, 54
"Sherry" 44
"She's Not There" 57
She's So Unusual 182
"Shining Star" 120
"Shop Around" 31, 32
"Shout" 21
"Silver Threads and Golden Needles" 44
"Simon Says" 81, 82
"Sixteen Tons" 179
Slow Train Coming 148
"Soft and Wet" 146
"So It Goes" 132
"Somebody to Love" 73
Some Girls 143
"Something" 91
"Somewhere" 56
Song Remains the Same, The 127
"Soul Sacrifice" 87
"Sounds of Silence" 66, 70
"Space Oddity" 86, 106, 154
"Spanish Harlem" 31, 33
Sports 182
Stand 174
"Stand By Me" 31
Station to Station 127
"Stoned Free" 71
Stranger, The 141, 154, *155*
"Stranger on the Shore" 37, 38
"Strangers in the Night" 66
"Street Fighting Man" 83
"Stroll, The" 17
"Sugar and Spice" 48
"Sugar Sugar" 81, 91
"Summer Holiday" 52
"Summertime Blues" 18, *18*
"Sunshine of Your Love" 162
"Sunshine Superman" 66
"Surfin'" 37
"Surfin' Safari" 41
"Surfin' Stomp" 51
Surrealistic Pillow 73
Sweet Baby James 94, *102*
"Sweets for My Sweet" 48, 53

T

Talking Book 117
"Talkin' John Birch Society Blues" 53

Tapestry 95, *95*, 154
Tarkus 100
"Teddy Bear" 12
"Teen Angel" 20
"Telegram Sam" 105
"Telstar" *40*, 42, 45
"That'll Be The Day" 13, 16, 17
"That's What You Get" 70
"There Goes My Baby" 25, 26
"There's Always Something There to Remind Me" 56
There's a Riot Going On 174
"These Boots are Made for Walkin'" 66, 70
This Year's Model 145
Thriller 133, 173, 179, 182, 185, *185*
"Tie a Yellow Ribbon Round the Old Oak Tree" 114
"Times They Are a-Changin', The" 58
"Together" 56
"To Know Him is to Love Him" 21, 33
"Tom Dooley" 25
Tommy 110
"Tonight's the Night" 132
"Tossin' and Turnin'" 36
Total Eclipse of the Heart 173
Transformer 110
"Travelin' Light" 23
"Travelin' Man" 36
Troutmask Replica 186
Tubular Bells 100
Tusk 136
"Tutti-Frutti" 9
"Twist, The" 21, 31, 37
"Twist and Shout" 28, 49
"Twisting the Night Away" 28
"Two Tribes" 182, 185

U

Undead 80
Upstairs at Eric's 166, 171
Up Where We Belong 171

V

"Valley Girl" 171
Van Halen II 150
Victory 182
"Virginia Plain" 106, *107*
"Volare" 21
"Voodoo Chile" 92

W

Waiting for the Sun 83
"Wake Up Little Susie" 17
"Walk Away Renee" 66
"Walk, Don't Run" 31, *38*, 42
"Walkin' Back to Happiness" 33
"Walk Like a Man" 48
"Walk on the Wild Side" 110
Wall, The 154
"Wanderer, The" 32
Welcome to the Pleasuredome 186
"Well Respected Man, A" 65
What's Going On 117
"When a Man Loves a Woman" 67, 71
"White Rabbit" 73
"Whiter Shade of Pale, A" 77
"Whole Lotta Shakin' Goin' On" 9, 12, 16, 112
"Who's Sorry Now?" 22
"Why Do Fools Fall in Love?" *12*, 14, 82
"Wild Thing" 69, *70*

"Will You Still Love Me Tomorrow?" 34, 170
Wings Over America 127, 133
"Wipe Out" 51
"With a Little Help From My Friends" 83, *90*
"Without You" 179
"Woodstock" 87
Woodstock 97
"World Without Love" 54, 58, *59*
"Wuthering Heights" *147*, *159*

Y

"Yakety Yak" 14, 21
Yes Album, The 100
Yesterday and Today 70
"YMCA" 150, 151, *151*
"You Ain't Seen Nothing Yet" 116
"You Don't Have to Say You Love Me" 70
"You Keep Me Hanging On" 71
"You Light Up My Life" 136, 141
"You'll Never Walk Alone" 53
"Young Blood" 16
"You Really Got Me" *59*, 162
You're Gonna Get It 145
"You're So Vain" 94
"You've Lost That Loving Feeling" 61
"You've Really Got a Hold On Me" 45
"Yummy Yummy Yummy" 81

Z

Zenyatta Mondatta 154

General

A

Abba 118, 133, 138, *141*
ABC 171, 172
AC/DC 156, 157
Adamson, Stuart *186*
Allman Brothers 103, 109, 124, 130, 176
Anderson, Ian 80, *83*
Andrea True Connection 130
Animals 54, 58, 76, 97, 173
Anka, Paul 16, 20, 23, *24*, 25, 29, 34
Ant, Adam *168*; and the Ants 156, 164, 166, 170
Archies 81, 91
Asia 160, *160*
Avalon, Frankie 17, 18, 20, 21, 23, 27, 34, 53
Average White Band 117, 119, 130

B

Bachman Turner Overdrive 116
Bad Company 116, *119*
Badfinger 88, 102, *117*, 124, 179
Baez, Joan 31, 52, 53, 64, 79, 140
Baker, Ginger 84, 101, 151
Ballard, Hank, and the Midnighters 21, 31
Bananarama *176*, 186
Band 82, 83, 84, *90*, *118*, 124, 127, 133, 141
Band Aid 186, *186*
Barrett, Syd 74, 82
Bay City Rollers 116, 125, 131, 170, 179
Beach Boys 22, 37, 41, *43*, 51, 53, 61, 67, *77*, 82, 97, 132, 176, 179
Beatles: as Silver Beatles 27, 31;

German gigs 31, 45; at Cavern 34, 37, 44, 53; Epstein takes on 37; rejected by Decca 43; TV debut 43; team up with Martin 44; first single 45; first three No. 1s 48; in Royal Command Performance 53, 109; five records in US Top Ten 54; first US LP 58; first US visit 58; *A Hard Day's Night* 58, 59; awarded MBEs 64; *Help!* 65; retire from live gigs 66; records banned in South Africa 71; US tour (1966) 71; acid rock phase 72; campaign for legalization of marijuana 77; *Magical Mystery Tour* 78, 79; sever US connections 82; and Apple 82, 83; last public appearance 88; disband 92, 96; decline offer to reform 130; all singles rereleased (1976) 131; early albums rereleased (1984) 182; other references 13, 16, 29, 41, *41*, 42, *44*, *46*, 49, 51, 52, 53, 59, 60, 61, 64, 65, 70, *71*, *76*, 90, 91, *94*, 110, 170, 183
Beck, Jeff 61, *61*, *63*, 64, 93
Bee Gees 76, 82, 88, 120, 133, *133*, 136, 144
Bell, Freddie, and the Bell Boys 8
Belmonts, Dion and the 20, 25, 32
Benatar, Pat 158, 160, *164*, 170
Berry, Chuck 9, 16, 18, 21, 26, 108, 153
Berry, Jan 22; *see also* Jan and Dean
Best, Pete 44, 58
Big Brother and the Holding Company 73
Big Country *186*
Bilk, Acker 33, 37, 38
Birkin, Jane 84
Black, Bill *8*, 18, 27, 31, 65
Black, Cilla 53, 56, *57*, 59
Black Sabbath 96, 146, 162
Blackwell, Chris 76, 123
Blind Faith 84
Blondie 128, *131*, 155, 157, 171, 173
Blood, Sweat and Tears 83, 111
Blue Cheer 80, 162
Bolan, Marc 105, *105*, 106, 141, *141*
Bond, Graham 118
Bonds, Gary US 28, 52
Bonham, John 'Bonzo' *114*, 158
Bono 185, 186
Bono, Sonny 62, 65, 118
Booker T and the MGs 41, 65, 125
Boomtown Rats *150*, 165
Boone, Pat 9, 16, 20, 30, 136, 141
Boston 126, 133
Bowie, David (David Jones) 58, 70, 86, 88, *88*, *104*, 106, 108, 110, 120, 125, 127, 131, 141, 154, *155*, 156, 158, 162, 165, 177
Bow Wow Wow 156
Box Tops 73
Boy George 172, 185, 186
Bread 93, *119*
Brown, James 9, 21, *60*, 88, 109, 151
Browne, Jackson 95, 146, 165
Buckingham, Lindsey *136*, *137*
Buffalo Springfield 73, 77, 84, *84*
Burdon, Eric 97, 101
Bush, Kate *147*, *159*
Byrds 61, 62, 64, 77, 79, 84, 88, *108*, 114, 115, 128

Byrne, David 128, *133*

C

Canned Heat 99, 164
Carpenters 93, 176
Cars 145, *146*
Cash, Johnny 9, 11, 96, 153
Cassidy, David 111, 118
Chad Mitchell Trio 119, 124
Chantays 42, 51
Charles, Ray 25, 37, 43, 65, 71, *90*, 151
Checker, Chubby 25, 28, *29*, 31, 37, 38, 52, 53, 97
Cher (La Pier) 62, 65, 118, 124, 125, 158
Chic *142*, 143, 150
Chicago 111, 146, *184*
Chiffons 52, 164
Chipmunks 25, 108
Clapton, Eric 61, *61*, 64, 84, 87, 91, 97, 102, 116, *120*, 123, 151
Clark, Dave, Five *46*, 49, 54, 58, *59*, 65
Clark, Dick 17, 27, 28, 43, 82
Clark, Petula 27, *59*, 60, *63*
Clash 123, *139*, 146, 157, 170, 179, 183
Coasters 14, 16, *16*, 21, 27
Cochran, Eddie 18, *18*, 30
Cocker, Joe 83, *90*, 171
Cohen, Leonard 97
Cole, Nat 'King' 70
Collins, Phil 100, *103*, 182, 186, *186*
Commodores 174
Contours *44*, 49
Cooke, Sam 17, 26, 28, *37*, 59
Coolidge, Rita 114, 115
Cooper, Alice 107, *107*, 109
Costello, Elvis 141, 145, *146*, 151
Country Joe and the Fish 73
County, Wayne 124, 151
Crazy Elephant 81
Crazy Horse 98
Cream 61, 74, 80, 83, 84, *120*, 162, 176
Creedence Clearwater Revival 84, *87*
Creme, Lol 169
Crickets 13, *15*, 25
Croce, Jim 110, 115
Crosby, Bing 31, 141
Crosby, David 79, *84*, 170
Crosby, Stills and Nash 79; and Young 84, *84*, 87, 90
Crystals *34*, 37, 41, 45
Culture Club 166, 171, 172
Curtis, King 102

D

Dakotas 48, *52*, 54
Dali's Car 186
Daltrey, Roger *64*, 70
Dammers, Jerry 164
Damned 132, *139*, 140
Darin, Bobby 18, *21*, 26, 27, 43, 45, 115
Davis, Miles 111
Dawn 98, 114
dBs 153, 183
Dean, Jimmy 44
Deep Purple 82, 93, 133, 162, 185
Def Leppard *160*, 162, 173, 184
Dekker, Desmond 86
Denny, Sandy 146
Denver, John 95, 110
Derek and the Dominoes 97

Devo 145, 153
Dexy's Midnight Runners 172, *173*, 177
Diamond, Neil 29, 67, *106*, 132, 185
Diddley, Bo *8*, 9, 21, 53
Dire Straits 148, *153*
Domino, Fats 11, 16, 17
Donegan, Lonnie 16
Donovan 64, 66, *66*, 82, 101
Don't Look Back 77
Doobie Brothers 104, 150
Doors 17, *72*, 73, 77, 78, 83, 88, 90, 102, 118
Dorsey, Tommy 11
Dr Feelgood 120
Dr Hook and the Medicine Show 112
Drifters 25, 26, 28, 29, 31, 53, 102
Duran Duran 168, 172, 176, 186
Dury, Ian 132, 145, *147*
Dylan, Bob: *Bob Dylan* released 37; *Freewheelin' Bob Dylan* released 44; radio debut 44; records BBC radio play 52; first major concert 52; first UK hit 58; 'goes electric' 61, 65, 164; marries 65; crashes motorbike 71; *Don't Look Back* 77; receives honorary doctorate 97; *Tarantula* published 97; *Pat Garrett and Billy the Kid* 114; *Basement Tapes* released 124; divorced 140; *Renaldo and Clara* 146, 171; 'born again' 153, 165; other references 26, 34, 37, *38*, 41, 53, 64, *65*, 79, 82, 84, 87, *90*, 91, 101, 102, 103, 115, *118*, 120, 132, 133, *145*, 148, 150, *153*, 170, *180*, 185

E

Eagles 104, *108*, 125, 158
Earth, Wind and Fire 120, *125*, 174, *186*
Easton, Sheena 160, *165*
Eddy, Duane 18, *21*, 27
Edmunds, Dave 98
Ed Sullivan Show 11, 17, 52, 53, 58, 59, 65, 78
Electric Light Orchestra 110, *110*
Elliot, Cass *69*, 119, 155
Emerson, Keith *91*, 93
Emerson, Lake and Palmer *91*, 93, 100, 109, 118, 160
Eno, Brian 106
Entwhistle, John *64*
Epstein, Brian 37, 44, *44*, 45, 48, 52, *53*, 56, *57*, 59, 64, 78
Equals 172
Eurythmics 172, 185
Eva, Little 29, 44
Everly Brothers 13, *13*, 17, 21, 28, 30, 36, 37, 53, 177; Don 43

F

Fabian 18, 21, 23, 25, 30, 31
Faces *92*, 93, *93*, 114
Faith, Adam 23, 30
Faithfull, Marianne *57*, 59, 78, 90, 153
Fame 166, *166*
Family 84
Farndon, Pete 170, 176
Ferry, Brian 106, *107*, 170
Fire and Rain 114
Fixx 166

Flack, Roberta 104
Flamin' Groovies 91, 132
Fleetwood Mac 97, 136, *136*, *137*, 140, 153
Flock of Seagulls, A 166, *171*, 172
Flying Burrito Brothers *108*, 115
Fontana, Wayne 60
Foreigner 138, 150, *153*
Four Seasons 44, 45, *45*, 48, 59, 144
Four Tops *55*, 56, 61, 66, 71, 184
Frampton, Peter 84, 103, 126, *131*, 132, 146, 171
Francis, Connie 17, 20, *22*, 23, *29*, 30, 97
Frankie Goes to Hollywood 48, 182, 184, 185, 186
Franklin, Aretha 31, *72*, 73, 101, 155
Frantz, Chris *133*, 171
Freddie and the Dreamers 49, 57, 64
Free 93, 116, *119*, 131
Freed, Alan 8, 10, 11, 14, 16, 20, 21, 22, 27, 64
Fun Boy Three 165, 170, *176*
Funicello, Annette 23, *25*, 27, 51, 53
Fury, Billy 23, 178

G

Gabriel, Peter 100, *103*, 125
Gaines, Steve and Cassidy 141
Gainsbourg, Serge 86
Garfunkel, Art 20, *66*, 165; see also Simon and Garfunkel
Gaye, Marvin *32*, 41, 45, 52, 117, 174, 185
Geldof, Bob *150*, 186, *186*
Generation X 133, 151, 173, *174*
Genesis 100, *100*, *103*, 125, 182, *186*
Gerry and the Pacemakers 31, 48, 53, *53*, 54, 64, 182
Gibb, Andy 144
Gilmour, Dave 82, *159*
Glitter, Gary (Paul Raven) 107, 133
Godley, Kevin 167
Goffin, Gerry 29, *95*
Go-Gos 166, *171*
Golding, Lynval 165, 170
Goldsboro, Bobby 80
Grand Funk Railroad 84, 162
Grateful Dead 65, 72, 77, 97, 112, 147, 158
Grease: movie 144; stage 109
Green, Peter 97, 140
Guthrie, Arlo 82, 96
Guthrie, Woody *66*, 79, 82

H

Hair 79, 109
Haley, Bill, and the Comets 8, 9, 10, 11, *11*, 16, 18, 164
Hall, Terry 164, 165
Hall and Oates *116*, 117, *117*
Ham, Pete 124, 179
Hancock, Herbie 111
Harder They Come, The 112
Hardin, Tim *42*, 159
Harrison, George: before Beatles 21; marries Patti Boyd 70; solo career 98, 112; and Concert for Bangladesh 102, 108; autobiography 158; other references 37, 59, 64, 71, 91, 119, 146, 151, 164; see also Beatles
Harry, Debbie 128, *131*, 155, 158, 165
Harvey, Alex 170

Havens, Richie 82, 87
Hawkins, Ronnie 84, 132
Headon, Topper 146, 170
Heart *128*
Heartbreakers *127*, 128, 145
Heartbreakers, Tom Petty and the 145, 151
Hell, Richard 118, 128, 132, 133, 145
Hendrix, Jimi 74, 75, *75*, 77, 79, 90, 92, 97, 170; Experience 71, 76, 77, 158
Herd 84, 126, *131*
Herman's Hermits 54, 60, 77
Holiday, Billie 26, *115*
Hollies *46*, 49, 84, 172
Holly, Buddy 13, *15*, 17, 21, 22, 25
Hooker, John Lee 31, 34, 185
Hopkins, Mary 83
Hopkins, (Sam) Lightnin' 170
Horn, Trevor 171, 184
Howlin' Wolf 130
Human League 152, 159, 166, 173
Humble Pie 84, *84*, 103, 126
Hurricanes, Rory Storm and the 31, 44, 109
Hyland, Bryan 28, 31
Hynde, Chrissie 154, 155, *155*

I

Idol, Billy 173, *174*
Iggy and the Stooges 84, *87*, 162
Impressions 32
Ink Spots 14, 120
Iron Butterfly 80, *81*, 162
Iron Maiden *160*, *162*
Isley Brothers 16, 21, 28, 49

J

Jackson, Joe *127*, 183
Jackson, Mahalia 108
Jackson, Michael 93, 104, 109, *133*, 168, 173, 174, 179, 182, 184, 185, *185*
Jackson Five (later the Jacksons) 93, *96*, *101*, 127, 174, 182, 185, 186
Jagger, Mick 18, 43, *51*, *57*, 59, 64, 78, *78*, 90, *98*, 102, 146, 151, 165, 176, 179, 184
Jam 133, 140, 171
James, Tommy, and the Shondells 66, 71
Jan and Dean 22, *23*, 27, 51
Jefferson Airplane 65, 71, 72-3, 77, 90, 124; Starship 124, 146
Jethro Tull 80, *83*
J Geils Band 114, 166, *170*
Joel, Billy 141, 151, 154, *155*, 170
John, Elton 101, 109, 110, *112*, 115, 131, 153, 165, 173
Jones, Brian 43, 90
Jones, Grace 155, *157*
Jones, Kenny *64*, 147
Jones, Mick *139*, 150, 179
Jones, Tom 61, 71
Joplin, Janis 73, 75, *75*, 91, 97, 155
Judas Priest 162, *162*

K

Kajagoogoo 172, 177
Kansas 146, 150
Kasenetz-Katz Singing Orchestral Chorus 81
Kidd, Johnny 29, 71; and the Pirates 29, *31*
King, Ben E 25, 31, 33
King, Carole 20, 27, 29, 95, *95*, 108,

114, 155
King Crimson 116, 150
Kingsmen 58, 65, 69, 70
Kingston Trio 25, 31, 36
Kinks 54, *59*, 64, 65, 70, 162, 173
Kirshner, Don 29, 44, 67, 81
Kiss 130, 143, *144*, 162, 164, 179
Knopfler, David and Mark 148, *153*
Korner, Alexis 43, 184
Kramer, Billy J 48, *52*, 54
Kristofferson, Kris 114, 115, 151

L

Lake, Gregg 93, 118
Lauper, Cyndi 182, *183*
Led Zeppelin 61, *61*, 80, *83*, 101, 114, *114*, 124, 125, 127, 136, 141, 158, 160, 162
Lee, Alvin 80, *83*
Lee, Brenda 23, 34, 45
Leiber, Jerry 14, 16, 29, 31, 33
Lennon, John: before Beatles 16, 17, 21; marries Cynthia Powell 44; 'Jesus Christ' remark 70, 71; and Yoko Ono 83, 88, 91, 103, 108, 109, 160; and Plastic Ono Band 87, *88*, 91; returns MBE 91; and Elephant's Memory Band 101; and David Bowie 120; son by Yoko born 125; releases last single 159, 160; murdered 159, *159*, 160, 165; other references 36, 53, 82, 90, 96, 98, 116, 119, 132; see also Beatles
Lennon/McCartney songs 45, 48, *52*, 53, 54, 58, *59*
Lennox, Annie 172, 185
Lewis, Jerry Lee 9, 11, 12, 16, *16*, 17, 18, 20, 21, 43, 77, 78, 112, 133, 177
Lewis, Walter 'Furry' 165
Little Feat 98, 151
Loggins, Kenny 182
Loggins and Messina 127
Love 73
Love Sculpture 98
Lovin' Spoonful 61, 62, 71
Lowe, Nick 132, 153
Lwin, Annabella 156
Lydon, John (Johnny Rotten) *139*, 140, 146, 147, 151, 159, 164
Lymon, Frankie, and the Teenagers 11, *12*, 14, 16, 17, 82
Lynyrd Skynyrd 132, 141

M

Madness 150, *153*, 168, 173
Mahavishnu Orchestra 111
Mamas and the Papas 62, 66, 119, 162; see also Elliot, Cass
Manfred Mann 54, 173
Manilow, Barry 124
Marketts 51, 70
Marley, Bob 123, *125*, 132, 133, 159, 164, 171
Marriott, Steve 60, *64*, 84, *84*, 126
Martha and the Vandellas 52
Martin, Dean 58, 148
Martin, George 44, 45
Marvelettes 32, 36
Marvin, Lee 92
Matthews Southern Comfort 87
Mayall, John: Bluesbreakers 120, 137
Mayfield, Curtis 32
McCartney, Linda 88, 98, 124

McCartney, Paul: before Beatles 17; admits to having taken LSD 77; marries Linda 88; rumored death 91; solo career 96, 98, *98*, 116; and Wings 108, 125, 132, 133, 156; other references *11*, 37, 54, 83, 124, 151; see also Beatles; Lennon/McCartney songs
MC5 75, 84, 103, 157, 162
McIntosh, Robbie 119, 130
McLaren, Malcolm 138, 156
McLaughlin, John 111
McPhatter, Clyde 10, 25, 102
McVie, Christine *136*
McVie, John *136*, *137*
Meat Loaf 142, *145*, 158, 177, 186
Melvin, Harold, and the Blue Notes 104, 170
Men At Work 168, 173, *176*, *179*, 183
Michael, George *182*, 186
Midler, Bette 184
Miles, Buddy 101
Miller, Steve 124, 133, 166, *166*
Mingus, Charles 151
Miracles 31, 32, 45, 53; see also Robinson, Smokey
Mitchell, Joni 87, 95, *96*, 97, 133, 171
Mitchell, Mitch 158
Monkees 58, 67, 70, 71, *71*, 77, 79, 81
Moody Blues 54, 160
Moon, Keith *64*, 115, 131, 147, *151*
Moroder, Giorgio 127, 138, *138*
Morrison, Jim 17, *72*, 73, 78, 88, 91, 102, 118, 125
Morrison, Van 61, *63*, 117, 133, 185
Morton, George 'Shadow' 56
Mott the Hoople 116
Move 76, 78, 83, 110, *110*

N

Nash, Graham *84*, 165
Nash, Johnny 123
Nelson, Ricky 16, 18, *21*, 23, 36, 103
Nevins, Al 29, 44
Newman, Randy 95, 119
Newton-John, Olivia 144, 166, *168*
New York Dolls 107, *108*, 109, *117*, 127, 128, 138, 162
Nicks, Stevie *136*, *137*
1910 Fruitgum Co 81, 82
Nugent, Ted 116, 119, 125, 162, *163*
Numan, Gary 20, 150, 157, 165, 170
Nyro, Laura 95

O

Ochs, Phil, 53, 131
Ofarim, Esther and Abi 82
Ohio Players 120, *123*
O'Jays 104, 140
Oldfield, Mike 100
Oldham, Andrew Loog 52
Ono, Yoko 83, 88, 91, 103, 108, 109, 112, 125, 159, *159*, 160
Orbison, Roy 18, 28, 31, *37*, 43
Osbourne, Ozzy 162, 170, 184
Osmond, Donny 17, *102*, 103, 108, 109, 164
Osmonds 98, 101, *101*, 111, 112, 115, 116

P

Page, Jimmy 61, *61*, 80, *114*, 158, 160
Pappalardi, Felix 176

Parker, (Colonel) Tom 10, 12, 17, *26*, 30, 141
Parton, Dolly 25
Partridge Family 101, 111
Perkins, Carl 9, 10, 11, 185
Peter and Gordon 54, 58, *59*
Peter, Paul and Mary 53, 96
Petty, Tom *142*, 145, 151
Phillips, John 164
Phillips, Sam 8, 9, 12, 18
Pickett, Bobby 'Boris' 45
Pickett, Wilson 'Wicked' 61, 62, 71
Pink Floyd 71, *72*, 74, 78, 82, 100, 133, 154, 157, *159*, 179
Pitney, Gene 29, 32, 41
Plant, Robert *114*, 125, 141, 160
Plasmatics 155, *157*, 158, 164
Plastic Ono Band 87, *88*, 91
Platters 8, 10, 14, 16, *16*, 21, 26, 36, 44
Police 123, *145*, 148, *148*, 154, 157, 172, 183
Poole, Brian 49, *51*
Presley, Elvis: start of career 8-9; TV debut 10; gains Parker as manager 10, 12, *26*; signed up by Paramount 10; on *Ed Sullivan Show* 11; movie debut 11; army service 16, 18, 20, 21, 22, 30; released from army 30; *GI Blues* 30; contracts with Hal Wallis 34; *Wild in the Country* 36; edition of *American Bandstand* devoted to 43; *Spinout* 71; marries 77; *Clambake* 79; birth of daughter 82; *Trouble With Girls* 91; divorced 115; records last hit 133; death 138, *140*, 141; other references *8, 15,* 17, 25, 27, 28, 31, *31,* 37, 38, 45, 48, 65, 83, 91, 102, 131, 140, 157
Preston, Billy 102, 124
Pretenders 154, *155*, 170, 172, 176
Pretty Things 65, *66,* 127
Price, Alan 54
Prince 146, 174, *174*, 182, 185, 186
Proby, PJ 56, 64
Procol Harum 77
Public Image Ltd 147, 164
Purple Rain 174, *174*, 182, 186

Q

Quarrymen 16, 17, 21, 27
Quatro, Suzi 110, *111*
Queen 110, *112*, 147, 154, 165, 185
? and the Mysterians 69, 71
Quiet Riot 173

R

Ramones 33, 118, *127*, 128, 132, 133, 145, 151, 177
Redding, Noel 158
Redding, Otis 52, 62, 73, 75, *78,* 79, 87
Reed, Lou 92, 99, 110, 112, *128,* 156
Reeves, Jim 58, 110
REO Speedwagon 160, *160*
Revere, Paul, and the Raiders 34, 66, 102
Richard, Cliff 21, 23, *27,* 29, 30, 52, 127, 132, 156, 165
Richard, Keith 43, *51, 57,* 59, 64, *78,* 128, 132, 151, 165, 171, 179
Richard, Little 9, 11, *11,* 16, 17, 18, 153
Richie, Lionel 174, 186
Ridgeley, Andrew *182*

Riley, Jeannie C 80
Robinson, Smokey 32, *49,* 58, 77, 176
Robinson, Tom 153
Rock Around the Clock 8, 11, *16*
Rock'n'Roll Trio 153
Rodgers, Nile *142,* 143
Rogers, Kenny 138
Rolling Stones: stage debut 44; Oldham takes on 52; first single 53; TV debut 53; on *Juke Box Jury* 58; US TV debut 58; refuse to tour South Africa 59; adversely compared with Dave Clark Five 59; banned by BBC 59; rival Beatles in US 60; US tour (1966) 70; behind Iron Curtain 77; Altamont 87; departure of Brian Jones 90; departure of Mick Taylor 119; other references 49, *51,* 53, *63,* 64, 65, 83, *98,* 109, 110, 127, 132, 140, 143, 145, 165, 184
Ronettes *34,* 65
Ronson, Mick *104,* 106
Ronstadt, Linda 141, *157*
Rose Royce 136
Ross, Diana *55,* 83, 110, *115,* 124, 143
Roth, David Lee *148,* 150
Rotten, Johnny *see* Lydon, John
Rowlands, Kevin *173,* 177
Roxy Music 106, *107,* 170
Rundgren, Todd 116, *117,* 132, 142
Rydell, Bobby 23, 27, 34, 44

S

Santana 87, 140, 150
Saturday Night Fever 136, 141
Saxon *160,* 162, 165
Schenker, Michael 140, *173*
Scorpions *173*
Searchers 48, 53, 54
Sedaka, Neil 27, 29, *29*
Seeger, Pete 52, 82, 165
Seger, Bob 127, 154, *155*
Sex Pistols 125, 131, 132, 133, 138-39, *139,* 140, 141, 145, 146, 156, 164
Shadows 29, 30, 38, 42, 52, 115
Sha Na Na 87, 116, 118
Shangri Las 56, 59
Shankar, Ravi 75, 79, 102, 119
Shannon, Del 32, *32,* 54
Shapiro, Helen 33, 52
Shaw, Sandie 56, 59, 184
Shirelles 26, 29, 34, 170
Showaddywaddy 116, 151
Simon, Carly 94, 109, 146
Simon, Paul 20, *66,* 146, 165
Simon and Garfunkel 66, 70, 77, 96
Sinatra, Frank 31, 66, 90
Sinatra, Nancy 66, 70
Siouxsie and the Banshees *157*
Slade 98, 125, 173
Sledge, Percy 67, 71
Sledge, Sister 143, 150
Slick, Grace 65, 71, 73, 96, 146
Slik 130, 153
Sly and the Family Stone 87, 108
Small Faces 60, *64,* 84, *84,* 93
Smith, Mike 49, 65
Smith, Patti 128, *128,* 132, 140, 147, 155, 157
Soft Machine 114
Sonny and Cher 62, 65
Spandau Ballet 172, *174,* 186

Specials 123, 150, 164, 165
Spector, Phil 21, 31, 33, *34,* 37, 41, 45, 60, 61, 66, 92
Spencer Davis Group 61, 76
Spirit 80, 132
Split Enz *142*
Springfield, Dusty 44, *55,* 56, 70
Springfields 44, *55,* 56
Springsteen, Bruce 70, 120, *120,* 125, 131, 132, 143, 146, *159,* 165, *168,* 171
Starr, Ringo 44, 82, 83, 88, 98, 102, 109, 151, 164; *see also* Beatles
Status Quo 162, 170, 184
Steele, Tommy 11, 20, *26*
Steely Dan 104, 165
Stewart, Rod *92,* 93, *93,* 114, 132, 165, 173
Stills, Stephen 73, *84,* 151, 165
Sting *145,* 148, *148,* 183
Stoller, Mike 14, 16, 29, 31, 33
Stone, Sly 108, 118, 119, 174
Storm, Rory 31, 44, 111
Stranglers 130, 132, 139, 140, 158
Strummer, Joe 131, 146, 157, 170
Styx *160,* 160
Sullivan, Ed 11, 59, 78, 91
Summer, Donna 86, 127, 130, 138, *138*
Supremes 36, 45, *55,* 56, 61, 65, 71, 83, 110, 130
Surfaris 42, *42,* 51
Swinging Blue Jeans 49

T

Talking Heads 128, *133,* 145, 153, 171
Taylor, James 94, 95, *102,* 108, 109
Taylor, Mick 90, 119
Teddy Bears 21, 33
Television 118, 128, *133,* 145
Temptations *33,* 61, 70, 104, 115
10cc 132, 167
Ten Years After 80, *83,* 87
Terrell, Tammi 96
Tex, Joe 171
Them 61, *63,* 117
Thin Lizzy 153, 162, *164*
Thirteenth Floor Elevators 69, 128
Thompson Twins *170,* 172
Three Dog Night 93, 124
Thriller 179
Thunders, Johnny *127,* 145
Tornados *40,* 42, 45
Tosh, Peter 123, *124*
Townshend, Peter *64,* 70, 90, 115, 124, 179
Traffic 61, 76, 84, 176, 171
Travolta, John 136, 144
Tremeloes 43, 49, *51*
T.Rex/Tyrannosaurus Rex 88, 102, 105, *105,* 141
Troggs 69, *70*
Turner, Ike 28, *29,* 31, *37,* 66, 70, 118, 133
Turner, Tina 28, *29,* 31, *37,* 66, *69,* 70, 133, *183,* 180
Turtles *22,* 61, 65

U

UFO 140, 162, *173*
Ullman, Tracie *179*
Ultravox 130, 167
Undertones 177
Ure, Midge 130, 153, 186, *186*
Uriah Heep 160, 162, 177
U2 172, 185

V

Valens, Ritchie 22, 25, 37
Valli, Frankie *45,* 48, 144
Vangelis 166
Van Halen *148,* 150, 151, 171, 177, 184
Vee, Bobby 23, 29
Velvet Underground 92, 97, *97,* 110, 128, 162
Ventures 31, *38,* 42
Verlaine, Tom 118, 128, *133*
Vicious, Sid 16, *139,* 140, 146, 147, 151, 156
Village People 150, 151, *151*
Vincent, Gene 9, *9,* 10, *11, 15,* 16, 18, 27, 30, 103
Vinton, Bobby 56, 109
Voorman, Klaus 91

W

Wailers 123, 159
Walker, Aaron 'T-Bone' 124
Walker Brothers 61, 76
Warwick, Dionne 29
Waters, Muddy 16, 138, 147, 165, 176
Weavers 43, 165
Weil, Cynthia 29, 155
Weller, Paul 171
Wells, Mary 31, 32, 45, 58
Wham! 177, 182, *182,* 186
Who: first chart entry 64; Woodstock 87; *Quadrophenia* 110; *Tommy* 110; certified loudest rock band ever 132; Pete Townshend leaves 179; other references 60, *64,* 65, 70, 71, 75, 77, 90, 109, 115, 131, 147, *151,* 153, 162, 164, 166
Wilde, Kim 31
Wilde, Marty 23
Williams, Wendy O 155, *157,* 164
Williamson, Sonny Boy 64
Wilson, Brian 41, 114, 132
Wilson, Carl 77, 91, 114
Wilson, Dennis 41, 114, 179
Wilson, Jackie 34, 125, 184
Wings 108, 109, 118, 125, 132, 133, 153, 156
Winwood, Steve 61, 76, 84
Wizzard 110
Wonder, Stevie 45, 48, *49,* 53, 110, 115, 116, 117, 127, 174
Wood, Ronnie *92,* 93, *93,* 165
Wood, Roy 110, *110*
Woodstock Festival 80, 86-7, 91, 94, 96, 112
Wray, Link 18

Y

Yardbirds 61, *61,* 64, 65, 71, *120,* 132, 173
Yazoo (Yaz) 166, 171
Yes 100, *102,* 132, 160, 182, 184
Young, Neil 73, *84,* 90, 132, 133, 134
Young Rascals 65, 66

Z

Zager and Evans 86
Zappa, Frank 90, 103, 108, 171
Zombies 54, 57, 64
ZZ Top 127, 162, *163,* 168

Phil Collins showed phenomenal talent and energy
as producer, soloist and member of Genesis.

PICTURE CREDITS

Camera Press 94 top left, center left, bottom left **Colorific!** 64 bottom, 160 right, 167 bottom, 174 bottom, Contact/Annie Leibovitz title page bottom right **London Features International** title page top left, 6-7, 35, 36 left, 43, 46-47, 46 bottom, 54, 67 bottom, 70 74, 77 right, 78, 92 left, 92-93, 117, 120, 123-125, 126-127, 127, 131, 138 right, 139 left & center, 140, 141 bottom, 142 left, 143, 150 left, 151-152, 152 bottom, 155 top, 156, 157 left, 159 bottom, 161 top, 168, 172 to 179, 182, 183 right **Michael Ochs Archives** 8 to 19, 20 to 25, 26 right, 28, 29, 30 left, 32 to 34, 36 right, 37 to 39, 42, 44 left, 45, 49, 55 top & bottom, 58, 60, 63 bottom, 65 bottom, 66, 69, 73, 80-81, 84-85, 86, 95, 96, 119, 133 **Pictorial Press** title page, 31, 53, 57, 64 top, 65 top, 68, 71 right, 115, 118, 124, 125, 148, 149, 154, 161 bottom, 162-163 bottom, 163, 164, 165 left, 167 top, 169, 170 left, 184, 186 left, 186 top right **Barry Plummer** 85, 101 left, 113 bottom, 142 right, 152-153, 166 **David Redfern** title page center & bottom left, contents page, 62, 101 right, 83, 145, 147 right, 154 left, 165 right, 177, 183 left, Richard E Aaron 129 bottom, 132 left, 137, 144 left & top right, 146, Peter Cronin 162, 162-163 top, 171 right, Colin Fuller 122, Rafael Macia 160 left, Stephen Morley 159 top, Andrew Putter 116, Alison Turner 126 **Rex Features** title page top right & bottom center, 26 left, 27, 30 right, 40, 41, 44 right, 47 inset, 48, 50, 51, 52, 56, 59 top, 61, 63 top left & top right, 67 top, 71 left, 72, 75, 76, 77 left, 79, 82, 87 to 91, 93, 94 bottom right, 97 to 100, 102 to 108, 110, 113 top, 114, 121, 129 top, 130, 132 right, 134-135, 136, 138 left, 139 top right & bottom right, 141 top, 147 left & center, 150 right, 152 top, 157 right, 158, 171 center, 173, 180-181, 185, Eugen Adebari 111, Clive Dixon 112, John Rogers 144 bottom right **Frank Spooner** Pictures 186 bottom right.

Front cover: **Rex Features** full page **London Features International** insets
Back cover: **London Features International**
Endpapers: Phil Collins **Pictorial Press**
          The Police **London Features International**

Multimedia Publications (UK) Limited have endeavored to observe the legal requirements with regard to the rights of the suppliers of photographic and illustrative material